DAWN OF A NEW STEEL AGE:

Bill Cowher's Steelers Forge Into the '90s

Ed Bouchette

Sagamore Publishing
Champaign, Illinois

Production Manager: Susan M. McKinney
Dustjacket and photo insert design: Michelle R. Dressen
Editors: David Hamburg, Russ Lake
Proofreader: Phyllis L. Bannon

Publisher's Cataloging in Publication
(Prepared by Quality Books Inc.)

Bouchette, Ed J.
    Dawn of a new steel age: Bill Cowher's Steelers forge into the
'90s/ Ed Bouchette.
    p. cm.
    Preassigned LCCN: 93-84957.
    ISBN 0-915611-81-3

    1. Pittsburgh Steelers (Football team)   I. Title.

GV956.P57M45 1993   796.33'264'0974886
                                      QBI93-1129

Printed in the United States

To my wife, Debbie; and our children: Scott, Danielle, and Brittany. They are the best team anyone could have.
And to my Mom and Dad, who started the franchise.

Contents

Acknowledgments vi

1   A New Beginning 1

2   The Emperor Has No Players 9

3   Noll's Last Hurrah 19

4   Walton's Mountain: Goodnight, Chuck 27

5   Big Footprints to Fill 45

6   A Fine Predicament You Got Me Into 55

7   Lightning Rod 69

8   A Different Bill Sets Sail 77

9   Convincing the Doubters 85

10   Another Tough Irishman 99

11   Not Yet Ready for Prime Time 107

12   The Bigger They Are, The Harder They Fall 119

13   The Future: Another Art Rooney 133

14   All He Wants is a Foster Home 147

15   No Steel Curtain Call 155

16   On Their Scouts' Honor 163

17   The Meanest Man in the NFL 177

18   Limping Home 185

19   A Room With No View 195

20   Unfinished Business 203

Acknowledgments

Although I've covered the Steelers off and on since 1974—mostly on since 1985—this book would not have been possible without the help and support of others.

First, to my editors at the *Pittsburgh Post-Gazette*, notably John Craig and Fritz Huysman, for allowing me to pursue this project and for keeping me employed and on the beat during a devastating newspaper strike in 1992.

Bob Labriola, the editor of *Steelers Digest*, encouraged the idea for the book and offered insight, suggestions and corrections. Vic Ketchman, sports editor of the *Irwin Standard Observer*, guided me in certain areas that only someone with his perspective and interest in the Steelers could. Mike Prisuta, who covers the Steelers for the *Beaver County Times*, eagerly provided material that was helpful. Peter King of *Sports Illustrated* furnished advice and information.

Dan Edwards, the Steelers' public relations director, as usual, answered all my questions, looked up stats and helped check facts. The Pittsburgh Steelers—the front office, the coaches, scouts, players and other staff members — were more than kind with their patience, time, and openness during my research for this book. The Rooneys, of whom there are many, graciously helped me understand their family history and were accessible and candid in the fashion of the family patriarch, Art Rooney, the Chief.

Others provided help from stories they had written or information they passed along. These include my colleagues at the *Post-Gazette*, Gerry Dulac and Ron Cook; Jeff Legwold of the *North Hills News Record*; Mike Ciarochi of the *Tribune-Review*, Ron Musselman of the *Johnstown Tribune-Democrat*, and Teresa Varley of *Steelers Digest*.

Several people, although they did not contribute directly to this book, guided me along a path that ultimately led to it being written. Randy Jesick and David Truby, professors at Indiana University of Pennsylvania, discovered a spark and fanned it a long time ago. Dave Ailes, sports editor of the *Tribune-Review*, saved me from leaving my profession and put me in a creative environment that was invaluable. Bruce Keidan, a gifted columnist with the *Pittsburgh Post-Gazette* and its former sports editor, hired me and taught me a thing or two about reporting and writing.

To all of you, thanks.

1

A NEW BEGINNING

Revolutions altered its air, its skyline and its industry, but if you lived in Pittsburgh or were simply among the other 80 million or so Americans who seemed to call it home, you were certain about four matters.

The Allegheny and Monongahela would meet to form the Ohio. A parade would clog the Boulevard of the Allies on every obscure holiday. The most memorable moment in baseball history had occurred in Oakland — Pittsburgh's Oakland.

And Chuck Noll would coach the Steelers.

Washington, D.C. had its presidents, Los Angeles had its movie stars, San Diego had its weather, but Pittsburgh had Chuck Noll. He brought the city four Super Bowl titles, a pro football revolution that altered the town's image. Nothing mattered more to Pittsburghers than their image. Before Noll, that image nestled somewhere between Cleveland and Birmingham — dirty town, dirty rivers, dirty air, dirty people. At least Cleveland and Birmingham had great football teams. Pittsburgh had the losingest franchise in the NFL.

Noll helped change all that. As he built the Steelers into a pro football dynasty in the 1970s, the national spotlight peeled away Pittsburgh's filthy reputation and discovered a jewel. Much of America, while watching Noll's Steelers, learned the truth about Pittsburgh — its air was clean, its rivers were getting cleaner, its skyline was spectacular, and its people were warm, friendly, and capable of much more than forging steel.

Then, the old ways returned, not to the city, but to its football team. The stars faded, the losses mounted, the playoffs became only a memory. But because of Chuck Noll there was always hope. He would bring them back, pull them out of the inevitable down cycle all championship teams must experience. As he seemed about to do just that, to coax the Steelers back toward the top, he somehow boxed himself into a corner and escaped the only honorable way. He retired.

There would never be another Chuck Noll. Never. Then, along came Bill Cowher, a native son, 34 years old when he was hired to coach the Pittsburgh Steelers on January 21, 1992. A kid, for crying out loud. A naive one, too. He informed skeptical reporters at his introductory press conference that the Steelers had a "wealth of talent" and they had "no glaring weaknesses."

He did not stop there.

"Our goal this year," he later dumbfounded witnesses, "is to put a fifth trophy in the case outside in the hall."

It was a good thing he did not say those things at a banquet. People might have choked. Chuck Noll, who was elected to the Pro Football Hall of Fame 11 months after he retired, helped put those four Lombardi Trophies in the Steelers' foyer. He ranks fifth in victories among coaches in NFL history, yet he had managed to get the Steelers in the playoffs only once in the previous seven seasons.

Now here is young Bill Cowher in his first days on the job, and he says the immediate goal is a Super Bowl title? How ludicrous, how unrealistic, how gutsy, how . . . how . . . how . . . interesting. Why *not?* Noll said similar things in his first year. "Losing," Noll declared, "has nothing to do with geography."

Cowher burst back into Pittsburgh the way author James Parton in 1868 described the city — "Hell with the lid taken off." Cowher lit a fire under everyone — fans, players, team executives. He captivated them, converted them, made them believers. Why shouldn't they try to win the Super Bowl? What were they in this for, anyway?

"I've heard people say to me, here's a guy putting a lot of pressure on himself, setting such high goals," Cowher said. "I don't think that's pressure. Isn't that the goal of every National

Football League team? If your goal is to just have a winning season or win your division, and you lose after that, then what do you say? We've accomplished our goal and we're satisfied with losing? I've never believed that you should ever set a goal for failure.

"So I kind of wondered why people would say I put pressure on myself when, in essence, my expectations are that."

They called that Cowher Power, and it brought the city of Pittsburgh to its feet in 1992. The slumbering Steeler Nation had reawakened and roared in anticipation. All around the city, Hollywood producers made movies in droves while the real drama went on in Three Rivers Stadium. In fact, actor Danny Aiello, in town to film a picture, walked into the Steelers locker room after a victory and was treated like any other big star without permission to be there — equipment manager Tony Parisi tossed him out on his ear. "Who was that guy, anyway?" Parisi asked.

That is what they said when Bill Cowher first arrived, but it was the same question asked of the new coach 23 years earlier, too. "Chuck who?" Neither was asked to leave. But only his immediate family knew that on the very day Bill Cowher was introduced to the people of Pittsburgh, he had a panic attack that caused him to wonder why he ever took the job.

Nothing came easy that first year, from the time he plowed his 1992 Chrysler New Yorker into the back of another car on Route 30 on his way to open training camp, to the near blowup between his two quarterbacks at the end of the season. Cowher was challenged by Pro Bowl linebacker Greg Lloyd before they ever hit training camp. He managed to ease that problem and defuse two other powder-kegs involving Barry Foster and Hardy Nickerson.

The team overcame the bitterness that surfaced when starting veterans Louis Lipps and Thomas Everett were forced out because of contract demands and cheered Cowher's decision to cut unworthy but highly paid No. 1 draft pick Huey Richardson. The subject of money persistently hovered in the locker room because, for the third time in four years, Pittsburgh was the lowest-paying team in the National Football League, according to union figures, and because free agency was on the doorstep.

The Pittsburgh Steelers helped teammates get through family emergencies in 1992 — the death of Rod Woodson's father in the spring, a heart attack suffered by the father of John Jackson, the debilitating stroke that struck down quarterback Neil O'Donnell's father on the eve of the first exhibition game, and the severe damage to David Little's home in Florida by Hurricane Andrew in August.

The Steelers were troubled again by a drug suspension, their third in two seasons. Jackson and Dermontti Dawson were devastated to learn their agent had ripped them off for hundreds of thousands of dollars.

The Steelers inevitably drew comparisons to the Super Bowl teams of the 1970s, even as they tried to carve their own identity. And four players who helped form the core of the team and its future — Woodson, O'Donnell, Foster and Lloyd — demonstrated how their family circumstances continued to affect their drive on and off the field.

While all this went on, Pittsburgh's two daily newspapers did not. They were idled by a strike on May 17 and did not resume publication for the entire '92 season. Bill Cowher admitted the blackout helped his football team, turning a normal honeymoon period for a new coach into a unique opportunity. Instead of having to deal with reactions to stories — both positive ones and negative — Cowher saw potential problems quickly dry up and disappear. Distractions became less distracting.

"No question it allowed us to take this one week at a time," Cowher said. "Based on the success we were having, you could get caught up in reading how good you were, get caught up in feeling a sense of accomplishment. We didn't experience that.

"From another standpoint, when we were 3-2, there would have been a sense of 'Here's what's wrong with your team,' and now you get caught up with maybe getting too low. We talked about not getting too high or too low. Without a paper, we were able to do that. I think it's been a big plus for us."

The newspaper blackout did not end until January 18, 1993 By then, the *Pittsburgh Press* had died, bought and closed by its smaller competitor, the *Pittsburgh Post-Gazette* in an upset more stunning than the Steelers' turnaround in 1992.

The new era of the Steelers actually began several years before Chuck Noll retired. It started when Dan Rooney, the team's president, fired his younger brother Art as the long-time head of the Steelers' scouting department in October of 1986, marking the end of a long period of front-office stability. "I was told that I was a little bit too large" in the organization, Artie said.

The transfer in power from Noll to Cowher dramatically changed the Pittsburgh Steelers. But more changes had been evolving behind the scenes for several years, and they could eventually transform the franchise.

Before Cowher ever became coach, plans were being made to possibly transfer ownership from the five Rooney brothers and Jack McGinley to Dan Rooney and/or his son, Art Rooney II, with possible corporate ownership involved.

Art Rooney II is the eldest grandson of the team's late founder, Art Rooney, Sr. He could well be the next president of the Steelers, and his uncles would gladly see him take on that job. But they wished he had taken another job when he had the chance — that of United States Senator, which could have put him on a track to the White House.

During the late '80s and early 1990s, the Steelers went through more changes in the front office than they had in the previous 15 seasons. They employed four different controllers in seven years. Dick Haley, the long-time director of player personnel, was promoted to replace Art Rooney Jr. as head of the entire personnel and scouting department in 1987. Haley then left early in 1992 for the same position with the New York Jets.

Tom Donahoe, a high school coach in 1984, rose from scout to the most powerful man in the organization without the Rooney surname. He became the director of football operations in '92—in essence the team's general manager, which is a title Rooney detests and vowed never to issue. For two decades, the Steelers' management team consisted mainly of Rooney and Noll.

Rooney, who prides himself on being a "football man," was the unnamed general manager of the ball club and Noll was its unnamed director of football operations. Now it was Rooney, Donahoe, and Cowher, with a younger Rooney on the horizon.

Much of the scouting and personnel staff has changed during the past several years, with Tom Modrak moving from pro personnel director to college scouting coordinator to director of scouting. Charles Bailey was promoted from scout to pro personnel coordinator. Joe Gordon, for nearly 20 years the team's public relations director, moved higher into the organization but seemed to have a new title every other month. His most recent is director of communications.

For all their changes, however, the Pittsburgh Steelers remain a family-run business, one of the most stable and respectable in a league which itself is undergoing upheaval. Dan Rooney became intimately involved in trying to manage the league's emergence into its new era. He was the central figure for management in forging a new agreement with the NFL players, ending 5 1/2 years without a collective bargaining agreement in the league.

The trick now is for the Steelers to remain competitive — even win more Super Bowls — as a small-market team in the new era of NFL free agency.

"There are some interesting years coming up here," Art Rooney II said.

The spring of 1993 turned interesting quickly for the Steelers when, barely one month into the NFL's new free agency, they faced several momentous decisions on personnel. They had to decide whether quarterback Neil O'Donnell would sign as a free agent with Tampa Bay or to match his offer worth a whopping $8.2 million over three years (they matched). They lost two starting linebackers—Hardy Nickerson and Jerrol Williams—to free agency, but added pass-rushing linebacker Kevin Greene of the Los Angeles Rams.

Bill Cowher's rookie season as head coach certainly provided a boost of optimism for the future. His style as well as his results energized a franchise and its fans. Pittsburgh, favored only to be out of the race by Halloween, ran away with its first American Football Conference Central Division title in eight years with an 11-5 record. It was the Steelers' best record since 1979, when they went on to win their fourth Super Bowl. The excitement that built before the Steelers' first home playoff game in 10 years was something once taken for granted. It had been too long.

Cowher knew what it was like to be a fan, knew what it was like to lose. He had held his father's hand while walking up Cardiac Hill in the 1960s to watch John Henry Johnson toil for the Steelers in Pitt Stadium. He had seen them make their debut in Three Rivers Stadium in 1970. He had sat next to a young Terry Bradshaw at a Crafton midget banquet and peppered him with questions. Jut-jawed Bill Cowher was one of them.

"The biggest (satisfaction) I had was to see the way this city reacted," said Cowher. "To see the excitement that's generated by playing home playoff games — that's why we're in this business. To go through something like that is kind of the motivating force to get us back."

The Mon and the Allegheny still churn into the Ohio River, the parades steadily march down the boulevard and Bill Mazeroski, who hit the home run to deliver the 1960 World Series victory to Pittsburgh, still owns the town. Chuck Noll doesn't coach the Pittsburgh Steelers anymore, but he's in the Hall of Fame.

And the new guy looks as if he knows his way around.

2

THE EMPEROR HAS NO PLAYERS

Chuck Noll outlasted the Berlin Wall by two years. How perfect. Both German, both seemingly impenetrable, the wall and the "emperor" each stood strong for a generation, portraying contrasting ideologies. Noll was the arch-conservative coach of the Pittsburgh Steelers. His concept of a great president is Richard Nixon.

Noll, like Nixon, rose to power in 1969. He erected four Super Bowl champions in Pittsburgh, the certified birthplace of pro football in 1892, but host to the least successful franchise in history before Noll arrived. Before Noll, the Steelers were clods in black and yellow, bruising and amusing. A decade into Noll's tenure, they were the Steel Curtain, the black and *gold*, the Team of the '70s, and the best thing that happened to Pittsburgh since steel.

He was known as the Pope, the Emperor, all knowing, all seeing, omnipotent. He said "jump" and not only the Steelers, but all of Pittsburgh asked, "Off which bridge?" Noll was a rock in Pittsburgh. While sports figures came and went in the city, there was always Noll, an unflappable link not only to the town's glories of the '70s but what it hoped would be a football renaissance in the '80s and '90s.

Now, nearly two years to the day after thousands poured freely through Berlin's Bradenburg Gate, two years after he was proclaimed American Football Conference Coach of the Year, Noll was crumbling in Pittsburgh.

The day after Christmas, 1991, was a day many thought would never come. Noll was Coach for Life, one of few men who could name his price and his duration, as few other contemporaries could — such as his friend, Don Shula, and Joe Paterno, who turned down the Steelers before they turned to Noll in '69.

He was the subject of respect and contempt in Pittsburgh in the '80s and early '90s. Revered for bringing those four gleaming Lombardi Trophies to Pittsburgh, Noll was knocked for allowing the game to pass him by as playoff appearances eluded him in the '80s. By Christmas of '91, the Steelers had not made the playoffs in six of the seven previous seasons, had not won their division championship in eight years, had not been to a Super Bowl in a dozen years. Chuck Noll's record since his team won its fourth Super Bowl, on January 20, 1980, was 95-95. His record from 1985 through '91 was 52-61.

Any other coach with that docket would have been shown the exit ramp at Three Rivers Stadium. Noll wasn't any other coach. He remains the only one to have won four Super Bowls, and that achievement more than carried him through the down times, as it should have.

New York Giants general manager George Young coached with Noll in Baltimore and is one of his closest friends in the NFL. He believed that Noll was in a no-win situation in the 1980s, that his teams achieved so much success in the '70s, it was impossible to satisfy the Pittsburgh fans thereafter.

"Chuck was fighting his own legend every Sunday," Young said.

Noll's situation reminded Young, a former high school history teacher, of the political fall from grace of two great 19th-century English soldiers.

"The Duke of Marlborough and the Duke of Wellington, they ran them out. Hell, they even voted Churchill out of office before the war was over. The same things happen to football coaches. When they become legends and they can't produce, they fall farther. People who climb the highest heights have the longest to slip."

Now it was the day after Christmas of '91 and Chuck Noll had tired of the fight. He came to a decision on his 23-year career with the Steelers voluntarily, as voluntarily as a man can when asked to choose between his job and his honor, his pride, his friends. It was the second time in four years he confronted this dilemma, and he chose a different course this time.

Chuck Noll did not want it to end. He proclaimed as much one week earlier when he said he still had the desire to coach. Yet there was no way out for him other than the one he was about to take as he strode into Dan Rooney's office on December 26, 1991.

What brought Noll to that brief but historic meeting was not merely his team's poor showing in the previous seven seasons. Part of it was an approaching loss of autonomy over the Steelers football operation; most of it, however, could be traced to one abrupt decision he made when he was on top of the football world two years earlier. He hired an assistant coach after the euphoria of the 1989 playoff season, outwardly just another perfunctory personnel move by a head coach. But the decision to hire Joe Walton ultimately brought an end to one of the most successful coaching reigns in NFL history.

Marianne Noll tells the story of the time she and her husband went house hunting in 1969 shortly after their arrival in Pittsburgh. "The first house we looked at, we bought," she said. That same house, across the street from an elementary school in suburban Upper St. Clair, served as the Nolls's home for 24 years, expanded through several improvements.

Noll made a quick, emphatic decision on his house in '69, stuck with it, and shaped it to his liking. Too often, he hired assistant coaches in a similar manner, and he came to regret it.

Early on, hiring assistants was a snap. He was 37 years old in 1969 and had been a player and assistant coach in pro football for 16 years. He knew the men he was hiring, had been one of them. And when he got a bad one, he was quick to dispose of him. Not one member of Noll's original staff in 1969 was with him for the Steelers' first Super Bowl season in 1974.

In the 1970s, when he needed a coach, he leaned on his top lieutenants to help find one. Once he became a head coach, Noll got out of the loop. He wasn't one to gossip on the phone to others around the league as many coaches do. He focused on his team, and as a result, fell out of touch with the top young assistants around the NFL. He often allowed other assistants such as George Perles and Woody Widenhofer to hand pick new coaches. That worked for a while. But it turned disastrous in the 1980s.

Inevitably, the string ran out for the Steelers, and just when Noll needed the help of men like Widenhofer, Perles, and Rollie Dotsch, they moved on to head coaching positions either in the USFL or college. The players who fueled one of pro football's greatest dynasties grew old, and the Steelers did a poor job of replacing them. Much of the blame falls on the scouting staff and Noll, who had the final say on draft choices.

They produced two of the greatest drafts in NFL history three years apart, in 1971 and 1974. Their early drafts under Noll and scouting head Art Rooney Jr. became a preview of the Pro Football Hall of Fame: Joe Greene, Terry Bradshaw, Jack Ham, Franco Harris, Jack Lambert, Mel Blount, and others, such as Lynn Swann, Mike Webster, Mike Wagner, John Stallworth, L. C. Greenwood, Dwight White, Jon Kolb, etc.

The brilliance of their early '70s drafts dimmed in mid-decade, and as the early '90s wore on, the Steelers still hadn't lived down their inability to restock through the draft. Suddenly, as if flipping a switch, the system that produced such great players turned out flops. They drafted Greg Hawthorne and Sidney Thornton, Willie Fry and Zack Valentine, Bob Barber and Keith Gary, Walter Abercrombie and John Meyer, and a lot of other guys who couldn't help them.

Compounding the problem was Noll's stubbornness. He refused to look into other areas to restock his team, and his fondness for his aging superstars kept them around too long. Belying his public image, Noll was not as much a brutally cold decision maker as he was an old softy. He could not bring himself to dump the players who delivered four Super Bowls to his doorstep in order to make room for the young blood he needed to keep his team near the top.

"You get attached to guys and there's a loyalty," said Tom Donahoe, the Steelers' director of football operations. "You just hope, like with an L. C. Greenwood or Dwight White, 'Maybe I can squeeze one more year out of this guy. He's been so great for the team, the city; I just can't cut him.'

"Put yourself in his shoes. Could you do it? Could you imagine the feelings that you would have? Here's a guy who helped get us to the pinnacle of the National Football League, a record that probably would never be duplicated. Now, you have to sit down and tell the guy, 'You can't play anymore; we're cutting you.' It's tough."

Other coaching greats, faced with similar dilemmas, chose not to do it, either. Instead of waiving their old stars, they waved good-bye themselves. Vince Lombardi fled Green Bay after the 1967 season and coached the Washington Redskins in 1969. Shula left the Baltimore Colts in 1970 for Miami.

"In the coaching business," said Young, "as you get older many people think you get dumber, especially if you're a great coach. Every Sunday, a great coach has to fight his own myth. Lombardi is a great example of that when he realized he couldn't keep his legend going and he bailed out."

Noll was still riding the Super Bowl wave when he first made some critical personnel decisions that would hurt his team's future.

The example often cited was that of defensive end Dwaine Board, another nugget Steelers scouts dug out of a small, black school, this time from North Carolina A & T on the fifth round in 1979. Board tore up training camp that summer and assistant coaches pleaded with Noll to keep him on the roster. But Noll refused to make room by cutting an older player, such as Dwight White. He waived Board, who was claimed by San Francisco, where he became a starter on two Super Bowl champions.

Other young talent was similarly wasted. Defensive back Dave Brown, the team's No. 1 draft choice in 1975, was left unprotected in the 1976 expansion draft. The new Seattle Seahawks plucked him off their roster. Fourteen years later Brown retired with 62 interceptions, fifth most in NFL history. There were others, like tight ends Walter White in 1975 and Brent Jones in 1986 during a period in which the Steelers desperately needed a tight end. Both were cut and never played in Pittsburgh. Jones, like Board, went to San Francisco, where he earned two Super Bowl rings and developed into one of the best tight ends in the NFL.

The Steelers also had incredibly bad luck. Not only did they join most of the NFL in making the monumental error of skipping over Dan Marino in 1983, the man they did select became a paraplegic six months later. Defensive tackle Gabe Rivera was playing well as a rookie when an October auto accident put him in a wheelchair for life. Another good player, tight end Chris Kolodziejski, injured his knee in 1984, and while it was healing, he slipped on ice in front of a supermarket, tearing it beyond help.

Also, when the United States Football League folded in 1986, Noll did not seriously consider signing any of its players for the Steelers. He firmly believed that the USFL, its players, its coaches, its scouts, its secretaries, and equipment managers were all traitors to the National Football League. He held a grudge against them. When the league folded, he celebrated openly, even showing no sympathy for those in his own profession thrown out of work.

"Don't give me hearts and flowers bullshit," he said in the summer of 1986 as the USFL died. "You can get hearts and flowers bullshit about everything in life if you want to. But the hard-fact rule is you have to survive as an individual. There's a rite of survival. If you want to feel sorry for someone else, *you* die. Go ahead, I'll let you do that. I have a little stronger survival instinct."

The bad luck, bad drafts, and bad personnel decisions caught up with Noll's Steelers in the 1980s. They lurched to and fro in the first half of the decade, like a great boxer on his last legs, occasionally getting off a dangerous hook. The Steelers slipped out of the playoffs after their final Super Bowl victory to consecutive seasons of 9-7 and 8-8 in '80 and '81.

Cleveland safety Clarence Scott smugly declared in 1980, "The Curtain . . . turned to draperies," after the hated Browns had savaged them.

The Steelers actually were rejuvenated in strike-abbreviated 1982, but a poor pass thrown by Terry Bradshaw late in the first playoff game at home led to a 14-point San Diego rally in the final nine minutes and a 31-28 Charger victory. Pittsburgh continued to play well in 1983, winning nine of its first 11 games as Cliff Stoudt replaced the injured Bradshaw at quarterback. But Stoudt self-destructed in the final third of the season. The Steelers needed a heroic effort off the bench by the sore-armed Bradshaw in what would be his final NFL appearance to beat the New York Jets and get into the playoffs, but they and Stoudt were rubbed out by the Los Angeles Raiders, 38-10 in the opening round.

By 1984, little was expected of the Steelers. Nearly all their stars from the 1970s had faded or retired. Important players such as Stoudt, Jim Smith, Ray Pinney, and Tyronne McGriff bolted to the USFL. Franco Harris held out of training camp and Dan Rooney shocked all of Pittsburgh by waiving him. Jack Lambert injured his toe that season and was finished. Mel Blount retired before the season. John Stallworth, Mike Webster, and Donnie Shell remained, the last of the four Super Bowl participants. There were not one, but two new quarterbacks in the lineup, David Woodley and Mark Malone.

It was time for Chuck Noll to rebuild, but one last blast caught everyone by surprise and postponed the much-needed rebuilding. The Steelers administered the only defeat San Francisco suffered in 1984. They won the AFC Central Division title with a 9-7 record and stunned Denver in the playoffs, 24-17, to reach the AFC Championship Game against Miami.

The Steelers were one game from their fifth Super Bowl visit. But Dan Marino made Noll and the Steelers pay for their decision in the draft a year earlier. He passed for 421 yards and four touchdowns and led the Miami Dolphins to a 45-28 victory over his hometown team.

Nevertheless, it appeared that the Steelers had reloaded for a new era of winning. Steeler fans dusted off their "One for the Thumb" bumper stickers. But 1984 was a mirage. The talent was not there and the Steelers were about to enter their darkest period of Noll's regime. The first half of the decade had actually reaffirmed Noll's coaching ability, although at the time he got no credit for it. He took teams of aging veterans and limited talent and seemingly through sheer determination kept them bobbing to the top, actually taking them to the playoffs three straight years.

That all ended in 1985. By then, Noll's great coaching staff of the 1970s was depleted. The USFL gutted Noll's staff, stealing Perles and Dotsch in 1982 and Widenhofer after the '83 season. Noll filled their jobs with others, some good, some bad. And it was primarily those hirings, combined with a stretch of mediocrity on the field, that would lead to his first showdown with Dan Rooney, the Steelers' president, part owner, and son of the revered founder of the ball club, Art Rooney.

The ride was over, extended by the playoff teases of 1982-84. Few could keep a team on top that long. Noll had coached four Super Bowl winners and had worked more magic in the early '80s.

"You stick around long enough," Perles said, "you go through cycles."

It was time for Pittsburgh's down cycle. The Steelers went 7-9 in 1985, their first losing season since 1971. They went 6-10 in 1986, their worst season since 1969. These were the days of Walter Abercrombie running wide and never turning the corner, of cornerback Harvey Clayton hopelessly chasing receivers, of David Woodley's mysterious retirement, of no passes to the tight ends, of a man driving his car up, up through the ramps at Three Rivers Stadium, crashing into a gate and then blaming it all on Mark Malone's play at quarterback.

The gold had turned a dull yellow again.

After the 1986 season, Dan Rooney fired his brother, Art Jr. as head of the team's personnel department. The drafts since 1975 were horrible, but that was not why the brothers became estranged. Dan Rooney believed that Art operated the scouting department as an island, apart from the organization. He said he wanted to improve communications among all departments, particularly between the scouts and Noll. So the man who oversaw some of the greatest drafts any team had in the history of pro football was fired by his brother.

And the bleeding did not stop, and the communications did not improve, and the drafts did not get better.

The Steelers wobbled to 8-7 in the 1987 strike season, then bottomed out at 5-11 in 1988. It was Noll's worst season since his first in Pittsburgh, and by the end of it he grappled with one of the most difficult decisions in his 20 seasons with the ball club.

Dan Rooney had seen enough. Rooney ranks among the most powerful, friendly, and open owners in the NFL. He rarely criticized Noll in public, or anyone else, for that matter. So it came as a shock when he knocked Noll and his staff to a reporter following a loss to Cleveland in 1988. He blasted the coaches for calling "stupid plays."

"This," said Rooney, "may sound like I'm putting a little extra pressure on the coaching staff, but you can bring in talent and they just don't develop. Now, whose fault is that?"

It was the first solid evidence that Rooney was unhappy with Noll. As losses continued to mount, Rooney turned his anger into a plan of action. By the end of the season, it became obvious he would make changes, but would they include the Big One — firing Noll?

"We were headed in a direction that was bad," Rooney says today. "I thought there were some real difficult situations here that had to be changed. I don't try to get in and coach the team, but there are things that if I think there's a problem, I'm going to step in."

On August 25, 1988, "The Chief, "Art Rooney Sr. died from a stroke he had suffered days earlier. The Chief had turned the operation of his club over to Dan, his eldest son, in the 1960s and given him the title of president in 1975. But right until the day he had his stroke in his office at Three Rivers Stadium, the father served as counsel to the son. The Chief had given his sad endorsement when Dan fired Art Jr. in '86. He had been there for the wrenching strike of '87.

But Dan would have to go it alone on this one. He sought advice from two of the men closest to him — Joe Gordon, who rose from publicity director to director of communications and business, and Dan's eldest son, Art II, a prominent Pittsburgh lawyer, the team's counsel, and Dan's heir apparent as head of the Steelers.

"At the end of the season," Rooney said, "we have to evaluate everything we're doing."

It took only three days after the Steelers concluded their worst season in 19 years for Rooney to inform Noll of his evaluation. Noll and Dan Rooney held a meeting in the Steelers' offices at Three Rivers Stadium on December 21, 1988.

"We've got problems," Rooney told him.

Noll agreed, and they discussed them. Rooney wanted him to make changes to his staff; in particular, Rooney wanted Noll to fire some coaches, including Jed Hughes, the linebackers coach.

Hughes was a favorite of Noll's. He had gotten Noll's ear and, to the chagrin of others, bypassed defensive coordinator Tony Dungy and went directly to Noll with many of his ideas for the defense. Noll became visibly upset anytime anyone knocked Jed Hughes, but the front office had grown weary of Hughes, and Rooney was adamant. He wanted him out.

They discussed the situation further. Finally, Noll said, "Well, I can't do that."

But it wasn't until he traipsed back down the hall, past the four Super Bowl trophies in the lobby, and reached the coaches' offices that his anger showed.

Noll was given complete control over the football operation by Rooney and his father when they hired him. He had the final say on draft picks, trades, and anything else involving his football team. Never had Rooney told him what coaches to hire or fire. Not until December 21, 1988, that is.

It had to stun Noll that after 20 seasons of unquestioned authority he was being ordered to make changes on his staff for the first time.

Noll turned to several coaches and said, "They want me to fire some guys." A few blanched, realizing it might be them. Noll told them he would quit first.

Noll's two senior assistants, Dick Hoak and Tom Moore, quickly offered to tender their resignations in order to save Noll. "No," he told them, "you're not the ones they want."

A cloud hung over the staff. Will McDonough of CBS-TV and the *Boston Globe* reported on Christmas Day, 1988, that Noll would resign.

3

NOLL'S LAST HURRAH

Before Noll could resign rather than being forced to fire two of his coaches, Joe Greene walked into the owner's office.

Greene was Noll's first draft choice in 1969, a man of great size and heart who played a ferocious defensive tackle during the Super Bowl era and was swept into the Pro Football Hall of Fame in the first year of his eligibility.

After his retirement from the Steelers in 1982, Greene tried the restaurant business back home in Dallas. When it failed, he expressed an interest in coaching, and Noll leapt at the chance to give him his first job in the business. Greene became the Steelers' defensive line coach on February 19, 1987.

Now, less than two years later, he was about to play an unexpected role in extending the career of the man who had drafted him first, gave him his first job in coaching, and introduced him at his Hall of Fame induction ceremony in Canton. Greene asked Rooney what was going on, that Noll had informed his coaches he would resign.

Rooney, struck by the abruptness of it, asked Noll to meet with him again. They talked and Rooney told his coach: "Think about this over Christmas. Come back then and we'll discuss it, because it's too important a thing for the organization, for everybody."

On December 26, Noll and Rooney again gathered in the Steelers' offices. They talked about the future. Rooney assured Noll that he wanted him to stay, but changes in his staff were necessary. Rooney offered to fire the coaches if Noll did not want to.

Rooney insisted on some basic changes, but was willing to discuss compromises. Noll finally agreed to rearrange his staff, and saved a job or two in the process. He strongly believed he had a team on the verge of a new era of winning. What would quitting at this point solve? Instead of costing several coaches their jobs, his entire staff would be out on the street and he would forever be known as the four-time Super Bowl coach whose career ended on a sour, 5-11 note. He still had something to prove in Pittsburgh.

"Yeah, I guess I did come pretty close," Noll admitted a few year after his near-resignation. "I enjoy coaching, and I want to coach for a while yet, that's all."

The Steelers called a news conference for the morning of January 3.

Typically, Noll had not informed his coaches of what was to come. He detested that part of the job, which is why he rarely told players when they were cut, relegating the duty to others. It hurt him too much.

So his coaches learned of their fates the previous night from a reporter. Special teams coach Dennis Fitzgerald refused to believe it and accused the writer of making it up. But in the next morning's *Pittsburgh Post-Gazette*, the news of the dismissals broke.

Belatedly, Noll informed the coaches of his decision right before the news conference. There, Noll announced that Hughes, Fitzgerald, offensive line coach Hal Hunter, and strength coach Walt Evans would not return for 1989, and that Tony Dungy had resigned. Dungy, at 33, was the NFL's youngest coordinator and one of the highest-ranking black coaches in the league. Just two years earlier, he had been a candidate to become the NFL's first black head coach when the Philadelphia Eagles interviewed him for a job that Buddy Ryan eventually got.

Dungy was one of the league's brightest young coaches. He made the Steelers as a rookie free agent safety in 1977 and led them with six interceptions during their third Super Bowl season of 1978. Noll hired him in 1981 to coach the secondary and elevated him to defensive coordinator in 1983, when he was only 27.

But Noll had allowed linebackers coach Jed Hughes to usurp Dungy's authority over the defense. Hughes, an energetic coach, went over Dungy and directly to Noll with his suggestions on defense. Hughes, for example, convinced Noll that defensive end Aaron Jones, the Steelers' top draft pick in 1988, should play linebacker with the Steelers. Jones, who played at Division 1-AA Eastern Kentucky, was overwhelmed by the move and it set him back immeasurably.

Noll encouraged Hughes and, as a result, Dungy's voice on defense was compromised. Asked to take a demotion during the '88 purge, Dungy correctly surmised he had little to lose by resigning. He became the secondary coach under Marty Schottenheimer's new regime in Kansas City, where another young man had just been elevated to defensive coordinator of the Chiefs — 31-year-old Bill Cowher. Dungy then rose to defensive coordinator again in 1992 under Dennis Green with the Minnesota Vikings.

Tucked into the epic black-and-gold press release announcing the firings were two other items: Not only would Chuck Noll return for the 1989 season, he would also remain with the Steelers the rest of his career. What did that mean? Neither Rooney nor Noll was forthcoming at the time.

It did not mean he would remain coach forever. Many read into it that Noll would become general manager when his coaching days ended. Those who believed that did not know Chuck Noll.

"I'm not a packager," he said. "I'm a product man. To me, the most important thing is the product. The presentation is important in this business, the packaging is important. But that's not my thing. I'm the engineer."

No, Noll would remain with the Steelers the rest of his career because, in exchange for agreeing to the reforms, Rooney gave Noll two enticements:

1) A new, three-year coaching contract at slightly more than $700,000 annually that would extend through the 1991 season, and

2) Provided he remained coach for the next three years, Noll would receive, upon his retirement, a $1 million bonus spread over 10 years.

It was Dan Rooney's way of saying thank you.

The other crucial announcement that day: East Coast scout Tom Donahoe was elevated to director of pro personnel and development. The pro personnel part was easy to understand, but the development? Donahoe, a Pittsburgh native, was about to embark on a strange journey no man had taken since Noll became coach in 1969. Not only was Donahoe to supervise the scouting of pro players and other teams in the league, he was also to scout the Steelers and "advise" Noll and his staff. It was the first time Noll had such an adviser.

Rooney gave Donahoe one more important duty. He was to assist Noll in hiring his coaches, another first.

The word spread through the same NFL grapevine that Chuck Noll disdained: Noll sold out his coaches to save his neck. Never mind that it was not true, the image was tarnished.

His absoluteness as a leader began to erode, at least in the minds of others.

Donahoe fervently approached the task of finding the new assistants. He compiled a list with Noll, then arranged interviews between the candidates and the head coach.

The top candidate to become linebackers coach was Dave Wannstedt, a Pittsburgh native and Pitt graduate who was defensive coordinator at the University of Miami. During the interview, Noll asked Wannstedt if he could give him the name of anyone in the NFL as a reference, someone who knew his work.

Wannstedt told him to call Don Shula of the Miami Dolphins. Noll and Shula were close friends. Their wives talked often, and when Dorothy Shula died of breast cancer in 1991, Chuck and Marianne Noll took it hard. When Shula was the head coach of the Baltimore Colts, he recommended his assistant, Noll, for the Steelers coaching job in 1969.

So Noll was more than happy to call Shula about Wannstedt. After the two friends and head coaches talked, Shula himself contacted Wannstedt. Shortly thereafter, Wannstedt accepted the job as the linebackers coach of the Miami Dolphins before Noll could offer him the same job in Pittsburgh. If Noll felt betrayed by his good buddy in Miami, he never let on.

Another team's shake-up provided more coaching candidates. Rod Rust was the Kansas City Chiefs defensive coordinator when Frank Gansz was fired as head coach after the 1988 season. Some of the Chiefs' assistants were technically kept on the staff, but they all received permission from the team to seek other jobs.

Donahoe wanted Noll to interview Rust. Noll said he could not, because Rust was still employed by the Chiefs. Donahoe explained the situation to him, and Noll agreed to talk to Rust. The interview was arranged for the week of the Senior Bowl in Mobile, Alabama. But again Noll balked. He is under contract with the Chiefs, Noll told Donahoe. Finally, Donahoe convinced Noll that everything was on the up-and-up. The interview went off, and Noll hired Rust as his new defensive coordinator.

Noll also agreed to let Rust bring Dave Brazil with him from Kansas City as his linebackers coach. The rest of the coaching staff was filled out, and the Steelers entered 1989 with a renewed spirit, hoping to put the unpleasantness of 1988 behind them.

"Potentially," Noll said in August of 1989, "we have a good football team."

Yeah, but he had a potential disaster on his hands when that team opened the season by getting thumped 51-0 at home by Cleveland. Cincinnati followed by snuffing the Steelers 41-10. The count read Opponents 92, Steelers 10, after two games. Combined with 1988, that left Noll's teams 5-13 over the past two seasons, and a flock of vultures circled above Three Rivers Stadium.

Dan Rooney called a meeting with Noll in his office on September 28. He was joined by his eldest son, Art Rooney II, and Joe Gordon, the Steelers' director of communications and business at the time.

The town was in an uproar. Writers suggested it was time for Noll to exit. Instead of a pink slip, Rooney gave Noll a pep talk.

"Hey," Rooney told Noll, "let's not be influenced about what's happening around us."

Thought Noll: "I don't need a pep talk."

"The people who were in on that meeting," Noll said later, "get the vibes of the city probably more than I do. I may be oblivious to some of the goings-on . . . they thought I was being affected, I guess. I've got thick skin. Maybe I'm not as sensitive."

The crisis passed when the Steelers, one-touchdown under-dogs, went out and upset the Minnesota Vikings at home, 27-14, to begin a modest two-game winning streak. But by Thanksgiving, they had slipped to 4-6, and attacks on Noll came from another front.

"The players don't like being around the stadium," former Steelers running back Rich Erenberg said on the Steelers' pre-game TV show, of all places. "They're kind of miserable. It's a miserable atmosphere. The assistant coaches don't like (Noll), the players don't like him, and he's not a very good motivator.

"I would get rid of the coach . . . put somebody else in there . . . who can create an atmosphere so the players want to win."

Other former players had criticized Noll, including Terry Bradshaw and Rocky Bleier. But Bradshaw had a personal vendetta against Noll that dragged on for years. Bleier's comments came at a small gathering in the Mon Valley, and they were picked up by a local paper. But they were not as cutting. Erenberg's blast was different, though. It was a serious raking from a recent player who still knew the territory, an attack using unnamed assistant coaches and players as the weapon. But, again, Noll and the Steelers turned things around in dramatic fashion. They reacted to Erenberg's criticism by winning five of the final six games of the season to make the playoffs, magically, as a 9-7 wild card team.

The accolades then poured in for Noll.

"To start the season the way he did and come back the way he did, there's got to be greatness in you to do that," former Cleveland Browns executive Ernie Accorsi said. "In my opinion, there has been no better coach in my 20 years in this league."

Noll and the Steelers had another shocker left. They went to the Astrodome for their first playoff game in five years and upset the Houston Oilers, 26-23, on Gary Anderson's 50-yard field goal in overtime.

Their impossible dream of making it back to the AFC Championship game, though, ended in Denver when the Broncos scored a touchdown with 2 1/2 minutes to go and won, 24-23. Otherwise, Pittsburgh would have played in Cleveland the following Sunday for the right to go to its fifth Super Bowl.

Nevertheless, Chuck Noll's Steelers so impressed the entire National Football League with their coming of age in 1989 that they were dubbed the team of the 1990s. It was another religious experience. They had their Immaculate Reception in 1972. Now it was the Resurrection in 1989.

"The 1990s," quarterback Bubby Brister said, "are going to be bright for this team. I can see that."

"Let's play the '90s," Noll cautioned, "and find out."

4

WALTON'S MOUNTAIN: GOODNIGHT, CHUCK

Chuck Noll was riding high again in Pittsburgh. The Pro Football Writers named him Coach of the Year in the American Football Conference, an honor he never received while winning four Super Bowls.

The good times seemed to be on their way back. But at the height of Noll's renewed popularity he would make a hasty, fateful decision that would eventually push him into retirement: He hired Joe Walton and yielded control of his offense to him.

Joe Greene, an eyewitness to Noll's First Reich in the 1970s, had been forecasting another.

"He's had a pretty good run at it," Greene said early in 1990. "He put together a good football team, a *real* good football team that lasted the better part of a decade. And he's in the process of putting together another one. He knows how to do it.

"He's putting together one that's going to be remembered very fondly. Our team is being put together with the fibre that cannot be shaken in one season. It's the same kind of fibre that was put together and won in the '70s."

Noll's fibre displayed itself anew during a press conference in January 1990 after the close playoff loss to Denver ended the season. Instead of serving as a wake for 1989, it was an upbeat affair that focused on the promise of the 1990s.

Near the end, someone asked Noll if all of his coaches would return the following season, and he said they would.

Asked if he had talked to Dan Rooney about it in light of what happened a year earlier, Noll said he had not. Things were much different after the 1989 season than they were after '88.

"I'm the head coach," he assured everyone. "I'm in charge of the coaching staff."

When that comment appeared in the paper the next morning, Art Rooney Jr. circled it in red and mailed it to longtime Steelers scout Bill Nunn with this comment: "The Emperor's back!"

They had seen it before. Noll, vulnerable during down years, re-emphasized his authority during the good ones. Nobody was going to tell Chuck Noll what to do with his coaching staff this time. Dan Rooney did not even try.

But Noll was wrong. All of his coaches did not return. Rod Rust, his defensive coordinator, was hired by the New England Patriots as their head coach. Noll wanted to maintain Rust's defensive system so he elevated David Brazil, Rust's hand-picked linebackers coach, to fill the job.

Now he needed a linebackers coach and he wanted no help in finding one. Without much consultation, he hired Denny Creehan, a Pittsburgh native who had talked previously to Noll about jobs with the Steelers.

The Steelers proudly announced that the hometown kid was leaving his assistant's job at the University of California to join Noll's staff. Problem was, Creehan wasn't an assistant at Cal. The next day, the *Pittsburgh Post-Gazette* reported that Creehan actually had been hired as the head coach at San Francisco State two months earlier, and officials there were surprised and angered that the Steelers had hired him without notice.

Noll had no idea.

"He wrote to me on Cal stationary," a dumbfounded Noll said. He had believed Creehan was still an assistant there. Apparently, references were not checked in this matter. Embarrassed, Rooney talked with the president of San Francisco State and they worked out a deal that day: Creehan would return as head coach of the school's football team, and the Steelers would have nothing more to do with him.

This fiasco emphasized Noll's increasing weakness in hiring assistants. He was more out of the loop than ever. As humiliating an experience as that was, though, it did not hurt Noll. But his hiring of Joe Walton as the team's offensive coordinator would . . . mortally.

Tom Moore had become Noll's first offensive coordinator in 1983, having started as an assistant with Noll in 1977. Moore was loyal to a fault and that is what some in the front office were finding with his offense. It was the same trapping offense, with certain variations, Noll had used in the 1970s. But when Franco Harris, Terry Bradshaw, Lynn Swann, John Stallworth and the rest departed, that offense suddenly became stodgy and unimaginative.

Quarterback Bubby Brister wounded Moore when, at a public meeting in '88, he declared Moore's offense "complicated," a term few others had ever used to describe it.

"Sometimes, I think it's too complicated," Brister complained. "We have so many words just to call the play. And then I call the play and the guys say, 'What the hell are we doing?' We may as well punt on first down and get it over with. I think right now we are almost playing conservative and trying not to make mistakes. You have to be aggressive in this game. You have to go for it."

Moore grabbed Brister after that and they went out for a few beers to discuss the facts of life, the Steelers, and their relationship.

The two became closer, but by February of 1990, Moore had heard enough. He felt he was getting no respect inside the Steelers organization, other than from Noll and some fellow assistants. When his old buddy Jerry Burns offered him the job as his top assistant with the Minnesota Vikings, Moore left.

The announcement of Moore's departure came February 12, 1990. Two days later, Chuck Noll drove to the airport to pick up a passenger from New York, a candidate to replace Moore. Normally, a scouting intern or PR assistant would make the 36-mile roundtrip to the Pittsburgh airport to haul a player or coach to the office. But Noll told no one about this.

Those close to Noll say hiring coaches is the one job he detested, almost as much as he hated firing them. He was not comfortable doing it and did not thoroughly examine their backgrounds or their suitability for the jobs. It was strange, because when it came to drafting college players, Noll immersed himself in it, investigating everything about the players. But with coaches it was like houses, one look was enough.

Some people held the theory that college players were mere numbers to Noll; he could objectively rate them because he did not know them. A coach, on the other hand, was one of his own. He had to talk to him face to face, get to know him. And if Chuck Noll liked him, even if he may not have been a good coach, he had a difficult time saying no to him. That is why many of Noll's assistants were the only ones he interviewed for the job.

So when the latest coaching candidate spent February 14, 1990 with Noll, it was reasonable to assume the job was his if he wanted it. They discussed offensive philosophies and finally, midway through the afternoon, Noll introduced Joe Walton around the office as his new offensive coordinator.

Dan Rooney, Tom Donahoe, Dick Haley, and everyone else were surprised, but they weren't particularly unhappy about it at first. Walton, who just had been fired after seven years as head coach of the New York Jets, was a native of Beaver Falls, Pennsylvania, and a Pitt graduate. He had two years left at $400,000 annually on his Jets contract. The Steelers made him their highest-paid assistant coach at $120,000 a year and the Jets picked up the rest.

"Everybody thought that Joe was a good pick," Rooney said. "Everybody felt, here's a guy who was a head coach. We had really not hired former head coaches before."

The hiring would later be called by some, the St. Valentine's Day Disaster. But at the time, all seemed well.

"I see it as the perfect place for me right now," Walton said.

Dick Hoak had uttered a quiet caution as he left Three Rivers Stadium that day that turned prophetic. He had been the Steelers' best running back in the late '60s and coached the running backs under Noll since 1972. He knew the Steelers' offensive system better than anyone. In fact, he should have been the logical choice as offensive coordinator. He is a good coach and one of the most loyal members of the organization; he even turned down the Pittsburgh Maulers of the USFL when they offered to make him their head coach because he could not do it to The Chief, Art Rooney Sr. Noll had promoted Brazil to defensive coordinator, why not Hoak, as offensive coordinator? But Hoak realized Noll was reaching for something different, he just hoped it wasn't too different.

"We have a good thing going here," Hoak said. "The offense began clicking halfway through the season, we made the playoffs and did pretty well. I just hope we don't dump the whole thing for something else."

Walton ran a sophisticated offense that featured scads of formations, hundreds of plays, and men in motion more often than not. It did everything but shoot lasers and play the music from Star Wars.

On paper, Walton's offense was dazzling. It had an answer for every defensive trick and would make opposing coaches batty trying to formulate a gameplan for it. If the front office did not like Tom Moore's offense, here was its antidote.

A former coach under Noll said, "It was directly opposite what Chuck had always been. It was so atypical of what the Steelers always did. They ran the football, controlled the clock, played great defense and got big plays from the passing game.

"I think Chuck thought, 'Maybe we need to explore something else because that's what they want around here. If that's what you want, that's what we'll give you. If they want a flashy offense, he has it.' We became something altogether different under Walton."

Donahoe noticed a similar motive.

"I think Chuck was a little bit frustrated with the offense. I think he was trying to do something to kind of propel the offense into modern-day football, which maybe was a mistake. He tried to open things up, be a little more creative, more imaginative. As a result, he hired Joe and sort of gave him full handle to do whatever he wanted to do."

Donahoe knew they were in trouble "when I read the playbook." It was jam-packed with so many combinations of plays and formations, it confused many of them. The Steelers' entire terminology was scrapped and Walton's introduced. It was like telling 50 football players and 10 coaches to forget speaking English and learn Japanese — and they had all of several months to be proficient in it.

"We kind of went lock, stock, and barrel into this whole new world," Donahoe said. "And the players didn't respond to it. Ever. Not in the beginning, not in the middle, not in the end."

The offense looked great to Noll on paper. In practice, it was a circus. Players moaned when they were introduced to it during an extended minicamp. But Brister praised the offense that spring.

"It's fun. We do so many good things and it's going to be important for me to get it down pat so we can come out moving the ball, come out pretty hot, because we have the offense to do it now. There's no doubt about it. When we're not pounding the ball and running traps and stuff, we do have a good pass offense now, something that was a little predictable before. Now we'll be all over the place — motion, shifting. We're going to be dictating now. It's going to be fun. Fun!"

Brister's attitude changed quickly once he got elbow deep into the playbook with all its waggles and think-and-dink philosophy. Brister does not hide his emotion, but what he was doing on the practice field at St. Vincent College that summer of '90 was unprecedented for a quarterback and leader of the team.

The offense frustrated and befuddled him. Often, Brister would drop back in the pocket, turn and spike the ball into the ground angrily because something had gone wrong. Other times, he'd fire a pass in disgust far over the snow fence that ringed the practice field.

"There are no geniuses in this game," Brister spouted after another bad day with Walton and the new offense. "But some people think they are."

After a pathetic performance on offense in a 20-9 loss to Dallas in the third exhibition game of the 1990 season, Brister stormed out of the locker room, smashing his forearm into the door on the way out. The following week, Brister, with the backing of some veterans, appealed to Noll and Walton to simplify the offense, and they did get some of it reduced.

But nothing worked, including the offense. The Steelers did not score a touchdown on offense in the first four games of the 1990 season, a rare feat.

The team was as close to anarchy as any had been under Noll as players bickered in the locker room and on the field. Brister ripped Walton publicly and Noll threatened to bench him because of it. They held a players-only meeting on October 2 to discuss the deteriorating situation.

"Maybe," Noll said, "we're trying to do too much."

Before Walton, the Steelers signalled plays in by hand from the sidelines. Walton believed in shuttling his plays in and out with messengers. That created another problem because the terminology was so long and complex that by the time the messenger arrived in the huddle, he often forgot part of the play or got it wrong. Noll got Walton to make another concession: Send in the plays with a messenger and signal the formation in by hand, an order that did not please the offensive coordinator.

For the second time in six weeks, Noll ordered Walton to cut back on the offense. That worked for a week or two, before it was right back to the same thing. There were too many plays, too many formations, too many combinations. Plays were called in the heat of a game that hadn't been practiced since training camp.

Noll went to each offensive coach and told him to sell the players on what Walton was trying to do. He told them he was thinking about approaching the team himself. But some of his assistants did not know what they were trying to sell. The philosophies that were always clear-cut under Noll were now muddled. They weren't trying to run the ball much, which was always a Noll staple. There was no consistency in the offensive philosophy, so how could they expect any in a game?

The offense had no focus. People in the front office, on the coaching staff, and in the locker room were stunned that Noll had turned over the entire offense to Walton. For years, Noll was his own offensive coordinator and kept Tom Moore on a tight rein when he slipped him the title. But now he took a back seat and let the fate of the team unfold. Noll had become an administrator. While his coaches were in meetings with players, Noll could sometimes be seen out in the hall, chatting with people. He even had more time for reporters.

It was a strange sight to behold. It might have worked, too, had Noll used an offense that fit his team better. Even before Noll arrived in 1969, the Pittsburgh Steelers played hard-nosed football. They won four Super Bowls with that as their personality, and maintained it through 1989 when they nearly made it to the AFC Championship game again.

But they became a finesse offense under Walton and not a very good one, partly because they did not believe in that style of play.

"I hope to hell this isn't our personality," Joe Greene seethed. "I don't want it to be mine."

Tempers flared between coaches. They screamed at one another through headphones during a game in Los Angeles and there was some shouting in the locker room afterward.

Walton confided to people that he did not think the Steelers had much talent on offense. After losing his job in New York, Walton wanted to resurrect his career. He made no secret of the fact he wanted to be a head coach again.

Walton had turned into the bad guy, but was it all his fault? He talked to Noll about a job, laid out his system for him, told him what he planned to do, and was hired. Walton did nothing more or less than what he was employed to do. He didn't order Chuck Noll to scrap his terminology, and it wasn't as if Walton did not have a track record with his offense. Walton, in fact, maintained that some of the old Steelers' offense was integrated into his. That may have added to the confusion about its philosophy.

He did not believe Bubby Brister should be the quarterback. He favored Neil O'Donnell, but Brister was forced on him. In light of what would happen in 1992, it could be said Walton was a man of vision.

Walton wanted to win as badly as anyone; he just may have been on the wrong team at the wrong time.

"Even Chuck's coaches felt that maybe he gave him too much authority," Donahoe said, "that maybe he didn't step in enough to say, 'Hey, we used to do it this way and it worked.' Probably what we should have done is take a combination of what we had done that was successful and combine that with some new ideas to try to improve our passing game, try to improve our third-down package, whatever needed to be improved."

The offense actually had its moments in 1990, mostly during a mid-season spurt when Pittsburgh won four of five games and scored 111 points in three of them. Brister was voted the AFC Player of the Week, then the AFC Player of the Month for October. The players presented Walton with a game ball after one victory, and he broke down and cried.

But the inconsistency continued and the season was being salvaged by the No. 1-ranked defense in the NFL. The Steelers had allowed only six touchdown passes after 15 games, three fewer than the NFL record. But that defense had one dreadful game and it came in the finale in Houston. Had the Steelers beaten the Oilers and backup quarterback Cody Carlson on December 30, they would have won their first AFC Central Division title in six years.

Instead, Tim Worley fumbled on the first series, and the life was sucked out of the team. Carlson, making his first start in two years for the injured Warren Moon, completed 22 of 29 and flipped three TD passes, half of what the Steelers had allowed to that point all season.

Pittsburgh lost, 34-14, finished 9-7 and out of the playoffs.

No changes were made after the season. The entire staff returned, including Walton. But if 1990 was controversial for the Pittsburgh Steelers, '91 was a catastrophe.

It was a sweltering training camp, both on the field and in the disposition of the ballclub. Guard Terry Long failed his steroids test and tried to kill himself after Chuck Noll told him about it in July. Noll criticized the rookie holdouts, as usual, and also took aim at a few underachieving former No. 1 picks — Aaron Jones and Tim Worley. Rookie first-rounder Huey Richardson somehow broke his nose in a no-pads, non-contact walk-through drill, then broke his right thumb in a real practice. Cornerback Rod Woodson, their best player, held out all camp in a contract dispute.

The crowds at the St. Vincent College training site in Latrobe had dwindled to a few hundred, often a few dozen. A decade earlier, thousands jammed the tiny campus daily to watch the Steelers practice in the summer.

Noll, however, was buoyed by his team's two scrimmages against the Washington Redskins and a victory in the first exhibition game against them. As the season began, even Bubby Brister and Joe Walton were singing in the same key.

"I feel great about it," Brister said of the offense.

Said Walton: "I don't think they really grasped the whole thing last year. But now . . . I think they've grasped everything pretty well. That's the difference."

The Steelers began the season with a 26-20 victory over San Diego. Bubby Brister left the game in the fourth quarter with a concussion as the fans in Three Rivers Stadium cheered.

The real headaches, though, were to come. And one that had a profound effect on Chuck Noll happened following their 52-34 loss in the second game of the season at Buffalo.

The Tuesday after that setback, Noll, his staff and the players were shaken by a column Joe Greene had written in *Steelers Digest*. The paper is partly owned by the Steelers and is headquartered in their offices. Editor Bob Labriola hand delivers copies of *Steelers Digest* throughout their offices every Tuesday around noon.

Joe Greene's words made for a lousy lunch that September 11. He had talked to Labriola on Monday morning, and he was angry at what he saw in Buffalo.

"We have to try to find some way to simplify and minimize what we do. The guys have to be able to go out and play, instead of thinking . . . we stepped out of our class . . . last year, we were a mediocre football team . . . We were mediocre the year before, and the year before. We've only been able to be competitive with mediocre football teams . . . Some of what was lacking was the week's preparation, and some of it was gameday strategy . . . What do I do with the guys who still think football is a big party? You play someone else. But . . . there's no one else to put in . . . I can't recall a time, in recent memory, when I was more personally devastated . . ."

No one was more devastated by Greene's critique than Chuck Noll, although he shrugs it off today.

"I don't remember," he says.

The loss in Buffalo had been tough, but not a disheartening one considering the Steelers had one of the youngest teams in the league, had gone to Buffalo and given the Bills a game until midway through the final quarter. The Bills had just lost the Super Bowl the previous January by one point on a missed field goal. They would go to the Super Bowl again that season. A lot of teams went to Buffalo and came back more tattered than the Steelers.

Inevitably after a loss like that, Noll would be upbeat with his team. He would tell them they had gone to the home of the AFC Champs and done a good job, that they were 1-1 and had every reason to be proud of themselves.

"That was the thing about Chuck, he was always so steady as a head coach," Donahoe said. "That's important because your players are constantly looking at you and they're constantly saying, 'OK, we didn't play very well, now how did this affect this guy? Is he going to come in here and go hara-kiri on us or is he going to take it in stride?'

"Sometimes, you have to go hara-kiri. But with a young team, going to Buffalo, playing the team that everybody expected to go to the Super Bowl, we probably would have been better to emphasize the positives, knowing the coaches to a large degree screwed up that game, not the players."

Instead, Greene went hara-kiri before Noll had a chance to soothe his team's psyche. Greene took the thunder away from Noll in the exact opposite manner in which Noll would have reacted. His words struck Chuck Noll in the stomach harder than Greene had punched Paul Howard of Denver 14 years earlier on the playing field.

The players had Monday off and when they arrived Tuesday to see the Greene column, it was a downer. Greene had not intended it to be that way. He had hoped to light a fire under them. The last thing he wanted to do was undermine Noll, the man who meant so much to him and his career.

Had it been any other coach on the staff, Noll would have hauled him in for a harsh rebuke. But that did not occur. Other coaches on the staff noticed a mix of bewilderment and disappointment in Noll over Greene's actions. They say Noll was never the same after that. He lost some of the fire. He denies that, too. "I don't recall it having a big effect," Noll says.

The Steelers weren't the same either. They won two of their next three, beating New England and Indianapolis, two of the worst teams in the league. Then they lost four straight and stood 3-6.

The individual as well as collective misfortunes piled up in '91. Starting guard Brian Blankenship's career was ended by a neck injury in the fourth game. Halfback Tim Worley was put on injured reserve, then went AWOL for two days, then was suspended for using cocaine. Long was suspended for using steroids. Brister injured a knee and was replaced by O'Donnell, a move Walton had wanted to make anyway.

Then came a most unusual occurrence. Both Donahoe and player personnel director Dick Haley, speaking separately, ripped the coaches for not developing the younger players.

"We've got to try to get guys to be successful or else trade all 12 draft choices," Donahoe said. "If you're not going to have a commitment to them, why pick them?"

Haley was upset because rookie wide receivers Jeff Graham and Ernie Mills weren't playing much.

"We drafted them to play and I think they're very capable. But they have to get the opportunity to have more than one or two balls thrown at them. You're not going to make it one way or the other on two passes."

Despite the rare public criticism by front office members of the coaching staff, Dan Rooney dismissed a notion that there was a rift in his organization. The personnel department, however, had become more vocal about their displeasure with the way Noll used certain players. Several times, Donahoe appealed to Noll to sign a long-snapper, but Noll had no use for such a one-dimensional player. Yet the Steelers lost two or three games in 1991 because of bad snaps, wins that would have put them in the playoffs.

Through all the losses and controversies, Noll remained loyal to Walton.

"He's in charge of (the offense). He's done a good job," Noll said in mid-November. "I have a great deal of confidence in what they're doing. Joe does a great job of studying the stuff and tying the things that we're trying to do together, making the calls, and I have confidence in him."

Noll was painting himself into a corner that he would later not be able to escape. His relentless support of Walton came as Dan Rooney was deciding that Walton had to go. Reports surfaced that Walton would be out at the end of the year.

The morale on the team struck bottom. Coaches again screamed at one another. Once when a play didn't work on third-and-one, Joe Greene gritted his teeth on the sidelines and cursed, "That guy is going to get us all fired."

As evidenced by Greene's season-long reaction, the problems on offense affected the defense. Ranked No. 1 in 1990, it had slipped to No. 22. The Steelers' top-ranked pass defense in '90 was now ranked third from the bottom of the NFL.

Linebacker Bryan Hinkle had been with the Steelers since 1981, was their former MVP and one of their best linebackers for nearly a decade. He was a captain and took a no-nonsense approach to the game. He could see what was happening and he did not like it.

"Our offensive players did not pick up Joe Walton's system and understand it, perform and execute it. They didn't do it and it hurt us week-in and week-out. You can candy-coat it anyway you want to, that's the bottom line."

Those problems then spread to the defense.

"After two years of it," Hinkle said, "it not only affects the offensive players, it starts to affect the defensive players. I mean, you're out there busting your ass and you can say, 'Yeah, keep busting your ass' and you do. But I know it starts creeping in the back of your mind, 'It's the same shit again.'"

Noll either did not notice, or thought they could overcome it. Others knew the problem ran too deep even for one of Noll's patented sheer-of-will resolutions.

"If you were Chuck, what would you have done different?" Donahoe asks today. "I think I would have had some long talks with Joe Walton and said, 'Hey, Joe, this isn't working. We had a pretty good team when you came here. Now, I like some of the things you're doing, but there are also some good things we were doing. Let's put them together and see if we can get something going here.'

"But that just wasn't Chuck's way. Chuck was a very loyal guy. If Chuck Noll's in your corner, you've got a friend for life, and you never have to worry about your job. If Chuck thinks you're working hard for him and you're doing the job, then he'll support you to the Nth degree."

The more people criticized Walton, the more Noll defended him. To this day Noll backs that offense. He subtly puts the blame on Brister and admits the defense was part of the problem.

"It wasn't Joe. His offense worked pretty well. I think our quarterback stats improved. A lot of things you can't blame on Joe, because I thought Joe did a pretty good job. We had problems with the quarterbacks handling it, but for the most part it still worked, and we moved the football and did things.

"Of course, we made mistakes too, which killed us. You eliminate the mistakes, then it comes. But again it's trying to get everybody on the same page, and we had difficulty doing that."

One reason they couldn't, the reason so many mistakes were made is the offense confused them so much.

"It wasn't Joe's offense that killed us," Noll insists. "That's a bad rap. There were some things we could have changed there but also on defense, the whole structure. We probably weren't as aggressive defensively as we should have been. We didn't play aggressive enough defense, and you need to do that."

But as the '91 season tripped along, the rest of the coaches noticed a continuing change in Noll.

"I could see a change in Chuck his last year," said Hoak. "He just wasn't the same person. I thought things were bothering him. He was just different than he normally was, and I don't know if that was to hide his feelings or what. Maybe he was struggling with his decision, maybe it was all the rumors and everything going around that started to wear on him. I don't know what it was, but he was just different his last 8-10 games."

Those who worked with Noll noticed that things that once upset him no longer did. Little details that would have bothered him once were ignored or put off.

At one point during the '91 season, Noll went to Walton and said, "We have to simplify things. It isn't working, they're too confused."

Walton replied, "We'll do it in the offseason."

Noll did not push the matter, and the offseason was about to become permanent for both coaches.

Noll continued to praise the talent on the Steelers. He said he had better talent in 1991 than he had when they made the playoffs in 1989.

"He made that statement a number of times," said Dick Hoak.

But if they had better talent, why were they losing more games?

"Hey," Noll snapped, "let me put it this way, all right? Players win, coaches lose, and it comes down to that. And the losses are mine."

In other times, people would dismiss that, as Noll tried to deflect criticism of his team onto himself. But by late '91, they accepted his statement as reality.

The first real indication that Noll might be nearing his final days as the Steelers' coach came on Monday, December 2. The Cowboys had beaten Pittsburgh, 20-10, four days earlier on Thanksgiving, thanks in part to two wayward long snaps on punts.

Noll was asked if he planned to return in '92.

"That is something that we will talk about after this is all over."

Asked if it would be his call, he said: "I think so. I don't know. If they want me to move aside, it is that way. I have never had a big deal one way or the other with that.

"When you have lost as many games as we have lost, the blame comes right here on me. I am the only one who has to answer for it."

It was a startling reply. When he was asked a similar question about his future in 1988, Noll got up and walked out of the press conference.

There was to be one final controversy involving Walton. Brister's knee healed enough for him to return to practice, but O'Donnell remained the starter, and Brister his brooding backup for eight games. Then, with Houston holding a commanding 24-6 lead in the fourth quarter in the third-to-last game of the season in the Astrodome, Walton told Brister to warm up. Brister refused.

"I'm no bleeping relief quarterback," Brister declared after the game. "I don't mop up for anybody."

O'Donnell finished out the 31-6 loss. But instead of tearing Brister a new earhole, Noll inexplicably gave him the job back for the final two games of the season. It was Walton who reluctantly delivered the message to the two quarterbacks.

Humiliated by the whole experience, Walton cried when he told Brister and O'Donnell of Noll's decision.

"He was very emotional about it," said O'Donnell, who liked Walton's offense. "It was very hard on him, and he was hearing a lot of heat here after he got a lot of heat in New York. I really felt bad for him because he was trying hard and he was trying to do his best."

With Brister at quarterback, the Steelers beat Cincinnati and Cleveland to wrap up a 7-9 season, one of the most tumultuous in their history. Had they won another game, they would have been a wild-card playoff team at 8-8. But the focus for the final few weeks shifted from the field to Chuck Noll's future.

Would he or would he not be back?

Noll said he did not know, but acknowledged "It's different than any other year." Before the final game he said he still had the desire to coach, but he could not say whether he'd be back. He said his decision would not depend on what Rooney said to him at their year-end meeting.

What then? All of Pittsburgh fretted over Noll's decision. The five Rooney brothers discussed it at their board meeting at the end of the year. They had no more idea what Noll would do than his assistant coaches did.

"I wanted him back. Definitely," Dan Rooney said.

He wanted him with strings attached, though. Rooney had decided long ago that Walton must go. He never actually told Noll that, but Noll got the idea. It was mentioned often enough in the press.

"The rumors went around," Hoak said. "I know Chuck supposedly didn't read the papers or do this or that, but there was no way he couldn't have been aware of the things around here."

Noll was tired of strings. He reluctantly agreed to them in 1988. A second time was out of the question.

There was no way out. He still wanted to coach, believed he had the talent to win and loved the challenge of getting his team back on top. But he would not fire Joe Walton on orders. That would diminish him in the eyes of everyone — his colleagues, players, the fans, himself. Also, Rooney was about to elevate Tom Donahoe to the post of director of football operations and make him Noll's immediate boss. The only bosses Noll ever had with the Steelers were the late Art Rooney Sr. and his son, Dan.

It was too much to ask a man of Noll's stature.

A few coaches and scouts suggested the only way out was for Joe Walton to resign, to walk into Dan Rooney's office and tell him, 'Thanks, sorry it didn't work out, I'm moving on.' That was what Dick Hoak and Tom Moore offered to do in '88 to save Noll's skin. But Walton was oblivious to the situation. He, like many others, believed the job was Noll's forever and since Noll had supported him, it would be business as usual in 1992.

One report late in the season listed Walton as a candidate to become head coach of the Indianapolis Colts, and his response showed how he misread the looming situation.

"I've said all along that I'd be interested in being a head coach again," Walton said. "But I'm not looking to leave here. I'm happy here, especially with Chuck."

The season ended December 22. Dan Rooney casually told Noll he'd see him after Christmas.

"I said, 'Hey, we have to get together and talk about things.' It was prevalent there was a need to talk about things and get it straightened out."

So on the day after Christmas, Noll strode into Dan Rooney's office at 10 a.m.

"OK," Rooney said, "we have to talk about this."

But in Noll's eyes there was no need to talk. In 10 days he would turn 60.

"I think it's time," he responded quickly.

He had arrived at his decision earlier that morning. There was no way out. It was time. In his heart, Dan Rooney believed it too, and was relieved that Noll had chosen that course.

Noll left Rooney's office and began calling his shocked assistant coaches to inform them of his decision. Then he walked back to the kitchen, where a small group of reporters on the watch had gathered. He poured coffee for them and discussed various topics, football and his job status not among them. He was in a good mood and laughed easily.

At one o'clock, Dan Rooney came back and said, "It's time."

The mood turned somber as everyone walked down the hall and into the press conference. There, Noll announced his retirement.

"It would have been great to have had 10 victories and been in the playoffs and have gone all the way, and then said, 'Goodbye,' but it didn't work out that way."

The press conference lasted 20 minutes before Noll, near tears, broke it off. "You've got enough now, before it gets tougher."

With that, Noll pulled on his black overcoat and moved toward the door. He shook hands with several reporters, one of whom once asked him how he would like to be remembered.

"Don't leave anything on the beach but your footprints," he answered.

He walked briskly down the hall, out the front door, hopped in his car and was gone. He never glanced at the four gleaming Super Bowl trophies in the lobby as he passed them.

Those are Chuck Noll's footprints.

5

BIG FOOTPRINTS
TO FILL

Now what?

The sports landscape is littered with men who tried to follow legendary coaches without success: Phil Bengtson (Vince Lombardi), Gene Bartow (John Wooden), and Ray Perkins (Bear Bryant), to name several.

Someone would now get the chance to follow Chuck Noll in Pittsburgh, the only coach to win four Super Bowls. Who would want to? If, as George Young said, Noll was chasing his own legend, imagine how difficult it would be for someone else.

Dan Rooney and the Steelers were somewhat out of practice at hiring head coaches. They had not done it in 23 years. Rooney ran that search himself, but this time he turned the job over to Tom Donahoe, who upon Chuck Noll's retirement, would soon be placed in charge of the football operation. Rooney gave Donahoe, 44, the same advice his father gave him 23 years earlier when Art Sr. put him in charge of hiring a new coach: Don't screw it up.

Seven years earlier, Donahoe was a high school football coach who had not played the game in college or the pros. Now, here he was going to lead the search for Chuck Noll's successor with the Pittsburgh Steelers.

He is a bright man who began as a Blesto scout and rocketed to the top of the Steelers organization. Shortly after Noll retired,

Rooney put Donahoe in charge as the director of football operations. It was an unprecedented move. The new coach would answer to Donahoe, and Donahoe would answer only to Rooney. The changing of the guard would involve more than Chuck Noll's retirement.

Soon thereafter, Dick Haley, for 20 years the Steelers' director of player personnel, resigned to accept a similar job with the New York Jets. He had been Donahoe's superior and was unwilling to continue as his subordinate.

Donahoe knows the game of football, but he did not know many people in the league nor all the various offensive and defensive strategies and systems it held.

Rooney would take care of that. This would not be merely a search for the Steelers' next head coach, it also would serve as Tom Donahoe's education — a touring, intense NFL classroom experience for the Steelers' new de facto general manager. The interview process would be a two-way street: Donahoe evaluating coaching candidates and picking their brains as well.

"It's been a long time since we've had to look here," Donahoe said. "Everyone had to dust their notes off and see what to do."

Rooney wanted nothing to do with retread coaches or fancy Dans, as his dad would have called them.

"We're not looking for a savior. We don't need saved," Rooney said, dripping Pittsburgh-ese.

He set forth his priorities: "A good person, a person with character and intelligence, a person who has the ability to teach, a person who has the ability to motivate the team."

It sounded a lot like Chuck Noll.

"I think it's unfair to say that we're going to go out and try to get a guy who's exactly in the mold of Chuck Noll. That might be impossible. But as far as some of his basic characteristics, yes."

And one other thing. Rooney wanted someone who "has an appreciation of Pittsburgh."

"We've had coaches here who looked down their noses at Pittsburgh and I don't think you can do that. Pittsburgh is a good place and the Steelers are special."

Some scoffed at that statement because it sounded so small-townish. Yet whether or not they believed it, the Pittsburgh Steelers are different. They operate unlike any other NFL franchise. They have few employees compared with other teams and theirs are mostly native western Pennsylvanians.

You can still walk through the front door, wander around the lobby, get your picture taken in front of four Super Bowl trophies, and damned near waltz into Dan Rooney's office without anyone so much as asking who you are or where you're going. There are no guards and the doors aren't locked, unlike many pro teams' offices, where you practically need a tank to get into the place.

There aren't as many characters hanging around headquarters as there were when Art Rooney Sr. ran the offices from the Roosevelt Hotel, but there are still quite a few. In no other city would you find the owner sitting in the lunch room chatting with reporters, secretaries, coaches, and scouts over coffee, almost on a daily basis.

You bet a new coach should have an appreciation for that.

Noll comprehended that, and he and the franchise thrived under it. Noll's tenure began before man walked on the moon, before the Steelers had ever won a playoff game, when the moon seemed more within reach than the New York Jets. It ended 23 years and four Super Bowls later.

The Steelers did not think their next coach would last a generation, but they weren't used to coaches passing through every three years either. They wanted someone who could take them into the next century.

Nine head coaching jobs opened in the NFL in 1991, and Pittsburgh filled its post last. The thorough search included interviews by Donahoe with 10 men — nine assistant coaches in the NFL and one head coach in the World League. The Steelers also wanted to interview Bobby Ross, the head coach at Georgia Tech, but he already had accepted a position as coach of the San Diego Chargers. Dennis Green, the head coach at Stanford, was the only other college coach on their list, but he backed out of two interviews with them and then asked that his name be removed.

Several coaches begged to be put on the list, including George Perles of Michigan State, and Joe Walton, who just didn't get it. Neither was interviewed. The Steelers also gave a courtesy interview to their old friend, Woody Widenhofer, the defensive coordinator with the Detroit Lions, after they had chosen their final four candidates.

Art Rooney II, Dan's eldest son and one of three men involved in hiring the coach, took one look at the original long list of coaches and came to a fast conclusion.

"I saw Cowher, at 34, was the youngest by far on this list. I said, 'We're not going to interview this guy who's only 34 years old.' That was my first comment about Bill Cowher."

Donahoe's education and the cross-country search for a coach began in the early days of the new year and brought him to Chicago, where he talked to both Bears coordinators, Vince Tobin on defense and Greg Landry on offense. He talked in San Francisco to 49ers offensive coordinator Mike Holmgren, the hottest candidate in the league. Holmgren impressed Donahoe, but the two sides never got much beyond the flirting stage. Holmgren had an agent who seemed to do much of the talking for him. The Steelers generally are not fond of agents and believe it distasteful for coaches to have one. Anyway, Holmgren appeared headed for Green Bay from the start.

Scratch Mike Holmgren.

Others contributed both to the coaching search and to Donahoe's learning experience: Dave Wannstedt, a Baldwin native and Pitt graduate who coached the Dallas Cowboys defense; Cowher, a native of nearby Crafton, Pennsylvania, who coached the Kansas City defense; Mike Riley, coach of the World League's San Antonio Riders; Steelers assistants Joe Greene, John Fox, and Dick Hoak; and former Steelers defensive coordinator Rod Rust, who had just been fired as head coach of the New England Patriots.

So many coaches, so little time. But Rooney insisted that they not rush the process. It also took a little longer because the two main candidates, Wannstedt and Cowher, were involved in the playoffs. Donahoe kept hoping the Cowboys and Chiefs would lose so he could get going on it. Both teams were rubbed out on January 5 in the quarterfinals, Buffalo routing Cowher's defense, 37-14, and Detroit spanking Wannstedt's, 38-6.

Soon, the list of 10 was whittled to a Final Four late in the second week of January: Joe Greene, Kevin Gilbride, Dave Wannstedt, and Bill Cowher.

Greene was a sentimental choice, a man who meant as much to the franchise as any player in its history. In the 1970s, the Steelers did not need motivators on their coaching staff; they had Joe Greene in their locker room. He was the heart and soul of the Super Bowl teams, and his spirit and physical presence dominated the atmosphere.

What he lacked in coaching experience, he more than made up for in attitude, intensity, and forceful personality. Greene could set a tone for the whole franchise. His candidacy was an exciting possibility to many.

"I want it," he said simply. "I'm very confident I can get it done. I'm very excited. I'd be a good head coach."

Gilbride's standing as a finalist seemed odd. He coached the run-and-shoot in Houston, the last offense the Steelers wanted to run.

"I really like Kevin, he's a good guy," Rooney said. "But I got the opinion that he is a run-and-shoot guy and he's not going to change. I told him right out. The more he talked, the less he convinced me. With him, we may not have been putting four wide receivers out there, but we were going to be a finesse team. Maybe it's my upbringing, but I just don't think you're going to win in Pittsburgh with a finesse team."

Gilbride convinced Donahoe that he was more than a run-and-shoot coach, but his choice as a finalist was provoked by something else.

At first, the Oilers denied the Steelers permission to talk to Gilbride. They had seen it for what it was, partially: A division rival picking the brains of its top lieutenant. It was an old Al Davis trick. What better way to gain knowledge of the way Gilbride and his offense tick than to make him a finalist and interview him at length for the job?

Gilbride pressed the Oilers and they reluctantly gave the Steelers the OK to talk to him. He came to Pittsburgh, where he spent seven hours on January 12 at Three Rivers Stadium.

Each finalist met with Dan, Art Rooney II, and Donahoe, the trio who would select the coach. They also met with Joe Gordon, one of the league's best PR men throughout the '70s and '80s before he became the Steelers' director of communications.

"Dan, Art, and myself felt those guys were all good head coach candidates," Donahoe said. "I personally feel at some time all those guys are going to be head coaches. But the trick was we had to come up with the best guy for the Steelers. Which guy we felt was most ready, which guy might be something special. They were all young, so you were kind of rolling the dice on that. They didn't have experience as head coaches other than Kevin, who had some collegiate experience."

The Steelers had settled on their final two: Cowher, 34, and Wannstedt, 39, both natives of the Pittsburgh area, both top young defensive coordinators. Dan Rooney broke the news to Greene on January 17. The Steelers believed Greene was not yet ready to become a head coach. He had been an assistant for only five seasons, and they had all been under Noll in Pittsburgh. They also wanted a clean break from Noll's regime; they wanted someone from outside with different ideas. Greene and Gilbride remained finalists in name only.

Picking one was not easy.

At first, Art was in Wannstedt's corner and Donahoe was for Cowher. It was perfect for Dan because he could sit back and let his son and Donahoe debate the pros and cons on each coach.

No one from the Oilers' front office bothered to speak to the Steelers about Gilbride, but quarterback Warren Moon called Dan Rooney to recommend him. Jimmy Johnson made an impassioned plea for Wannstedt, and Marty Schottenheimer pushed Cowher.

The process was almost unbearable for the two men's parents in Pittsburgh — Ginny and Frank Wannstedt in Baldwin and Laird and Dorothy Cowher in Crafton.

The Cowhers are typical Steeler fanatics, former season-ticket holders in the 1950s who reverently place a Terrible Towel on their TV set during games. The wait practically drove them to gnaw holes in the sacred towel.

"It's hard to believe that little kid I registered for Pop Warner football in 1967 could be the next coach of the team I admired," said the elder Cowher, also known as Bill. "I'd probably end up down on the field after falling out of the stands. I don't think I'd even know what's going on. I'll be on Cloud Nine. I'll be ecstatic."

Said Mrs. Cowher simply, "It's like a storybook."

Donahoe traveled to the Senior Bowl practices in Mobile, Alabama, on Tuesday, January 14, to further investigate the candidates. There, he talked with Wannstedt for 45 minutes in the stands. Cowher was at the East-West Shrine Game in California, but Donahoe ran into Schottenheimer and Chiefs president and GM Carl Peterson in Mobile.

Peterson told Donahoe that Cowher, 34, wasn't ready for the job. Then Peterson left and Schottenheimer turned to Donahoe. "I hate like hell to lose him because I'm not going to be able to replace him," Schottenheimer told him. "But he's ready to be a head coach."

For two or three days it went back and forth: Wannstedt or Cowher, the kid from Baldwin or the one from Crafton.

Rooney had favored Cowher for at least a week but let the process unfold. In the end, all three men agreed Cowher was their man.

"The thing we talked about constantly," Donahoe said, "was who's the guy who might be something special? And it just seemed to always keep going back to Bill. Because of a lot of things that you've seen now — his enthusiasm, his intensity, his ability to communicate — we thought we might be in a position to get lucky twice. We got pretty lucky with Chuck Noll. And I think in the end, Dan felt we might get lucky again and get a guy who's the real thing."

One matter that bothered both Rooneys was Cowher's age, 34. He graduated from Carlynton High School in 1975, months after the Steelers had won their first Super Bowl. He was five years younger than Art.

"The only thing that kept sticking in my craw, the only question that kept coming back was age," Dan Rooney said. "When he wasn't here, his age was a problem. He was 34 years old! But when I was with him, I never had a problem."

"But the first time we met Bill, that sort of became a non-factor almost right away because he just had the maturity," Art said. "Age didn't matter."

So Rooney decided to get together with him again. On Friday morning, January 17, the day Rooney told Joe Greene he was out, he made two phone calls to Kansas City. The first was to Schottenheimer, a Fort Cherry, Pennsylvania, native whose opinion Rooney strongly respects. Rooney asked him about two points that concerned him: The fact that Cowher had coached under only one system with Schottenheimer in Cleveland and K.C., and his youth.

"I told him I didn't think either one of them would be a problem, that Bill Cowher is ready to be a coach," Schottenheimer said. "I said I have no doubt in my mind that he'll be very successful because he's an excellent teacher and he's well organized; I said his youth isn't going to be a problem, that he's got very strong beliefs and convictions, but on the other hand, he has an ability to resolve issues through discussion."

Rooney then phoned Cowher and invited him and his wife, Kaye, to Pittsburgh for the weekend.

"I think Dan had to keep talking with me, maybe for me to reassure him that it was the right decision," Cowher said. "I just felt there was always this sense that he wanted to keep talking with me."

Cowher's presence always put Rooney's worries about his youth at ease. He could focus on the man rather than the number 34. Once, Dan called John Rooney, one of his younger twin brothers in Philadelphia, and talked about hiring the new coach.

"This Cowher, I like him an awful lot, but he's awful young, you know," Dan told his brother.

John gave him some advice: "Dan, if the coach doesn't work out, you're going to be the one blamed, whether he's 10 years old or a hundred years old. So you might as well hire the guy you like, and not worry about how old he is."

The Cowhers arrived in Pittsburgh Saturday afternoon and went to dinner that night with Tom and Mary Donahoe, Art and Greta Rooney, and Dan and Patricia Rooney.

The job, head coach of the Pittsburgh Steelers, was not discussed.

"Knowing Dan Rooney as I do now," Cowher said, "I can just see the sincerity in what he was doing. He just wanted to make sure he felt comfortable in what he wanted to do."

On Sunday morning, the Cowhers were invited to Three Rivers Stadium. Dan Ferens of the Steelers' front office took Kaye to show her the head coach's family box while Cowher joined the two Rooneys and Donahoe in the president's office.

"It was hard to find anything wrong with him," Art Rooney said.

"Bill Cowher sold himself to me, sold himself to all of us," said Dan Rooney.

He offered Cowher the job, and Cowher accepted. It took them 10 minutes to agree on a four-year contract.

"Thank you for the opportunity," Cowher told them. "I hope I can do what we all want done."

It was January 19, 1992, nearly 23 years since Chuck Noll was named coach of the Steelers, 17 years and one week after they won their first Super Bowl.

"There was a great deal of excitement," Cowher said, "and

a great deal of anxiety because of what was ahead."

In the meantime, Greene became the defensive line coach of the Miami Dolphins, who would reach the AFC championship game the following season. Jimmy Johnson immediately promoted Wannstedt to assistant head coach of the Dallas Cowboys, who would go on to win the Super Bowl the following season. Wannstedt would then be hired to replace Mike Ditka as coach of the Chicago Bears. Kevin Gilbride went back to the Houston Oilers, who were a disappointment again in 1992. In December, Gilbride would have a cancerous kidney removed, but he is well on his way to a complete recovery.

6

A FINE PREDICAMENT YOU GOT ME INTO

If he was anxious before January 21, 1992, Bill Cowher was delirious by the end of it.

The Steelers had delayed naming their head coach for two days because Monday was the Martin Luther King holiday. So the official announcement would wait until Tuesday of Super Bowl week, but the news broke Sunday night: Cowher, a native son, would replace Chuck Noll as the Steelers' head coach.

Those tidings weren't greeted cheerfully by all sides in Pittsburgh. Wannstedt had been the favorite of many fans and media in town. Unlike Cowher, who played at North Carolina State because Pitt was not interested in him, Wannstedt played at Pitt in the early '70s, then coached there under Johnny Majors.

Many saw Wannstedt in the mold of Mike Ditka, a Pitt star who performed his postgraduate work on the Dallas Cowboys coaching staff before hitting it big in Chicago. There were also plenty of disappointed Joe Greene fans in Pittsburgh.

Some fine citizens were so incensed by Cowher's selection that they made obscene phone calls to his parents, Laird and Dorothy, in Crafton. Welcome to the NFL, Mr. and Mrs. Cowher. They had to change their life-long phone number and keep it unlisted.

Bill Cowher was back in Kansas City preparing a statement for the press conference in Pittsburgh. He and his wife greeted the lone Kansas City TV crew at the airport and Cowher memorized his brief speech on the flight.

"When I got off the plane in Pittsburgh, it kind of hit," Cowher said. "There was a multitude of people and reporters there."

At Three Rivers Stadium, he entered the same room in which Noll had retired nearly a month earlier.

"I walked in there and I could see all the media and just sense all the apprehension I think a lot of people had. 'Who is this guy and what's he going to say? What's he going to do?' It was a very intense atmosphere."

Cowher was so nervous that he introduced his parents, his brothers, and his sister-in-law but forgot about his wife, Kaye. He gave a short, unremarkable speech, and during a question-and-answer period, he talked about the Steelers' "wealth of talent," which opened a few eyes.

That took nearly an hour. Then they put him on a telephone to a press conference with the media at the Super Bowl in Minneapolis. After that, he spent the next hour lining up interviews for assistant coaches as Kaye took a flight back to Kansas City.

Cowher made two live TV spots for the five o'clock news, then hustled to WPXI-TV to tape a half-hour show with Sam Nover. He hadn't eaten anything. He finally reached his hotel at 9 p.m., where he would conduct his first interview for an assistant coach with Ted Tollner, who was seeking the job of offensive coordinator.

"I was just drained and beaten," Cowher said. "I called my wife and couldn't get ahold of her. She had taken the phone off the hook because there were so many phone calls."

He was tired, hungry, and growing frantic because of it. He phoned his father in Crafton.

"I said, 'You have to get ahold of my wife. I have to talk to my wife.'"

Kaye Cowher finally got the message and called her husband. She was surprised at his reaction. He was overwhelmed by the job on his very first day.

"I don't know if I can take this," Bill told her. "I don't know what I've gotten into. This is unbelievable. If every day is like this day I don't know if I can do this. Honey, I may have gotten myself in too deep over my head."

He remembered the moment clearly and the near panic he felt. His hands gestured as he recalled it.

"It was just so magnified. Everywhere I went, it was this, it was that. It seemed like it was just so much, an overwhelming amount of responsibility thrown on you — whoosh — at once. Suddenly you went from this very calm world to this."

It was good she got through to him because Kaye Cowher, a former pro basketball player who met Bill at North Carolina State, had a calming effect on her husband during his first crisis as coach of the Pittsburgh Steelers.

"She said, 'Hey, you're going to be fine. You know what you want to do.' I said, 'Well, you're right. I'm just going to take this one day at a time. There's a lot of time left.' I really calmed down afterward."

It would be the only sign of panic he would show, but it would not be his last crisis.

Hiring a staff was a priority, and it would not be easy. Cowher had worked for one coach in his life, Marty Schottenheimer, so his working relationships were limited.

Because of his defensive background, Cowher wanted to hire his offensive coordinator first. Tollner left San Diego for Pittsburgh, figuring the job would be his. But Cowher wasn't ready to hire his offensive coordinator until he interviewed several men. Tollner, armed with an offer from Chuck Knox to become quarterbacks coach of the Los Angeles Rams, chose not to gamble.

That left it between Ron Erhardt and Mike Shanahan. Cowher interviewed both of them in Pittsburgh before the Super Bowl. Shanahan was fired earlier that week as offensive coordinator of the Denver Broncos after a dispute with Coach Dan Reeves. Shanahan also had an interview scheduled with San Francisco coach George Seifert to become the 49ers' offensive coordinator.

Cowher, though, wanted to know how badly Shanahan wanted the opportunity in Pittsburgh. "The job is yours," he told Shanahan hypothetically. "What's your answer?" When Shanahan told him he still wanted to talk to Seifert, Cowher told him he would look elsewhere for an offensive coordinator.

"It worked out better, anyway," Cowher said. "I probably would have hired Ron, anyway. He was an East Coast guy, he ran the kind of offense I wanted, everything fit."

Erhardt got the job on January 27, and his simple power offense would be the biggest reason for the Steelers' turnaround. Erhardt, 61, coached the New York Giants' power offense for a decade, including two Super Bowl victories. His philosophy was simple: big linemen mush straight ahead for a power runner. The passing game would be simplified and include three tight ends at times.

"People think O. J. Anderson and Joe Morris got all those yards with the Giants," Erhardt said. "That was Jumbo Elliott."

Elliott, though, is a 6-foot-7, 305-pound All-Pro tackle, something the Steelers had not yet developed.

Erhardt had been one of the most popular assistant coaches in the league, a man who began coaching in 1956 at Wilson High School in North Dakota and rose to head coach of the New England Patriots for three years.

After 10 years with the Giants and two Super Bowl championships, he was relieved of his duties as offensive coordinator by new coach Ray Handley in 1991 and given the title of assistant head coach in charge of reviewing videotapes.

"I was just a consultant working on both sides of the ball," Erhardt said. "It was a nice job, no pressure. This is much better."

Handley fired him after the '91 season, the best thing to happen to the Steelers and Ron Erhardt. Handley was mired in controversy and losses in New York and was fired after the '92 season with a combined 14-18 record and no playoff appearances.

In Pittsburgh, they loved the good-natured, wisecracking Erhardt, and they loved his simple scheme on offense after the technological wizardry that Joe Walton gave them. This was football again. The playbook shrank to where an offensive lineman could carry it under his arm once more.

"With Joe's offense, everything was based on formations," center Dermontti Dawson explained. "And you had so many different personnel groups going in for different formations that you kind of lost the intensity, because guys had to think, 'Well, am I in this play or am I out?' Man, I cannot count how many formations we had. With this, it's just line up. We really don't change formations much. We only have three or four different ones and we have 12 plays — Coach Erhardt calls them the Dirty Dozen — that we practice and have in the game plan no matter what, and we grow from those. It's so much easier."

Even an old linebacker could see that. Jack Ham, the Steeler Hall of Famer, broadcasts their preseason games for WPXI-TV and covered them several times on Mutual Radio's Game of the Week.

"No question the biggest thing that happened to this team on the negative side was the infusion of Joe Walton and that offense in the last couple years," Ham said.

"It was a team on the rise, getting better in 1989. Bubby Brister was confident after that season and looking forward to the following year, and I think that offense not only set back the offense but after a point it even had an effect on the defense as well, and the whole thing started to break down. That took its toll on this team."

Ham believes that Walton's offense cost the Steelers two good years, 1990 and 1991.

"Sometimes people think that in football you have to be a member of Mensa to coach or play. The less complicated you make it for players and let them be aggressive, the better."

That was also Cowher's philosophy on defense. He hired Dom Capers, the secondary coach of the New Orleans Saints, to become his defensive coordinator. But Cowher made it clear he would be involved in the defense, which would chuck its old read-and-react scheme to become a more attacking unit. He hired long-time Cincinnati defensive coordinator Dick LeBeau to run his secondary, giving him three veteran coaches on the defensive side.

Chuck Noll, who still defends Walton and the offense, admitted the Steelers defense was not aggressive enough in '90 and '91.

"Defensively, you want to get the ball for the offense," Noll said, "and you'd like to get it quickly because you don't want to spend a lot of time on the field. And we probably spent too much time on the field."

Cowher filled out his staff with a coaching mix from the pros and college ranks. He hired Marvin Lewis, who left Pitt to become the linebackers coach; Bob Harrison, who left Georgia to coach the wide receivers; offensive line coach Kent Stephenson, who lost his job in Seattle when Chuck Knox left; Steve Furness, the former Steel Curtain member, who replaced Joe Greene as defensive line coach; tight ends coach Pat Hodgson, who had been with Erhardt on the Giants; special teams coach John Guy, who left Kentucky; and long-time Steelers assistant Dick Hoak, the only holdover from Noll's staff.

It was an amalgamation of men who had never coached with each other, except for Hodgson and Erhardt. Cowher not only would replace the legendary Noll, do it in his hometown, do it at age 35, but he would have to do it with a group of men who had never coached with him.

"That really didn't bother me as much as making sure everyone knew exactly what was expected of them," Cowher said.

Structure such as that is one of Cowher's trademarks. Noll gave his coaches and players looser guidelines and expected them to get the job done. Practices were different, too.

"Just the way practices are run and structured is a big difference," said linebacker Bryan Hinkle, a Steeler since 1981. "If you're supposed to work five minutes on one drill, it's five minutes and then you go to the next one. With Chuck, sometimes we'd be on a drill for half an hour when it was only scheduled for five minutes because he would get involved with it. It's quite a change."

The voluntary workouts in the spring were more intense.

"With Chuck," Hinkle noted, "we had a minicamp a month long and you had time. If you wanted to come in and work out you did; if you didn't, you didn't have to. It's optional now, too, but it behooves you to be here."

Cowher even created a strict fine schedule. Miss a meal at training camp, a treatment for an injury, a meeting, a bed check, it would cost you money — $200 for just skipping lunch. He installed alarms on the exit doors in the Bonaventure dorm where the players stay at St. Vincent College so they could no longer sneak out after 11 p.m. curfew. Several players tested the alarms; they worked. Cowher no longer allowed placekicker Gary Anderson to go off golfing in the morning at training camp as he and the punter had in previous years. Anderson was required to be on the field or in meetings like everyone else.

Cowher is a disciplinarian with the rare ability to win affection from his players.

"He takes a hands-on approach," cornerback D. J. Johnson explained. "He gets in there. He's the first to high-five you when you come off the field. He's the first one to come talk to you if you do something bad on the field."

Cowher could turn on the charm or the heat. As fans would soon find out, he held nothing back on the sidelines, shouting encouragement, punching his fist in the air, pumping his arms at the side to encourage crowd noise, and running onto the field to congratulate his players. He sometimes would yell at them in the heat of the game.

"Greg Lloyd. GREG LLOYD!!" he screamed once after a play as if ready to scold his linebacker. When Lloyd finally heard him and turned toward the sidelines, Cowher shouted back, "Great bleeping play."

After years of Chuck Noll stoicism, Cowher was a revelation. Watching him on the sidelines was a game in itself.

"Cowher and his coaching staff have pumped a new energy into the players," safety Carnell Lake said. "He talks to his players, he encourages his players. I didn't see that happen here before this year. I like that."

The personal touch, not one of Noll's strong points, was Cowher's forte. He used it to good advantage in the Plan B free agency period shortly after he joined the Steelers. Left guard was the Steelers' Achilles heel on offense, and they needed to find a good big man to stick there if Erhardt's power offense was to work.

Tom Ricketts, a first-round pick from Pitt in 1989, was certainly big, but he was not good. They needed someone else. The Los Angeles Rams failed to protect their starting guard, Duval Love, a 6-3, 291-pound veteran of seven NFL seasons. Cowher and Donahoe believed he could be their answer at left guard, and the coach made an extra pitch to get him in Plan B.

When Love came to Pittsburgh, Cowher took him to lunch at the Allegheny Club.

"We didn't talk too much about football," Love said.

"We talked about life in general—his family, about my wife who was about to have a baby, stuff like that. Shooting the breeze really, just getting to know one another.

"It was the first time we met and we got along real well. He made me feel at ease. It was snowing that day. And he said, 'Isn't it beautiful here?' And I'm saying in my mind, 'Hey, it's 80 degrees back in California.'"

A note to those who believe players will flock to the sun or big cities in free agency: Duval Love came from Los Angeles to Pittsburgh because of the coach's personal touch. OK, he also got a raise from $425,000 to a contract averaging $555,000, but he could have gotten that elsewhere.

"I went other places and the head coach didn't show up or he had only five minutes for me. Coach Cowher took time to spend with me and obviously that makes a difference because it makes you feel like you're wanted. Coach Cowher made me feel welcome. He's not one of those coaches who sits in his office or up in a tower. He's involved."

Not all player relations went so smoothly.

Tim Worley, who was supposed to be the franchise running back, flunked several more drug tests in February and was given a minimum one-year suspension by the NFL. Halfback Barry Foster, angry over the pace of contract negotiations, skipped the first three days of mandatory minicamp and was fined $3,000. Tight end Eric Green rarely turned up for the new offseason program. Players, at first, groused about the intense and structured workouts in the spring.

But the big test came when Cowher announced he had moved Pro Bowl outside linebacker Greg Lloyd to inside linebacker for the spring on an experimental basis. Lloyd didn't like it one bit. He weighs only 225 pounds. That's OK if you are a middle linebacker in the 4-3 with the big boys up front protecting you, throwing themselves in front of 300-pound offensive linemen. But there are no such guard dogs in the 3-4.

"Shit, we were lining up in a 3-4 defense and I was just the other inside linebacker," Lloyd said. "I said, 'Hey, I'm only 225 pounds going up against 290 and 300. That's going to take its toll on me. My body's built to be on the outside and move quick, not to keep running into people like that.'"

Cowher pushed the experiment. He wasn't sure about David Little's stamina at age 33 or of Hardy Nickerson's contract status. He hadn't seen much of outside linebacker Huey Richardson, but he figured if he was a first-round draft pick in 1991 he must be something.

"I looked at Greg and thought he'd be a great inside linebacker," Cowher said.

Lloyd and his agent, Dick Bell, balked. Outside linebackers make the big money. Lloyd had just made the Pro Bowl. He felt he would not last long taking on the brutes inside.

Bell worked the back room, discreetly trying to pry Lloyd out of the situation. He had a series of discussions with Dan Ferens, the Steelers' assistant controller who handles many of their contract negotiations.

"This," Bell told Ferens, "isn't very good." But because of his politicking, some in the Steelers' front office sarcastically referred to him as Coach Bell when they saw him.

"We were wondering what the hell was going on," Bell said. "Why would you take a Pro Bowl linebacker and move him? We didn't like it from the get-go, but we were trying to be polite about it."

Lloyd's good manners ended 10 days before training camp opened. It was the final day of minicamp and Lloyd decided to tackle the issue as if it were an opposing quarterback.

"My concern is my longevity in this league," he said. "If nobody else has that concern, that's their problem. So for the last couple days of minicamp I became very radical. Everything they said to do I did just the opposite of. I let them know how much I didn't want to be there. I think I screwed up every play on purpose. They knew."

Mishandled, the situation could have blown up in Cowher's face. Lloyd was the first to test the new player-coach relations, and others were watching to see his reaction.

"It would have been a problem," Lloyd said, "because if I would have come to training camp titled `Inside Linebacker,' I probably never would have shown up. It almost makes you want to say 'screw it.' You don't want me to play where I want to play, then I won't play at all."

With both the *Pittsburgh Press* and *Post-Gazette* on strike since May 17, Lloyd's June discontent never became a big public issue.

"We didn't want to challenge the new head coach," Bell said. "But I felt Bill, in some ways, backed himself into a corner."

If he had, he walked right out of it. Cowher called Lloyd into his office at the end of minicamp in June and told him he was moving him back to outside linebacker.

"If a player believes it's not going to work and doesn't want it to work, then it won't," Cowher said. "We moved him back, not trying to appease him. To me, it was over with. I don't think there was a message there. I didn't go into great detail interpreting it. He was a very successful outside linebacker. We asked him to go in there, he said he'd try it; he tried it, didn't like it, so we moved him back. I said in the beginning nothing was etched in stone."

Cowher's first big confrontation as a young, rookie head coach had dissolved. As it turned out, it was a good thing he did not move Lloyd inside because a real weakness had formed at outside linebacker. To their horror, the new coaches discovered that Huey Richardson, their expensive young pass-rusher, had two problems: At outside linebacker, he had all the dexterity of a blocking dummy; as a defensive end, he was not big or strong enough to get near the quarterback.

It became evident quickly in training camp that Huey Richardson, just one year after he became the 15th pick in the '91 draft, could not play a lick. He was called the Silence of the Lamb — he refused to talk to reporters and some front office people, and he played like Little Bo Peep. Cowher repeatedly promised that he would keep the best 47 players, and Richardson was not one of them.

By the end of training camp, Cowher asked Tom Donahoe, "Can we cut a first-round draft pick?"

Donahoe winced. He thought they should give Richardson one more year. He was hurt much of his rookie season and was moved out of position by the previous staff. But it had become obvious that he would never fit. Players made fun of the way he back-pedaled on pass coverage and how he ran stiffly. A familiar sight on brilliant July and August afternoons on the St. Vincent College practice field was Huey Richardson slapping the ground with his hand and shouting obscenities after he botched another play. His name came up every time they had a personnel meeting that summer, and it wasn't to praise his work.

Donahoe told Cowher to keep his best players, even if Richardson had already pocketed nearly a million and a half of the boss's bucks for nothing in return.

"If there's one thing Dan Rooney's ever emphasized to me," Donahoe said, "it's keep the best players, regardless of who they are."

Out went Richardson, peddled to the Washington Redskins, who thought they got a bargain for a seventh-round draft pick in

1993. The 'Skins cut him during the season and the New York Jets picked him up and cut him again during the season.

"I think it's a good opportunity to show people you mean what you say," Donahoe said.

Richardson wasn't the only high-priced talent flushed away by the new regime. Before it was over, they cut Tom Ricketts, a No. 1 pick in 1989, and Craig Veasey a third-round pick in 1990. The housecleaning prompted Donahoe to say, "My philosophy with draft picks is you get 'em good or you get 'em gone."

With veterans, it was, you get 'em signed or you get 'em gone. In mid-September they traded safety Thomas Everett to Dallas and cut wide receiver Louis Lipps after the pair refused to sign contracts offered to them by the team.

These were unpopular moves among their teammates. Everett is a small, but muscular free safety who played hard and was a leader on defense. He started since his rookie season in 1987. Lipps was the second-leading receiver in team history, a popular player with the fans, and a veteran on a team desperate for wide receivers.

But Donahoe believed Everett was past his prime, and he wanted more money than strong safety Carnell Lake had gotten in his new contract that averaged $583,000 annually. The Steelers refused and they received a fifth-round draft pick from the Cowboys for him. Everett went on to play a key role as a strong safety in Dallas and starred in the Super Bowl with two interceptions and a sack.

Lipps, at 30, was a different case. He had been one of the best wide receivers in the league during his first two seasons ('84 and '85), then became injury prone and missed games. He led the Steelers in receptions his final four years with them, but his average yards per catch declined, and he dropped a frightful number of them in 1991. When he skipped all of training camp, the Steelers got tougher in their contract negotiations and eventually released him outright. Lipps was never known as a work-out player, and without supervision, the Steelers did not believe he would be in shape to play.

"When you get to the point with a holdout that he becomes an injury risk, you have to do something," Donahoe said. "It's one thing to work out on a track and another with guys flying at your Adam's apple. That became our concern with Louis Lipps — what are you getting?"

Through the first four weeks of training camp, the Steelers had offered Lipps $1.8 million for two years. When New Orleans claimed him on September 22, he signed for $1.525 million for two years. He pulled a hamstring two weeks later and on October 27, the Saints waived Lipps. No one else picked him up in 1992.

"His agent kept telling us how many teams were interested in him," Donahoe said. "There's another guy victimized by an incompetent agent. Based on what he signed for in New Orleans, the agent didn't give him all the facts. It happens all the time. I feel bad for the guy." The Steelers, though, signed Lipps as a free agent on April 21, 1993.

Some players were upset that Everett and Lipps weren't signed. Linebacker Hardy Nickerson was the most outspoken. He was bitter because he and the Steelers could not agree on a contract in 1991. He felt he was forced to play for low wages that year and again in '92, when he signed a one-year deal for $268,000 rather than sit out or accept a three-year contract.

"I don't know what the mentality of the front office is," Nickerson said, "but in my eyes those are two of the best players on the team and they're gone now. I hate to face being paid $268,000 this year when they have guys on special teams in San Diego making $400,000."

Cowher talked to Nickerson about his situation and asked him merely to forget his contract problems on the field, which he did. Nickerson, in fact, would go on to have the best of his six pro seasons and eventually make out better financially. Because he joined in one of the several antitrust lawsuits brought by other players, Nickerson was paid handsomely with the damages awarded those players. He then signed a $5.1 million, three-year contract with Tampa Bay as a free agent in the spring of '93.

Cowher had other problems to contend with at training camp, which was plagued by so much rain at the end of July the practice field turned to muck. Chuck Noll would have either continued to practice on the field or move the players into the Kennedy Hall gymnasium on the St. Vincent campus for indoor, close-quarters, noncontact workouts.

Noll occasionally persisted with practice at St. Vincent as lightning flashed in the skies over Latrobe. He would explain that he could determine there was no danger by counting the seconds between the flash and the thunder. That was of little comfort one electric afternoon in the 1980s to Mike Rooney, the teenage son of Art Jr. who ran the scouting department at the time and is Dan Rooney's brother. Mike filmed practice from the 30-foot metal scaffolding at training camp but shut off the camera and began to climb down as lightning flashed near the end of one workout.

"Hey," Noll called to him, "get back up there, we're not finished yet."

Artie walked over to Noll and said, "If you want film of this, send *your* son up there."

Cowher, instead of losing practices or working in dangerous conditions, asked the Steelers to find a suitable site elsewhere. They quickly boarded the players on buses and drove them 45 miles to Pittsburgh, where they practiced for two days on the artificial turf at Carnegie Mellon University.

Training camp was not nearly the same. Noll had abandoned the twice-daily workouts the first two weeks, when camp rosters were reduced to 80. Cowher alternated, holding two practices every other day. He also held a handful of practices at night to break up the routine and get them used to playing under lights.

Cowher often showed a different side in training camp than the back-slapping, hand-pumping, smiling young coach that TV cameras would catch on the sidelines in 1992. Early on, he had to let his players know that the new guy, although nearly their age, meant business. He felt they were testing him on occasion, and twice within a week midway through camp he reached for the paddle.

He screamed at his players often on the afternoon of July 28 and extended practice from the customary two hours to nearly three. Then, on August 4, he gathered his whole team around him at the end of the practice field and blistered them for 90 seconds, shouting an occasional profanity to emphasize his anger.

"If you don't want to do what you're told, get the bleep out of here. On offense, we're dropping balls all over the place. On defense, we've got guys just standing around. Now get the bleep out of here," he ended, pointing toward the steps disgustedly.

"That," Cowher said much later in the season, "was the first time they'd seen this guy react that way to a situation."

The reactions from people outside his team were not good as Cowher's Steelers lost their first two exhibition games. They slipped to Philadelphia on a disputed call at home, then got rubbed out by the Saints in New Orleans, 26-0. Cowher had declared the job at quarterback wide open between Bubby Brister, the incumbent, and young Neil O'Donnell. The two combined for a paltry 83 yards passing against the Saints.

But the Steelers showed marked improvement over the next two exhibition games, beating the Bears and Giants, and were hopeful as they prepared to open the 1992 season. O'Donnell won the quarterback job with a smashing first-half performance against the Giants in the finale.

The start of the regular season, however, loomed like a Texan's boot on a June bug — four of the Steelers' first five games were on the road, including the opener in Houston's noisy Astrodome.

7

LIGHTNING ROD

In his final college football game, Rod Woodson rushed for 93 yards on 15 carries, caught three passes for 67 yards, had 10 tackles on defense, broke up a pass, caused a fumble, returned two kickoffs for 46 yards, three punts for 30 yards, and dragged Purdue to a 17-15 victory over Indiana.

It was nothing compared to what he did in Bill Cowher's first game as an NFL head coach.

Mere statistics no longer sketch the boundaries of Woodson's value to a football team. For one thing, his NFL coaches hold these old-fashioned ideas that he must limit himself to playing defense, returning punts, returning kickoffs, and forget about those radical offensive leanings.

To understand what Woodson means to the Steelers, picture a man of steel in a flowing red-and-blue cape with a big "S" on his chest (he actually appeared that way on the cover of *Steelers Digest*); then imagine the driving compulsion of Jimmy Stewart in *Mr. Smith Goes to Washington*.

Many consider Hall of Famer Mel Blount, who has four Super Bowl rings, to be the best cornerback who ever played the game. Blount thinks Woodson is better.

"Man, the guy's incredible. Rod Woodson is a special kind of athlete. He's a better player than I was. He's a better player now than I was in my sixth year. And if Rod Woodson continues to play on the level he's playing, people will forget about Mel Blount."

Woodson was not supposed to play in the Steelers' 1992 season opener against the Houston Oilers, because he tore a calf muscle two weeks earlier in Chicago. While a calf muscle tear would stop a mere mortal, Woodson belongs on a higher plane. Woodson did not just play, he dominated the Oilers. The Steelers went to the Astrodome 11-point underdogs, but the oddsmakers forgot to check Woodson's level of spiritual possession that day.

Ernie Holmes, a.k.a. Fats of the Steel Curtain, was once asked how he felt before a big game in the 1970s. Replied Fats: "I'm more pumped up than the U.S. Blimp."

That was Rod Woodson on September 6, 1992, in Houston.

The Oilers took the opening kickoff, and after three plays, they had two first downs and were steaming from their 44. There, wide receiver Ernest Givins juked outside on Woodson, then moved inside to take Warren Moon's pass. Excuse me? Woodson bumped past Givins and intercepted it.

The Steelers' offense could not take advantage of that and Pittsburgh eventually fell behind, 14-0, midway through the opening quarter of what fast appeared to be a blowout.

But Cowher showed a daring he would exhibit most of the season. Punter Mark Royals dropped back into formation and stunned the Oilers when he tossed a pass to Warren Williams, who carried it 44 yards to the one. Barry Foster scored his first touchdown of the season to put Pittsburgh back in the ballgame, 14-7.

Houston clung to a 24-19 lead in the third quarter and was driving in Pittsburgh territory when Woodson said, "No mas." On first down at the 43, he blitzed, somehow leaped over guard Doug Dawson and batted the pass away. Two plays later, on third-and-two, Woodson hurdled over another Oiler to grab Lorenzo White and throw him down for no gain. Moon then threw incomplete to end that threat.

Finally, with Houston leading 24-22 in the fourth quarter, the Oilers were proceeding to put the game away with a first down at the Steelers' three, White carried off tackle on first down and Woodson crushed through a pitiful block by Leonard Harris to stop him cold. On second down, Moon rolled to the right under pressure and threw across field to Givins in the end zone. Woodson stepped up, intercepted the pass on the goal line, and ran it back 57 yards.

This time, the Steelers offense took it the rest of the way to go ahead, 29-24. That was how it ended, a shocking Pittsburgh victory that set the tone for the entire 1992 season. The players presented Bill Cowher with his unexpected first victory and his first Gatorade bath.

And the legend that was Rod Woodson continued to grow. He knocked down three Moon passes, had nine tackles, two interceptions, and the fire in his eyes burned brighter than ever.

"You can tell," Cowher said admiringly, "by the look in his eyes."

That's something you can't put on a stat sheet, either.

"You always like to think that great players make great plays in big games," said Tom Donahoe. "That's what you expect those guys to do. And Rod's done that for us."

He would continue doing it right through the 1992 season, wrecking offenses as no cornerback should. He has 4.3-second speed in the 40, was a world-class hurdler, and at 6 feet, 200 pounds, is one of the biggest cornerbacks in the league. Most corners play *either* the run or the pass; Woodson excels at both.

"He can hit with any of the defensive backs in the league," Steelers defensive coordinator Dom Capers said.

Next up, the New York Jets, a surprise playoff team the previous season. Woodson had a sack, forced a fumble, and blocked a field goal attempt. He was named the AFC Defensive Player of the Week as the Steelers ran off to a 2-0 record with a 27-10 victory at home.

Rod Woodson and the Steelers were on their way to a memorable year, just as Woodson had planned. He had dedicated the season to his father, James Woodson, who died on May 19, 1992, of a massive stroke.

"His memory is with me at all times," said Woodson. "Even on the field. This season is dedicated to my father, and that's probably one of the motivating factors for me. If I'm not doing well, I just talk to my dad and say, you know, 'Give me a little help here.'"

Woodson was not even permitted to grieve in peace for his father, thanks to overzealous cops in Fort Wayne, Indiana. The

Woodson family decided to take James Woodson off life support on May 19 after doctors told them the stroke ended all brain function. Rod's brother, Jamie, was angry when the family told him on the phone about the decision. He would not allow it.

Jamie arrived at the Woodson home and fought with Rod over the decision to end their father's life support. The police came and arrested both of them.

"It was so stupid," Rod said. "When you get officers who have a badge, they're the law, but some of those guys never went to school to deal with certain situations and they only know how to react one way — and that's the way they reacted."

Woodson beat the rap in his hometown and he and his brother quickly ended their differences. Rod went to trial in March 1993, and testimony showed that some of the cops had lied and faked a report of the incident. It took only 20 minutes for the jury to find Rod not guilty, and he now plans a lawsuit. Charges against Jamie were dropped.

James Woodson died shortly after the police left that day.

"You just never know when you're going to lose somebody like that," Woodson said, "and you never know how you're going to react to it. Sometimes it wakes people up. It gives you that inner strength to do well. When you have that, it's hard to get beat."

Woodson displayed a burning pride in himself and his family long before he reached the pros. He was an accomplished swimmer in Fort Wayne before he ever tried out for football. When he finally did give it a go, he quit temporarily at Snider High his sophomore year because he could not take the coaches' constant harangue. "I didn't want to hear anybody else yelling at me but my parents," he said.

Woodson heard more than yelling as a kid in Fort Wayne. He was taunted because his mother was white and his father black. The family struggled after his dad got laid off by International Harvester. Rod went two and a half weeks during a vacation break his junior year at Purdue without anything to eat but canned corn and green beans provided by his parents. Pride forbade him to ask anyone else for help.

"All I had was a quarter in my pocket and training table didn't start yet. I would not spend that quarter. That was *my* quarter."

Woodson tarnished his reputation at Purdue through some minor pranks; he switched the price tag on a pair of window blinds at a Kmart, and was charged with stealing a bartender's tip jar. He agreed to perform community service; and neither case went to trial. Woodson and former Steelers cornerback Delton Hall ran together during their early years in Pittsburgh and once fought with some patrons outside a local pub. But Woodson matured quickly and stopped running around. The Steelers helped the process by matching him with two of their model citizens. He roomed with safety Donnie Shell as a rookie, and his locker was next to Dwayne Woodruff, cornerback and attorney.

"You have to take on different responsibilities," Woodson said. "You have to take on a different role in your own life. That's what happened to me."

He continues his recklessness on the field, a trait Mike Poehlein first noticed when he coached him in track at Purdue. He would find Woodson in the locker room after running the hurdles, bleeding from wounds on his legs, gashes that often required stitches. Rod preferred to bull his way through the hurdles rather than leap over them.

"Rod broke them all the time," Poehlein said, laughing. "We got those new, unbreakable hurdles and he broke them. He went through them all the time and one day I said, 'Rod, let's go *over* the damn things.' But he was so tough; he didn't want to be bothered by jumping over them, he'd rather go through them. It cost him tenths of a second. It didn't please me as a track coach, but if I was a football coach, I'd love it."

And they do. Shortly after the Steelers selected him with the 10th pick in the 1987 draft, Chuck Noll uncharacteristically blurted, "I'm in love with him."

Opposing coaches cherish him so much, they order their own players to keep away from him, which is one reason he doesn't ring up many interceptions. Quarterbacks throw the other way.

Atlanta Falcons coach Jerry Glanville claims he lost his job with the Houston Oilers because he did not order his team to stay away from Woodson. Houston had a first down on the Steelers' 45 in sudden-death overtime in a playoff game on New Year's Eve 1989 in the Astrodome. Lorenzo White ran a sweep left. Woodson slammed into him like an exploding champagne cork.

The ball popped loose and Woodson gobbled it up. A few minutes later, Gary Anderson kicked a 50-yard field goal to send the Steelers into the next round and Jerry Glanville back to Atlanta.

"It's unusual that you get such a great hitter at corner," Glanville said. "We used to have it with Ronnie Lott years ago, but then they moved Lott to safety. If you have a big-time hitter who is also a cover guy, it gives your team an edge over everybody else's. Most cover guys don't hit like he hits."

Woodson loves to hit. Receivers, running backs, high hurdles, anything.

"If you don't hit, you won't make it in Pittsburgh," Woodson said. "I like hitting; it's fun. If I tried just to be a cover man, it would take away the excitement of the game."

"Hurdlers have a mean streak," Poehlein explained.

The new coaching staff took advantage of that more than ever. In the Steelers' "dime" defense that deploys six defensive backs, they moved Woodson from cornerback and put him on the line of scrimmage about five yards wide of the defensive end. They call it the press or slot position, where he takes a receiver head-on. It put him more into the action and allowed him to blitz, a fierce weapon because of his size, speed, and closeness to the quarterback.

"I love it," Woodson said. "Those slot receivers are closer to the quarterback and they usually throw to those guys. That gets me more involved. You're in the action. You're right there. I'm reading the quarterback, I can blitz, I can play man-to-man, I can play zone. It's like playing linebacker. You get to get your hands dirty. That's something cornerbacks don't often get to do, blitz and get sacks."

He finished second on the team with six sacks in 1992.

"He can cover with the best of them," Cowher said. "He's big like a safety and can cover like an undersized corner and has the mentality of a linebacker. You really couldn't ask for anything else. He's also one of the most dangerous returners in the game, and he plays hurt."

Teams on occasion took advantage of Woodson's aggressive nature to burn him deep. The Los Angeles Rams did it twice in a Monday night game in 1990. The receiver ran a little hitch, the quarterback pumped, Woodson bolted up to cover his man, and the receiver then flew past him. But quarterback Jim Everett overthrew his wide-open receiver the first time, and Flipper Anderson dropped the pass on the second one.

Rod didn't have such luck against the Packers in 1992. Pittsburgh carried a 3-0 record into Green Bay and a growing reputation as the surprise team of 1992. For once, the Steelers were favorites. But young Packer quarterback Brett Favre caught Woodson on his worst pro day. Wide receiver Sterling Sharpe ran a hitch, blew past Woodson, and Favre hit him with a 76-yard touchdown pass. Later, Woodson muffed a punt that gave Green Bay the ball at the Pittsburgh eight. On the next play, Favre went right at Woodson. He pump-faked to Sharpe and hit Robert Brooks for a touchdown pass.

Woodson heaved his helmet across the field in disgust and afterward apologized to his teammates for the 17-3 loss.

"I have to rebound and get the respect of my teammates again and my coaches."

Ha! Those were the last people he had to worry about. Right after Brooks's TD catch, Cowher put his arm around Woodson alone behind the bench and told him to forget it.

"He's the best in the business, the best I've ever coached and I've been around some pretty good ones," said Cowher, who coached All-Pros Albert Lewis in Kansas City and Frank Minnifield in Cleveland. "Rod's had some double moves on him and he's going to keep getting people running double moves on him because he's made a lot of plays for this team by anticipating routes."

No one apologized in Green Bay, by the way, for dropping seven passes from quarterback Neil O'Donnell. Had they caught several, they might have rendered Woodson's mistakes moot.

The Steelers had a bye the next week, then a trip to Cleveland, where they lost their second in a row, 17-9, to slip to 3-2. Some accounts of the game noted that Woodson blew a coverage again that allowed Michael Jackson to catch a 47-yard TD pass. Woodson woes continue! Rod never said anything, but he did exactly what he was supposed to do on the play. It was Solomon Wilcots and Sammy Walker who blew it.

Woodson's flame ignited another victory, another big game in Kansas City, the seventh game of 1992. No one gave them a chance against the Chiefs, but Woodson opened the scoring with an electrifying 80-yard punt return for a touchdown. It silenced the Tomahawk Chops and sent the Steelers to a 27-3 upset.

If there is one thing that Pittsburgh must do in this age of free agency, it's assure that Rod Woodson does not get away. He will not turn 30 until 1995, which means he could play into the next century. Mel Blount retired after 14 seasons with the Steelers, even though he was still an above-average cornerback. Woodson's 14th season would come in the year 2000.

Rod's contract was set to expire after the 1993 season, and because he was one of the players who sued the league in an antitrust case, the Steelers could not use their exemptions to keep him. The only way to do so was to convince him to stay. Woodson makes an average of $1.45 million annually on a three-year contract. He could easily double that. Woodson could be the Reggie White of '94.

"I see a situation where teams are going to need to really show their players throughout their careers their importance to the organization and treat them well," said Woodson's agent, Eugene Parker. "The Steelers will have an opportunity to show that with Rod. Football-wise, he definitely wants to stay. As long as the business aspects don't stand in the way, I'm sure he will stay."

It is imperative to Pittsburgh's quest for another Vince Lombardi Trophy that he does.

8

A DIFFERENT BILL SETS SAIL

Visitors to Pittsburgh the weekend of October 23, 1992, might have wondered if the whole city hadn't lost some huge, cruel bet to Atlanta when the Braves beat the Pirates in the National League Championship Series.

The Bubbas had taken over Three Rivers Stadium.

Friday night, the Tomahawk Chop thundered from loudspeakers as the Steelers went through practice under the lights. Saturday morning, country-western megastar Garth Brooks invaded a Steelers practice and stopped everyone in his cowboy boots.

Were the Steelers paying for the sins of their fellow tenants, the Pirates?

Nope, just another fun-filled weekend with Steelers coach Bill Cowher. If a few days could show the difference in styles between Pittsburgh's new coach and its former one, these were the days. The surprising Steelers were 4-2, but flying into a brutal three-game stretch that could easily clip their wings and send them and their rookie coach spinning into disaster. They had to play at Kansas City, home to Houston, and then at Buffalo. They figured to be doing well if they could escape with one victory, but 4-5 seemed more realistic after they got through playing three of the best and most experienced teams in the American Conference.

The Kansas City game would be played on Sunday night. So Cowher ordered a Friday night practice in Pittsburgh — with some musical accompaniment. Cowher had coached in Kansas City for three seasons and knew the problems the fans there caused opposing teams with their constant Tomahawk Chop drone. Bob McCartney, the Steelers' sharp video coordinator, taped the Chop when Atlanta fans performed it during the NL Championship Series. He blasted it through the Three Rivers sound system during Steelers practices all week.

Chuck Noll, more the traditionalist who disliked distractions, resisted suggestions that he practice at night before games and that he pipe noise into the stadium before certain away games.

On the following Saturday morning, Cowher practically turned his special teams practice session over to Garth Brooks, who not only is the most popular country music star, but also its biggest Steelers fan. Brooks, who grew up in Oklahoma, fell in love when he saw the Immaculate Reception on TV as a kid. His road manager, Mickey Weber, and Chet Fuhrman, the Steelers' conditioning coordinator, are friends, and they arranged his visit before Brooks's concert that night at the Civic Arena in Pittsburgh.

Brooks wore a pair of white Steelers pajama-style pants with gold emblems, and it was hard to tell who was more impressed, the Steelers or the country music king. All of them acted like kids on Santa's lap. "Mr. Brooks," quarterback Bubby Brister asked, "can I take my picture with you?" Brooks posed for at least 50 photos with players, front office people, even Dan Rooney, who presented him with a football and later asked, "Who was that?"

Brooks tossed a football around on the sidelines and punted a few times. He stayed two-and-a-half hours, traded autographs, and received a boatload of Steelers T-shirts and other clothing. Later, he sent them $10,000 worth of Garth Brooks apparel through the mail.

Brooks, who would sing the national anthem at the Super Bowl, said as he left, "I'll see you guys in Pasadena."

The visit was reminiscent of one that occurred in 1972, when the Steelers spent the week practicing in Palm Springs before their final game in San Diego. Broadcaster Myron Cope had run into Frank Sinatra at a restaurant and arranged for him to appear at practice the next day so he could be inducted into Franco's

Italian Army. "What's this I hear about you planning this distraction at my practice?" Noll asked Cope. But Noll allowed Harris to walk to the sidelines during practice to have his picture taken with Sinatra and the officers in Franco's Italian Army, who had brought wine and cheese for the occasion.

Noll and Cowher were alike in many ways, and so different in many more. They were both able to put things behind them quickly — losses, victories, injuries, drug suspensions, what have you. Both were consumed with detail. Each had quit playing at a young age to become an assistant coach on defense in the pros. They are German, from blue-collar families in steel towns — Noll from Cleveland and Cowher from the Pittsburgh suburb of Crafton. Both often uttered, "Whatever it takes."

Cowher, though, was more outgoing, an emotional coach moved to giving pep talks and shouting encouragement on the sidelines. He joined the players' gauntlet during pregame introductions and slapped high and low fives with them. Chuck Noll would rather be caught in drag than do that. Players all over derisively refer to "rah-rah" coaches, but Cowher was able to rise above that because his enthusiasm was real, not forced.

Defensive end Donald Evans will never forget what Cowher told the team before the opener in Houston.

"He said, 'Look, I don't want any tight asses. Go out there and get after those people. No tight asses! Just don't be a tight ass! Just have fun!'"

"He talks to you like a player," defensive end Aaron Jones said. "Like he is a player. Like if he only could, he'd be out there with us."

Steeler players, for the most part, respected Noll; but they had grown stale, for whatever reason, and Cowher reawakened them.

"I don't believe Chuck was ever an enthusiast," said linebacker Bryan Hinkle, a Steeler since 1981. "He expected you to know what to do, to be mature enough to come out and be prepared. He expected a lot of things from his players. He gave his players a lot of freedom. I think that worked in the '70s. I believe in the '80s and '90s players changed, and you can't do that anymore. I believe the way things are structured down here is the way you have to do it. Guys need to be told what to do sometimes. They need a little more structure. Guys need less free time. It's just the way things have changed, the way society is as a whole."

Hinkle and the two other oldest veterans, tackle Tunch Ilkin and linebacker David Little, talked among themselves often about those changes.

"It's a new team, a new era," Little said. "The team we have now and the coach we have now fits in well because everybody's so young. Everything is more structured than under Noll."

Noll, standing on the sidelines, would try to quiet a noisy crowd at Three Rivers Stadium as it drowned out an opposing quarterback's signals. He did not think it was fair. At press conferences, Cowher twice invited fans to crank up the noise level to disrupt the opposition. He also urged them on by pumping his arms on the sidelines.

He did not have to worry about inciting the Cowher group in booth 399, though.

This fervor apparently runs in Cowher's immediate family, and his wife, Kaye, matches his energy. They're thinking of soundproofing booth 399, where Kaye, Cowher's mom and dad, his brothers, Dale, 41, and Doug, 34, and other family members watch the games at Three Rivers Stadium between shrieks. Someone said Kaye Cowher gets so excited during games, they should strap her in a seatbelt. His dad, too.

"If it wasn't for this glass," Laird Cowher said, pointing to the front of the box, "I'd probably have gone through it a couple of games."

Laird, 70, and his wife, Dorothy, 69, were Steelers fans long before Bill became the team's coach, before Bill became their son. Laird Cowher (also known as Bill, and with the protruding jaw to match) graduated from Duquesne University in 1951, got a job, and the first things he bought were season tickets to the Steelers. Section 209.

He was a fan of all Pittsburgh's teams and was disappointed when Johnny Majors did not recruit Bill to Pitt. Instead, Bill went to play for Lou Holtz at North Carolina State in 1975 after he graduated from Carlynton High School. This created a problem for his family. The Steelers were in the process of erecting a football dynasty, and no way Laird Cowher was going to miss it. So the Cowher family drove nine-and-a-half hours to Raleigh to watch Bill play on Saturday and drove back to Pittsburgh in time to see the Steelers kick off at 1 p.m. on Sunday.

"It used to be a pleasure," Mr. Cowher said.

The Cowhers could keep up with their son when he played in Philadelphia and Cleveland and then coached in Cleveland, but Kansas City was too far to travel. When he returned to Pittsburgh as coach, they were able to have a Thanksgiving meal as a family again for the first time in 15 years, and Bill and Kaye had ever-ready baby-sitters for their three young daughters.

Cowher's reputation as a wild-eyed, Jack Lambert-style linebacker was forged at tiny Carlynton, where they had only 22 players on the football team his senior season. Tom Donahoe coached at South Park High School then and never forgot him.

"He intimidated everybody on my football team," Donahoe said, "including half my coaching staff. He was one of the most intense players I've ever seen."

He was bitterly disappointed that he was not recruited by Penn State — at 6-3, weighing only 190 pounds had something to do with it — and when N.C. State played the Nittany Lions, Cowher was possessed. "It was easy to get him motivated," said Chuck Amato, then the Wolfpack linebackers coach.

Cowher could frighten his teammates as well as the opposition. Buffalo Bills guard Jim Ritcher, one year younger than Cowher, vividly remembers the nighttime raids he pulled on the incoming freshmen during training camp.

"He was crazy," Ritcher said. "He used to hang out with some of the older guys when he was a sophomore. I was a freshman, and those guys would go around and bang on your door at 2, 3, 4 o'clock in the morning. They'd tell you if you didn't open up the door, they'd break your windows. You know, windows cost like $11 back then, and that was a lot of money to a college student."

Ritcher could not believe it when Cowher began dating Kaye, his future wife, in Raleigh. Kaye Young and her twin sister Faye were All-American honorable mention basketball players at North Carolina State who went on to play together in the fledgling Women's Professional Basketball League and film a Doublemint gum commercial.

"She was so nice and polite," Ritcher said, "and then there was Billy. We all enjoyed him, but he was such a big hell-raiser. He had wild, crazy eyes, and we all thought he was partly insane."

Maybe he was. In Cleveland and Philadelphia, where he became an NFL special teams whiz, they had a nickname for him:

"Face," not only because of the fierce eyes and the frenzied look but his huge, protruding jaw, which is hereditary. Dentists and orthodontists know it as a classic prognathic mandible. If your daughter had one, you'd take out a second mortgage to have it repaired. But a prognathic mandible gives a macho, Dick Tracy look to a man, and the forceful image it presents can help, especially if you are a pro football coach.

Cowher signed as a free agent in 1979 with the Eagles, who cut him before the season. He went back to North Carolina State as a graduate assistant coach and first got the idea it might not be a bad job. He signed with Cleveland and played for the Browns and again with the Eagles until a knee injury ended his career at age 28 in 1984.

Cleveland coach Marty Schottenheimer hired him as his special teams coach in 1985 and his wildman antics, sprinting up and down the sidelines on punts and kickoffs, sometimes drew as much attention as the game. Browns kicker Matt Bahr said Cowher, the coach, hadn't changed much from Cowher, the player. "He was still the first one down on kickoffs."

He became a secondary coach in 1987, then moved with Schottenheimer to Kansas City in 1989 after resisting a pass by the Steelers to become their new secondary coach. Donahoe still hadn't forgotten, but Cowher told him his next step was to become a defensive coordinator, not move sideways.

Schottenheimer needed a new defensive coordinator and interviewed Bill Arnsparger and Joe Collier for the job. Cowher told him he was his man.

"Marty," he said, "if you don't get the guy you want, I can do the job."

Cowher kept on Schottenheimer like a beagle on a rabbit.

"He cornered me in a room one day," Schottenheimer said.

"I can do it," Cowher told him.

"How do you know you can do it?" Schottenheimer asked.

"I'm prepared; I'm ready to take this test. All I need is the opportunity."

Schottenheimer called it an unyielding determination and finally made Bill Cowher his defensive coordinator, his protégé.

"Marty Schottenheimer gave me an opportunity," Cowher said. "He gave it to an unknown. He's very special to me. He was the first man to believe in me."

Those who have seen both men coach say there is a lot of Marty in Bill. He adopted many of his mentor's coaching ways. One of them: He got Dan Rooney to let him rearrange the seating on the team's charter flights. The oldest players took over the first-class seats, and the coaches and team executives, including the Rooneys, moved back into coach.

Cowher also got Rooney to agree to upgrade some of the prehistoric training equipment in Pittsburgh. They installed new weight machines, new aerobics machines and a Jugs machine that passes footballs. He even put numbers on the practice jerseys, something that had never happened under Noll.

Many of the changes he brought to Pittsburgh were learned under Schottenheimer. The two men talked on the phone each week. In fact, two days after the Steelers' big season-opening victory in Houston, Cowher still had not talked to his father about it, but he had talked to Schottenheimer.

For those reasons, and more, the Steelers' October 25, 1992, game in Kansas City was special for Bill Cowher. He took pains not to admit it in the week leading up to the showdown, but he had let it be known long before then.

"I want to come back," he told the *Kansas City Star's* Kent Pulliam the previous March, "and I want to prove to Marty that he has trained me very well. I want to get a chance to prove to him that I learned the lessons well under him. I guess it will be different only in the sense that I want to be respected."

Chiefs All-Pro linebacker Derrick Thomas idolized Cowher and once had said that if his coach was going to Pittsburgh he wanted to go, too. Thomas said he hoped that he could throw the ball around with Cowher on the field before the game, as they always had done in Kansas City.

As the Steelers' bus pulled up, billows of smoke from the tailgate barbecues engulfed Arrowhead Stadium, which was bathed in red. You must need more than a ticket to get into Arrowhead, you must have to wear a Chiefs sweatshirt, hat, or coat, too. This was a Sunday night game, nationally broadcast by TNT; the Kansas City fans lit into the Tomahawk Chop early and often.

This was going to be ugly.

It was, too — for Schottenheimer and the Chiefs. Rod Woodson returned a punt 80 yards for a touchdown midway through the first period as the Steelers jumped to a 7-0 lead and never looked back. They got their *chops* in, too. The Steelers had grown so weary of hearing the Tomahawk Chop pounding them over the Three Rivers Stadium sound system in practice that they took their revenge on the unsuspecting Kansas City fans. When Barry Foster scored a touchdown in the third quarter, he performed the Chop, then gave the fans the old Italian salute. Eric Green did a wonderful Chop after his four-yard touchdown reception from Neil O'Donnell. That made the final, 27-3, Steelers.

The only drama remaining came with two minutes left as broadcaster Myron Cope pounded on the glass separating his booth from the Steelers coaches. They had taken Foster out of the game, not knowing he had 95 yards rushing. Defensive coordinator Dom Capers finally realized what the ranting Cope was trying to tell him. They put Foster back in, he carried one time for 10 yards, and came back out. He had 105.

"This," Schottenheimer said about the Chiefs, "is a good football team we have here, and we're particularly good at home. And they came in and cleaned us out. They just waxed us."

Pittsburgh and its young coach not only had shown they could keep winning, but that they could do so in the NFL's most difficult dens in a big way. Defensive ends Kenny Davidson and Donald Evans dumped Gatorade on Cowher again. They knew what this one had meant to him.

"It was like a homecoming victory for our coach," Evans said. "I think the players basically won it for the coach."

The pupil had returned home and taught the master a lesson.

Afterward, Bill Cowher and Marty Schottenheimer greeted each other warmly and Cowher told him, "I hope you win all the rest."

9

CONVINCING THE DOUBTERS

Walk through two black doors that swing open into the Steelers' locker room and you run smack into a bulletin board. A message from NFL commissioner Paul Tagliabue warns players against gambling or taking bribes. Red letters order "No Smoking."

It's a good thing the NFL has not banned foul language, because a steady stream of it flowed from the Steelers' mouths as they paused to look at the bulletin board during the week preceding their second game against Houston. The commissioner's message has been there so long, it gets as much attention as one of the thumbtacks stuck in the board. The players never give it a second look, just as they had come to ignore the faded sign that greeted them under Chuck Noll's regime: "Whatever It Takes."

What held the Steelers' attentions and stirred their emotions were comments made by the Houston Oilers the day they lost the 1992 season opener to Pittsburgh in the Astrodome, 29-24. The remarks appeared in small type in the next day's *Houston Chronicle*, innocently buried without a provocative headline.

Someone noticed, however, and realized the psychological impact those words might carry before the rematch on November 1, because the *Chronicle* clipping found its way to Pittsburgh. Originally three-and-a-half inches deep as a newspaper brief, it was blown up to a foot to grace the Steelers' bulletin board. Provocative phrases were accented in yellow to underscore the message.

Said defensive tackle Doug Smith: "We should've known they couldn't beat us straight-up. They had to trick us to beat us."

And these words of sportsmanlike concession from wide receiver Haywood Jeffires:

"We kept shoving it down their throats. We moved the ball. They couldn't stop us. We stopped ourselves."

The Steelers seethed. The Oilers had called their first-game victory a fluke. Since then, Pittsburgh had squashed Kansas City, 27-3, en route to a 5-2 record, and were tied for first place with the Oilers entering their epic rematch in Pittsburgh. Yet, again, they had to prove something to Houston, to the NFL.

"I don't think they respect us as a secondary," Rod Woodson sniffed. "It's just one of those things, I guess. You have to go out there and earn their respect. The only way you can get respect is by playing on the football field."

D. J. Johnson, Woodson's cornermate, laughed off Smith's remark. Tricked them? What, they greased their jerseys? Pulled the old hidden-ball routine?

The Oilers were miffed because Pittsburgh punter Mark Royals threw a 44-yard pass to Warren Williams from punt formation in the first game, setting up a 1-yard touchdown run by Barry Foster. The Steelers also ran two reverses to wide receiver Dwight Stone, which should not have come as a surprise because Chuck Noll ordered reverses against the Oilers all the time.

"That's part of the game," Johnson noted, "just like a receiver running a stop-and-go pattern. That's trickery. That's the exact same thing. Tricks are part of the game. I don't think a trick is a bad thing. A play-action is a trick. There are tricks throughout games."

The Oilers, too, were angry over remarks the Steelers made after the first game. Woodson declared they were more prepared, that they had the run-and-shoot figured out.

"Before," Woodson said, "we had our tendencies and whatnot, but these were more or less perfect."

Jeffires went crazy over that one. The Oilers had 434 total yards on offense in the opener. How could they have us figured out?

"They said they knew everything we were doing, but I don't believe that," Jeffires said.

But the Steelers *did* have Houston's run-and-shoot figured out as never before. There were three reasons for that: defensive coordinator Dom Capers, secondary coach Dick LeBeau, and a new microchip.

Along with the different weight equipment, the Jugs machine, and everything else, the Steelers' new regime acquired a computer that broke down opponents' tendencies visually and put them on tape. Now a video fanatic like Woodson could take two or three tapes home each night of the week, pop them into the VCR and study the Oilers' tendencies more precisely. One would show, for example, what Houston likes to do on third-and-short near midfield; second-and-long deep in their own territory; in goal-line situations.

This was more than a computer printout; these were videos of actual plays the Oilers (or whichever opponent that week) ran in specific situations — their tendencies.

Now, the human element.

LeBeau and Capers added two experienced hands against the run-and-shoot. LeBeau, 55 going on 45, intercepted 62 passes over 14 years at cornerback for the Detroit Lions, the fifth most in NFL history. He had been the Cincinnati Bengals defensive coordinator for eight years before he became their fall guy after a horrible 1991 season.

He may have been Cincinnati's scapegoat, but he was a hell of a secondary coach. With the Bengals, he faced Houston twice annually and developed some insight into the run-and-shoot.

Capers joined the coaching profession and saw the world. Only 42, he had 18 years on the job when Cowher hired him, including college stops at Kent State, Washington, Hawaii, San Jose State, Cal, Tennessee, Ohio State, then the USFL Philadelphia/Baltimore Stars, and the New Orleans Saints.

He majored in defense and wrote a dissertation on the run-and-shoot. Capers was first introduced to it by quarterback Jim Kelly and the Houston Gamblers when they played the Stars in the USFL. Then, in 1990, the New Orleans Saints played four games against run-and-shoot teams — Atlanta twice, Detroit, and Houston. Capers researched the run-and-shoot.

"I spent a lot of time with some run-and-shoot people trying to learn the offense. That one year, a quarter of our schedule was against the run-and-shoot. I spent an awful lot of time in the offseason, putting together cutups and studying that offense.

"It's obviously a different style of offense when you play a third-down attack on every snap. And everything they do is based off of where you are located. All their routes are going to be determined off of what type of coverage you're in and your position on the receivers."

Ergo, don't let them know what you're up to. It was no secret that Capers preferred to defend against the run-and-shoot with the dime defense — six defensive backs, two down interior linemen, two down outside linebackers, and one stand-up middle linebacker. But he mixed things up enough that the Oilers never knew what was coming.

In the dime, Woodson moved from cornerback to the slot or press position, a spot a few yards off the line, directly across from one of the Oilers' slot receivers, normally Ernest Givins in '92. Strong safety Carnell Lake moved to the slot on the other side in the dime. On occasion, Capers would send both on the snap soaring toward quarterback Warren Moon, at times dropping one of the interior linemen 10 yards deep into pass coverage, an unorthodox but highly effective scheme.

If nothing else, Capers believed you must follow two rules on defense when you played Moon and the Houston Oilers: (1) Push inside to disrupt his passing lanes; (2) Don't overdo the outside pressure.

"One of the worst things you can do is get your outside guys up the field too much, because Moon takes that five-step drop, sets, and if he has a window to throw, then you have problems. It's better, even if you don't get sacks, if you can get your inside guys to push up into his face where he's got to throw through somebody."

One glance down the hallway of the Steelers' offices in Three Rivers Stadium and it spelled B-I-G G-A-M-E. Prowling the corridor were ESPN's Andrea Kremer, O. J. Simpson of NBC-TV, crews from the Black Entertainment Network and Channel 4 of the United Kingdom, Bill Parcells of NBC-TV, and Paul

Zimmerman of *Sports Illustrated*. Where was Dan Rather? There hadn't been this much national interest in the Steelers since 1989.

Myron Cope also triumphantly walked the halls. The diminutive Steelers broadcast analyst is the most popular nonathlete in Pittsburgh, a 62-year-old bundle of energy and ego. His excitable voice sounds like a sow snagged on a barbed-wire fence. Somehow, it grows on you. Early in the '92 season, however, it had been failing him. The combination of a throat infection and too many cigarettes had produced a lingering rawness that scared him. No matter how popular, in his business, you lose your voice and your job goes with it.

But the unmistakable sound of Cope bounced off the walls as he walked out of Bill Cowher's press conference on Tuesday before the second Houston game. A caller to his talk show the previous night urged him to bring out the Terrible Towel on Sunday.

The only thing dearer to Cope than his voice and his family is the Terrible Towel. He conceived the idea in the 1970s, a gimmick that might have died had the Steelers not been in the midst of one of the greatest dynasties in pro football history.

Pure and simple, it was a towel. Some were black, most were gold. Some were black and gold. Fans waved them in the stadium or reverently draped them over television sets during games for good luck. Throughout the '70s, Three Rivers Stadium was awash in the things. Tight end Eric Green begged Cope for one shortly after he became the Steelers' No. 1 draft pick in 1990. Bill Cowher's parents, lifelong Steelers fans, still own an original Terrible Towel. Cope even authored a piece for *Sports Illustrated* about his baby.

The Towel, like the Super Bowl Steelers, ran its course. Cope twice tried to rally it in the latter years of Chuck Noll's regime, but it and the Steelers both failed to produce.

Now, he had the fever again. He argued loudly with a reporter who dared suggest that the Towel had lost its magic, then jumped him on the air that night for telling such damnable lies about it. In the meantime, some in the Steelers organization privately hoped Cope would take his Towel and stuff it back in his cedar chest.

"This is a new team, a new era," Tom Donahoe said.

Nobody, however, could deny Cope's effect on the town with his teenage-like enthusiasm for the Steelers. Big football games need no introduction, but, particularly with Pittsburgh newspapers silent, Cope had a way of stirring the pot. He was an Old Steeler who still had a home with the new regime.

A different kind of big game had developed in the Steelers locker room. It began early in the season with a few guys tossing balled-up tape into a wastebasket. By midseason, it grew into a regular post-practice competition. Players who only a year before would have run over their coaches to sprint for home after practice, now hung out and raucously played trashball.

Two baskets, two players separated by 25 feet, each took a turn shooting the wad of tape into the bucket at the other end. The low ceiling deflected many an arched shot. They played to five, or if nobody could score, one or two. Leroy Thompson claimed victory over Barry Foster. Then Carnell Lake jumped in, then Jerrol Williams, and D. J. Johnson.

"Guess who the best is?" Johnson asked. "I am."

"No," Foster insisted, leaping in front. "I am."

"I am," shouted Thompson.

It was like homeroom when the teacher walked out. It was also like nothing else seen in this locker room in a long time. In the mid '80s, a handful of players, including the aging John Stallworth, stuck around after Tuesday practices to play Booray, a gutsy and often loud card game. A few years later, Stallworth was gone and the post-practice locker room became a ghost town.

"Our team wasn't truly close," Woodson said. "We didn't really talk to each other."

Beginning in '92, however, the loud buzz returned, as did the camaraderie.

Western Pennsylvania, despite the Pittsburgh newspaper strike, quickly got caught up in the Steelers' revival and the showdown against Houston. It was to be the biggest football game played at Three Rivers Stadium in years.

"Our fans deserve this game," Donahoe said. "It makes you feel good for the people who've been with us and stayed behind us. You can't ask for any more loyalty than our fans."

Donahoe, a good high school basketball player in Pittsburgh in the '60s, exposed a desire all those fans could understand. "Sometimes, you wish you were younger and more talented and could go out there and play in it."

Back in Houston, Jeffires was still lathered over the Steelers' comments about the run-and-shoot. We had 500, 600 yards against them in the first game, he exaggerated, how can they say they have us figured out?

Even Jack Pardee, the normally taciturn Oilers coach, was worked up.

"We had over 400 yards against them in that first game, so if they've got us figured out, I'm glad to hear it."

On it went. They don't respect us, the Steelers said. They don't have us figured out, the Oilers countered.

But the thing that tore more at the Steelers was the thought that the Oilers believed they had somehow won a fluke game, won it by trickery down in the Astrodome.

OK, you don't want to be tricked? Let's play some old-fashioned football.

The Steelers had hoped for a blinding snowstorm and 18 degrees to welcome the Astrodome Oilers to Three Rivers Stadium. They settled for an overcast 47 degrees and a steady 10-mile-an-hour wind.

The stadium was filled and it was loud, lending the atmosphere of a playoff game, although few Terrible Towels could be seen. NBC-TV had interviewed old Steelers and Oilers about their fierce rivalry in the '70s, when Houston lost two straight AFC championship games in Pittsburgh to send the Steelers to their final two Super Bowls in 1979 and 1980. Those games prompted former Oilers coach Bum Phillips to proclaim the door to the Super Bowl went through Pittsburgh, and he had promised the Oilers would soon kick it down.

As of Sunday, November 1, 1992, Houston was still trying. Those games in '79 and '80 had been the closest the Oilers had ever come to the Super Bowl. Now, NBC-TV was highlighting those old classics and letting the former players reminisce on its pregame show.

In a few moments, a classic of its own would unfold between the two archrivals again.

The first message was sent, appropriately, by Woodson, the driving force behind Pittsburgh's opening-game victory in Houston. The Oilers had a third-and-four on their 26 when Moon dumped a short pass to Ernest Givins on the left side. BAM!

Woodson smacked into Givins, dropping him a yard short of the sticks. Woodson sprang up and began to tremble over Givins, mocking the shiver and Electric Slide dance Givins performs after touchdown catches.

Nevertheless, Houston jumped on top, 6-0, on two Al Del Greco field goals, the second when Pardee elected not to go for a touchdown on fourth down at the Pittsburgh one.

The Steelers offense kicked in midway through the second quarter. After four games, Pittsburgh had ranked 27th in the 28-team NFL in third-down efficiency. It was something that dogged them during the Joe Walton era. Now it bit them again early in 1992. But by the midway point of the season, the Steelers had steadily improved on third downs.

They made two key ones on their first touchdown drive against Houston. On the first, wide receiver Ernie Mills slipped through the middle of the Oilers on third-and-nine to catch a 15-yarder from Neil O'Donnell at the Oilers' 32.

But a moment later, O'Donnell made a rookie mistake. He scrambled to his left on second down from the 20. He pump-faked on the run, and the field opened before him. Wide receiver Jeff Graham drifted into the end zone. O'Donnell kept running and pumping his arm. He could have run 10, 15 yards, maybe even made it all the way. Instead, he flipped a pass to Graham, who caught it in the end zone.

Some fans cheered, but the Steelers were horrified. O'Donnell was four yards past the line of scrimmage when he threw it, an illegal forward pass that cost them a down. It was a silly mistake, and on the sidelines his coach spread his arms, palms up, and gave him a quizzical look.

"Why?" Cowher asked, shaking his head.

"I don't know if the coaches got into my head maybe a little there," O'Donnell said later. "You're always looking downfield and when you're watching tape on Monday they say, 'Instead of running here, you could have thrown it.' You see, when you watch tape the following day, it all looks great on tape. But when you're on that field, you don't see the guy coming across the middle backside when you have someone running you down from behind. I thought I had taken a five-step drop, but I was a little shorter than that."

As he scrambled to his left, the *real* Monday morning coaches were on O'Donnell's mind: *See here, Neil. Throw the ball, pass it, don't run. You're the quarterback; you're not Barry Foster.* They did a fine job of drilling *that* into his head. O'Donnell passed the ball.

On the next play, he gave them something better to review Monday morning. The penalty made it third-and-nine at the 21. Halfback Leroy Thompson swung out and O'Donnell snapped off a 20-yard pass to him.

From the one, Barry Foster crunched into the line three times before he scored, but it put Pittsburgh in front, 7-6.

Three Rivers Stadium thundered its approval. Above, in the Steelers' owners' box, Chuck Noll stood clapping and cheering with the rest of them.

"That," O'Donnell said, "is the loudest I've heard it in our stadium. People said it was like the '70s."

The stadium exploded on the next series when rookie free safety Darren Perry — the man who replaced hard-hitting Thomas Everett — slammed into tiny Leonard Harris as he tried to catch a Warren Moon pass. Harris wobbled off the field, never to return that afternoon.

"You know they're going to catch some passes underneath," Perry said. "You can't stop that. But when they catch them, you just have to make them pay for it. You get them thinking and they'll be a little hesitant coming across the middle the next couple of times."

At halftime, L. C. Greenwood, the frightening old Steel Curtain defensive end, whistled his praise of the Steelers' monster hits.

"He made *contact*," Greenwood said with a smile. "Next time the receiver goes over the middle, he'll remember that."

The Pittsburgh defense, now playing to those Steel Curtain standards, upped the ante early in the second half. Warren Moon was about to get that Leonard Harris feeling.

On the second play of the half, Woodson came flying on a blitz from Moon's left. Moon released a pass toward Haywood Jeffires and was immediately crunched by Woodson, who applied a near knockout blow to the chin. Woodson then fell on Moon, whose head bounced off the Three Rivers carpet.

It was lights out for Mr. Moon. He swayed to the sidelines with a game-ending concussion, joining Harris in a long coat.

"My whole 200 pounds was on him," said Woodson. "And

he was on his back, and his neck was bent back. He didn't look good at all."

"A lot of us," D. J. Johnson said, "have a kind of taste of blood in our mouths. You're a tiger in the wild, you taste the blood a little bit, and you get hungrier and hungrier."

Problem was, that brought on Commander Cody. Two years earlier, the Steelers went to Houston for the last game of the 1990 season, boasting a 9-6 record and the best defense in the NFL. Their secondary had allowed only six touchdown passes all season. All they needed to do was beat Houston, and they would win the AFC Central Division. Not only that, Moon was hurt and couldn't play. Houston would start someone named Cody Carlson at quarterback.

It would be a snap — for the Oilers. Carlson performed his best Dan Marino imitation that day. He completed 22 of 29 passes for 247 yards and three touchdowns, half the scores the Steeler secondary had allowed in its previous 15 games. The Oilers won, 34-14, and Pittsburgh, denied the playoffs again, tumbled into a year long funk that ended with Chuck Noll's retirement.

Now, Carlson was back and it looked like more of the same. He zipped them straight downfield, hitting newcomer Webster Slaughter with an 11-yard TD pass that put the Oilers ahead, 13-7, with 25 minutes left in the game.

A minute later, the Steelers were backed up on their 10 when O'Donnell flushed out of the pocket to his left. Defensive lineman Jeff Alm closed in from behind, reached out and punched the ball from O'Donnell's hand. It bounced right to All-Pro defensive tackle Ray Childress, who easily stepped into the end zone for a Houston touchdown.

"I was regrouping my feet to throw the ball to Eric Green," O'Donnell explained. "I go to wind up and throw it and the ball is knocked out of my hands. Now I'm down on the ground, crawling like a baby with someone on my feet, and I see Childress running for a touchdown.

"We're down, 20-7, and people were going, 'God, here we go again.'"

Just as they had in Houston, the Steelers trailed by two touchdowns. The crowd fell so silent you could hear a Terrible Towel drop.

"We're down, 20-7, and it doesn't look good," Bill Cowher said. "But, hey, we've been there before."

Early in the fourth quarter the Steelers got within striking distance. O'Donnell capped a long drive with a two-yard touchdown pass to tight end Adrian Cooper off the bootleg: 20-14.

The crowd's tempo picked back up. Deeeeefense, Deeeeefense. It was 1975 again. Twice the Oilers were penalized, once for delay of game and once for offside. The crowd noise bothered the Oilers. Again, two Oiler linemen jumped early for another five-yard penalty.

Houston was on its 45, facing third-and-15. The noise increased. Cowher pumped his arms at the sides, palms up, urging the home mob to higher decibels. Because of the din, Carlson spurned the shotgun to stand behind center Bruce Matthews. Linebacker Greg Lloyd shifted from the down end position to an inside linebacker.

Matthews snapped the ball, Carlson bobbled it, and Greg Lloyd burst in.

"A lot of times, you try to time up what's going to happen," Lloyd said. "We were hitting the A-gaps on this one and I saw the ball was just there and I went for it. There was no magic to it, no game plan to the ball being there."

Lloyd snatched the ball, fell on it, then held off two Oilers beneath the pile to keep it.

"One guy was pulling one of my arms apart, the other guy was trying to pull the other arm to get the ball out of there. But you don't let the ball go in a situation like that."

Lloyd carried his booty to the sidelines, stopped, and whirled it into the stands, a gesture that cost him a $1,500 fine from the NFL and gave someone a hell of a memento.

Ten minutes and 45 seconds left. The Steelers began at the Houston 38, trailing by six. When O'Donnell was sacked on second down, however, they sat on the 44, 16 yards to go for a first down and one down to get it.

O'Donnell, from the shotgun, took little time setting up and firing a laser over the middle to Eric Green, a 24-yard reception that gave the Steelers a first down at the 20. Those who had begun questioning the strength of O'Donnell's arm remained silent on that one.

Barry Foster worked it down to the five on three carries and a penalty against the Oilers.

From there, O'Donnell ran the bootleg again. Again the Oilers bit, and this time he hit Green for a touchdown. Gary

Anderson kicked the extra point, and the Steelers had come from 13 down to lead by one with 7:13 to go.

The place was in the kind of uproar that made home television screens shake. There hadn't been this much fun at a football game in Three Rivers Stadium since Cliff Stoudt was pelted by snowballs upon his return in 1984 with the USFL.

And it wasn't over.

Stumpy Howe, the fist-sized nose tackle, punched through the Oilers line and sacked Carlson back at the Houston 15, virtually ending the next series. With five minutes left, all the Steelers had to do was put together one of those clock-killing drives their offense was made for.

They couldn't do it, and Houston got a final chance with 3:53 left, starting way back at the 14. Down they came, Commander Cody and the new Slaughterhouse Five. Pass to Jeffires to the 33, to Givins to the 47.

A defensive holding penalty on Donald Evans on the next play so confused the officiating crew, it took them 632 midfield conferences and half the afternoon to get it right. Was this delayed halftime entertainment? They did everything but blow trumpets. They looked like Moe, Larry, and Curly in black-and-white stripes. They marked off one penalty. Nope, that's not right. Conference. They marked off another. Nope. Conference.

NFL officiating has deteriorated over the past decade, partly because of the absurd instant replay rule that subjected many of their decisions to further review from some retired ref with bad eyesight sitting in a pressbox looking at a small screen. It's no wonder the refs on the field lost their ability to make decisive judgments. They also seem to be getting older. In a game where size and speed prevail, the NFL has men in their 50s and 60s officiating.

"I'm not going to get involved in commenting on the officiating," Bill Cowher would later say. "I think the people who were at this football game saw it, and I think the effort spoke for itself."

Anyway, the refs, somehow, finally got it right, then marched off the wrong distance — a six-yard penalty against Pittsburgh instead of five. There was 1:57 left, and Houston was camped on the Steelers' 47.

Commander Cody kept it up. He flung one to Slaughter to the 33, another to Duncan to the 27. The Steelers allowed the clock to run. The Oilers called their second time-out with 19 seconds left. They came back and ran Lorenzo White into the middle, obviously setting up for a field goal try. White was thrown for a one-yard loss by Jerrol Williams.

Time out, Houston. The clock showed :06. Oilers kicker Al Del Greco walked onto the field to try a 39-yard field goal to win it.

Cowher called a time-out to ice Del Greco. He had two time-outs left, but NFL rules prohibit calling two in a row. Del Greco didn't know that.

"I thought they were going to call two," he said.

Because of it, the Houston kicker wasn't prepared mentally to kick right away. But the whistle blew and the Oilers lined up. The wind also blew at its steady 10 m.p.h. pace, slapping across the field.

Matthews snapped it and Rod Woodson, who had blocked a 37-yard field goal try against the Jets, roared in from the side.

"I was just running in blind. We felt we had to block it. You can't rely on the kicker or the holder or somebody to make a mistake. We just said everybody's going to try to get that kicker."

On the Pittsburgh sidelines, Cowher squatted. He was smiling. Smiling! His team was in danger of falling to 5-3, a game behind Houston. A loss could burst their bubble and shove them back toward the mediocrity that had been their lot the past decade. How could a rookie head coach, 35 years old, smile during such a pressure-packed moment?

"I've been there before as an assistant, and all three times the guy made the kick and we lost," Cowher explained. "I was just thinking, I guess I have the law of averages on my side."

He was thinking about something else, too.

"I'll tell you what went through my mind: 'Here we are, 59 minutes, 54 seconds. Guys laying it on the line and it comes down to a kick. This is the crazy business we're in. This is the kind of profession, Cowher, that you chose. The whole scenario just seemed . . . I don't know. Guys are getting taken off the field left and right, laying it on the line, and then it comes down to whether a guy's going to kick it, and we're trying to call time out to ice him.'"

Bill Cowher smiles again as he retells it.

"It puts everything in perspective of what a great game it is. It's a classic game."

Matthews's snap sailed a bit high, as the Oilers taught him. Greg Montgomery snatched it and neatly swung it in place. Del Greco kicked, satisfied he'd done the job. The mob, eerily quiet, watched. The wind blew.

Del Greco's kick hooked a few feet to the left of the upright. No good! Three Rivers rocked. Players in black and gold danced jubilantly. Adrian Cooper hugged his head coach, then lifted him triumphantly off the ground for a split second.

The Pittsburgh Steelers were 6-2, tied with Buffalo for the best record in the American Football Conference at the halfway point of the season.

10

ANOTHER TOUGH IRISHMAN

Quarterback Neil O'Donnell could not rejoice in the Steelers' giddy success. Two days after their euphoric victory over Houston, he went shopping on his day off. He had to buy a wheelchair for his father.

Jack O'Donnell suffered a near-fatal stroke three months earlier at home in New Jersey and his youngest son felt almost helpless in Pittsburgh.

"If I can't help my family by being there, I'm going to help them do all the other stuff," Neil insisted. "If I can help them out by sending a wheelchair home and other things my dad's going to need, it makes me feel like I'm doing my part."

Jack and Barbara O'Donnell raised three daughters and six sons, a warm Irish Catholic family fiercely loyal to each other. Five sons played college football. Neil was the youngest and the best athlete, and his parents never missed one of his games at the University of Maryland, home or away, even during Neil's redshirt season when they knew he wouldn't play.

Jack O'Donnell, 69, yearned for the day that his son would become a starting quarterback in the NFL. "He retired to play golf and watch me play football," Neil said.

But just as Neil was on the verge of his biggest success, his father was struck down by a debilitating stroke that required six hours of brain surgery. It happened August 8, the night before the Steelers' first exhibition game of 1992, at home against

Philadelphia. Neil was locked in a wide-open fight with incumbent Bubby Brister for the starting quarterback job, and they were to split halves against the Eagles the next day.

Regardless, Neil wanted to go straight home to Madison, New Jersey. His family urged him to stay put. His brother Michael lived and worked in Pittsburgh and talked him into playing the next day.

"Neil's first reaction was 'I have to go see my father.' We had to talk that through," Michael O'Donnell said. "Will he be able to recognize you? What can he do? What's the best thing? Neil really couldn't help my father's case. It was in the hands of the Lord."

"At this juncture," Michael told his brother. "It's in everyone's best interest for you to fulfill your duties as an NFL quarterback and address the other situation afterward."

The tight duel with Brister had only four exhibition games to run, and missing one could wound O'Donnell's chances. Offensive coordinator Ron Erhardt told him: "Don't worry about the game of football. Take care of what you have to with your family."

Neil stayed in Pittsburgh and flew home immediately after the game. "My dad was on my mind pretty much, but one place where he'd want me is on the football field."

Brister played three quarters against the Eagles before O'Donnell got his chance in the fourth. He entered the game thinking about his dad, but somehow was able not only to play, but to pass for 241 yards and three touchdowns.

The quarterback competition still had a long way to go, but that one quarter by O'Donnell burned an impression in the minds of the new staff. Coaches forever talk about "mental toughness." Now they had their perfect example in Neil O'Donnell. If he could play the way he did under those circumstances, what else could ever ruffle him?

"I think it was a lot bigger ordeal for Neil than anybody ever knew about," Erhardt said. "He handled it about as good as you could handle it without anyone else feeling anything was really going on. At the same time, he was trying not to lose any edge he may have had at quarterback. That doesn't happen very often with a young man."

O'Donnell and Brister split the duties at quarterback through the exhibition season before O'Donnell blew the competition away in the final game against the New York Giants. Playing the first half, he completed 11 of 15 passes for 150 yards and two touchdowns as the Steelers piled up a 17-3 lead on the way to a 24-3 victory in their final tune-up.

He had wrestled the job of starting quarterback for the Pittsburgh Steelers away from Bubby Brister. But there still was no joy.

"He was very somber, quiet," Erhardt recalled.

O'Donnell flew back and forth to New Jersey. Despite the support he received from his family, he felt some guilt about remaining in Pittsburgh the day after his dad fell ill. "I did not want to go home to bury my father," he said. He spent hours at his dad's side, talking, hoping he could hear him. Like Neil, Jack O'Donnell was a tough guy; who had risen from an auto mechanic to owner of a sprawling dealership, O'Donnell Buick, in the competitive northern Jersey market. "O-D" everyone called him.

"My dad had a lot of pride and never depended on anyone," Neil said, "and now he needs someone to help him."

Neil spent several days during the Steelers' bye week of September 28 with his father. It was a depressing time for a young man who should have been having the time of his life.

"He's at a rehab home in a horrible part of New Jersey, but [it's] one of the best in the country. It's like being in prison. If they don't get him out of there soon, I have a feeling they're going to lose him. There may be a shot he may not walk again, and that's something hard to take."

Neil's voice shook slightly.

"All he wants to do is sit in his own chair and watch his own TV. He's content just to have his own family around there. But then when it gets closer to going back, he starts getting depressed. He's very emotional."

O'Donnell decided there was one way he could provide a psychological boost to his father's long recovery.

"I keep telling myself the best therapy for my dad is to continue winning football games. That's what my dad really lives for is to watch me play football. If we just keep winning, I think that's great therapy for him."

The Steelers complied, winning more games than anyone could have predicted, winning their first division title in eight years and nailing down the home-field advantage for the playoffs for the first time in a dozen seasons. If the stroke that cut down Jack O'Donnell seemed ill-timed, the therapy beamed to his satellite dish each Sunday was a godsend. Jack O'Donnell continued to recover slowly but steadily. By the end of the season, he had returned home from the rehab center. He lost the sight in his left eye but had 60 percent use of his left leg. His speech improved markedly and he had full mental acuity. There was hope that wheelchair his son bought in Pittsburgh might be in use only temporarily.

Neil would finish third in the American Conference in '92 with an 83.6 passer rating and make it to his first Pro Bowl in just his third season in the NFL. He missed one game with a hamstring injury in November and three at the end of the season with a cracked fibula. The coaches never hesitated to put him back in the lineup when he was healthy.

O'Donnell played just over one full season in his first three in the NFL — not one snap as a rookie, eight games in 1991, and 13 in 1992 — but it was clear to everyone that he, and not Brister, would be Pittsburgh's quarterback of the future.

"He has a good presence about himself," Erhardt said. "He has vision, the ability to see things."

He cultivated that long ago at Madison High School. The O'Donnell family developed a tradition of success at Madison and beyond. Steven went on to play quarterback at Duke, Michael played wide receiver at Penn State, Peter played wide receiver at New Hampshire, and Matthew was a linebacker at Boston College. Oldest brother Jack did not play college sports.

Neil's brothers never played in a losing football game at Madison High under coach Ted Monica. But Monica lost his job in a dispute with the Board of Education in Madison, and Neil was stuck with four different coaches in his four years on some mediocre high school football teams. He played free safety and quarterback and was stronger than his linemen. O'Donnell ran the pro style, the veer, the option, and back to the pro-style offense in his four seasons, and he did not get much attention from the press or the college recruiters.

"My sophomore year, we were on the sidelines getting ready to play a game, and the coach just kind of slumped over. He had a heart attack right there. So my high school career wasn't very good. I wasn't even all-county as a senior."

O'Donnell excelled in basketball, averaging 28 points a game for Madison, and he was recruited by Kentucky and Connecticut, among other schools. But Neil wanted to play football. Although Ted Monica could not be his coach, he became his tutor. Monica took him to the gym on Sunday afternoons, locked the doors so no one would see them, and worked on technique with O'Donnell — mechanical things like gripping the ball, pass drops, releases.

"He wanted to be great," Monica said.

Monica and Neil became close, and the ex-coach urged Maryland's Joe Krivac to come take a look. O'Donnell wound up going to College Park, Maryland, and Krivac became Neil's guru for the next five seasons with the Terps. At Maryland, O'Donnell joined a long line of young men that Krivac helped turn into NFL quarterbacks — Boomer Esiason, Frank Reich, Stan Gelbaugh, and Scott Zolak.

"He was a big believer in techniques," O'Donnell said. "I'll never forget this drill we ran before practice called 'in the nets.' We'd go out there for 15 minutes and just take drops, drops, drops, and throw the ball at receivers standing still. Our arms would be dead tired. He was very hard on technique."

The long hours with Krivac and Monica were worth it.

"I watch Neil now," Monica said, "and I see total concentration on the release, on cocking the ball correctly, keeping his fundamentals true, and consistency. I know sometimes he's home at his condo and lays on the bed, releasing the ball over and over again, practicing his release that we worked on years ago in high school."

Those exquisite techniques eventually caught the attention of a coach who believed in mechanics so much, he could have passed for football's Mr. Goodtrench. Chuck Noll, who once admitted he fell in love with Rod Woodson when he saw him work out, swooned when he saw videotapes of O'Donnell at Maryland.

"Every film I looked at, he was doing exactly what you ask a pro quarterback to do," Noll says today.

Noll took a personal interest in O'Donnell and sneered at reports the scouts had written about him. He was a big (6-3, 230), tough quarterback who threw for nearly 5,000 yards in just over two seasons as the Terps' starter.

"I put a film together, a tape of all his games because when I read his reports, they weren't as high as I thought they should be," Noll said.

Noll wanted to draft O'Donnell on the first round in 1990, but others assured him he would last until the third. Heads would have rolled had he not. Pittsburgh had two picks on the third round and some scouts thought it was safe to wait until their second choice to grab O'Donnell. Noll insisted they take him with their first pick in the round.

Some questioned why the Steelers drafted a quarterback so high, since Bubby Brister was still in his 20s and had just come off a season in which he captivated Pittsburgh by leading the team within a whisker of the AFC title game. By now, most fans have forgotten, but after 1989, Brister was supposed to be *the* up-and-coming young quarterback in the NFL. Even Bill Walsh said it.

Two seasons, two offensive coordinators, and one major knee surgery later, Brister was supplanted by O'Donnell, who outweighs him by 25 pounds. Brister has a stronger arm, but O'Donnell's is above average for an NFL quarterback, and he has a better touch. Brister, the swashbuckler, is more apt to improvise, O'Donnell more willing to stick with the play. Brister plays at a high pitch, while O'Donnell works with almost cool detachment.

"We're different quarterbacks," O'Donnell said. "He's more emotional than I am. I'm more poised; I stay back there. I deal with everything the way I deal with everything in life."

They are that way on and off the field, in and out of the locker room or in a Pittsburgh nightclub.

"People love to interview Bubby," O'Donnell said, "because he may say some things that are outgoing; writers love that because that would sell papers. I never was like that."

Joe Walton loved O'Donnell as a quarterback and wanted to start him over Brister in 1991. He got the chance when Brister injured a knee, and he played O'Donnell for eight games before Noll made him go back to Brister for the final two. Brister fought Walton's new offense for two years, and many of his teammates took the cue. The battle lines were drawn, and in the end, Walton, Chuck Noll, the Steelers, and Brister all lost out.

"I didn't believe it was that tough of an offense because I studied it," O'Donnell said. "You put an offense in there, you have to believe in it, and if you work at it, I believe it will be successful. I felt comfortable running his offense. I put some time in off the field learning it.

"I believe after we started losing games, people didn't want to believe in the offense and didn't want to put the extra time in to study."

O'Donnell might have been pointing the finger straight at his friend, Bubby, but he never said it directly. He also was in the minority on the issue, and teammates kidded him by referring to Walton as Neil's "father."

But when O'Donnell was yanked for the final two games of 1991 in favor of Brister, he became even more determined.

"I didn't accept the change, but I didn't pout about it. I told myself when I come back I'm going to win the starting job. I knew coming here, I wouldn't sit too long."

Somehow, through everything, Brister and O'Donnell, the two opposites, managed to remain friends. They had lockers next to one another, palled around together, and O'Donnell confided in Brister more than anyone else on the team when he needed someone to talk to about his father. O'Donnell even got testy in 1992 when reporters asked him how the competition with Brister had affected their relationship.

"People try to make us enemies, the media especially," O'Donnell said. "I thought after we went through that big battle in training camp and remained friends, that would be the end of it. But you still hear writers come in and ask. Are we supposed to fight? Are we supposed to argue? This game's hard enough. You don't need any enemies on your own team.

"Bubby's a very good friend of mine; Bubby's been very good to me since I've been here. We're friends on the field, we're friends off the field. We spend a lot of time together. If you get a little pressure, Bubby's a good guy to have around and make you joke. He's been great to me."

By the end of the season, however, Brister would say a few things that slighted O'Donnell and would ruin their friendship. The Steelers eventually decided they would be better off without Brister. They waived him on June 4, 1993. There would be big things awaiting O'Donnell after the season, too, that few could have foreseen.

11

NOT YET READY FOR PRIME TIME

The shrieks from the Steelers locker room rattled down the corridor outside. It sounded like the floor of the New York Stock Exchange during a 45-point rally.

A fight among players? More bulletin board ammunition from the opponent, this time the Buffalo Bills?

No, this was more serious. It was trashball at its height. Players, with the delight of 12 year olds, screeched, moaned, shouted insults and challenges as they took turns lining up for their 25-foot duels with balled-up tape.

It became a ritual with accompanying chants. Cornerback D. J. Johnson, who wants to be a TV broadcaster when he grows up, took the microphone from one of the local camera crews and rapped out the play-by-play while his teammates cut loose.

Money wedged its way into the game. A $200 pot built up as Greg Lloyd, Rod Woodson, and Carnell Lake awaited their turns.

Barry Foster sank a linedrive. "Coach Cowher says you got to stay focused," Foster said in triumph.

At the midway point of the season, Foster had 865 yards rushing, on his way to obliterating Franco Harris's team record of 1,246 yards. No Steeler had surpassed 1,000 since Franco did it in 1983.

But Foster would rather talk about trashball than his rushing stats.

"Right now," he boasted, "I'm the best. Leroy beat me, but I won more games in the series.

"Me, Rod, and David Johnson started it about a month into the season, and a lot of other guys started getting in. It gets your mind off the meetings, the lifting and things we go through. It's just a little period we have to ourselves as players."

Albert Bentley took his turn shooting. He felt part of the team, even though he had not yet played a down with the Steelers. They picked him up September 16 after he was waived on the final cut by Indianapolis, where he long played second fiddle to Eric Dickerson in the one-back offense. Nevertheless, he was a productive back for the Colts until a knee injury early in 1991 ended his playing days in Indianapolis.

Every Tuesday, someone asked Bill Cowher at his news conference why Albert Bentley did not play on Sunday. Each week, Cowher answered diplomatically. What he wanted to say was, "Look, Albert Bentley was once a capable running back. He was never Jim Brown or even Jim Kiick, even before he had reconstructive knee surgery. We picked him up when both tight ends were hurt because we needed insurance. Would you like me to bench Barry Foster so we can play this guy?"

Bentley was popular in the locker room, where he got his only playing time with the Steelers.

"When practice is over, guys could be in the showers and then heading for home," he said after shooting a round of trashball. "Instead, they're hanging around each other. It's a way to stick together a little bit longer."

Bentley was more than happy to leave the losing in Indy to join the rebirth in Pittsburgh.

"This is a close-knit group. You see a lot of unselfishness here. Everybody's kind of picking up everybody else. Everybody's real excited when they see other people do well.

"It's a lot of fun. It gives you more of that college feeling. In college, you come in and you know the guys with you will be there four or five years, and that emotional bond is a lot easier to develop. In the pros, you don't know whether your friend is going to be there next year or next week, for that matter."

Bentley had that old college feeling in his new surroundings. That week, he would touch the ball for the first time as a Steeler, returning a kickoff 17 yards in Buffalo, only his second action in seven games on the roster. He was feeling more a part of the team. Six days later, the Steelers waived Albert Bentley to make room for wide receiver Mark Didio from the practice squad.

Bill Cowher did not hesitate to make personnel moves. Chuck Noll was reluctant to do so during the season unless he was forced into it, and then, more often than not, he would either elevate someone from the practice squad or sign a player familiar with the "system."

Under Noll, the "system" had become so unique on offense and defense the past few years that hardly anyone out there knew it. Hell, the Steelers themselves didn't know it. So if anyone got hurt or they proved merely incapable as the season progressed, there was no one to replace him. If you made Chuck Noll's team by the first week of September, you were almost guaranteed a paycheck the entire fall. Noll preferred players he knew over those he did not. He often said he did not want other teams' mistakes, and if a player was available, he looked at him suspiciously.

Cowher, though, signed 'em, cut 'em, sometimes signed 'em again and sometimes cut 'em a second time. Backup center Dean Caliguire was cut, re-signed, and cut without ever playing a snap. The Bentley and Didio moves were Nos. 27 and 28 since the 47-man roster was reached on August 31, and it was barely halfway through the season. The final count was 37. And that did not count the trade of Thomas Everett, the release of Louis Lipps, or the signing, cutting, and re-signing of practice squad players.

Garry Howe was one man cut at the start of the season, put on the practice squad, and activated on October 13 for the rest of the year. They list him as 6 -1, 288. He is more like 5-11, 300 — kind of stumpy, which is his nickname. This is a body that has never known a steroid. He plays the defensive line like an overweight groundhog burrowing for his next meal. He was All-Big Eight at Colorado, but went undrafted. The Steelers invited him to camp in 1991, and he made their practice squad. After that season, Stumpy played for the Frankfurt Galaxy in the World League in the spring and reported back to the Steelers in 1992.

Once activated, he slowly worked his way into the lineup and passed up a former Colorado teammate, Joel Steed, the Steelers' third-round draft pick in '92. With a friendly disposition, an unusual body shape, and a lovable nickname, Stumpy Howe became a cult favorite with the fans.

"I'll tell you, this Stumpy thing is catching on big," he declared after his sack on Houston's Cody Carlson in Three Rivers Stadium. A sign hung from the upper deck that day: "Howe does he do it. 78."

"I really enjoy it. I hang out with people. I try to get to know people outside of the team. I think it's what the old Steelers were doing. I'm proud to be in a city like this where the fans are so excited to be around us and things like that. It's great when the crowd's there, and you get to know them."

Steve Furness, the defensive line coach and one of those "old" Steelers, started using Howe more and more in key situations. He would start his first game in November against Detroit and start again the following week against Indianapolis. Against Seattle in December, Howe lined up as a blocking back on the one-yard line and bulled through the Seahawks' line in front of Barry Foster. Had Foster not slipped, he would have scored. They tried it three more times without scoring. The next day, Howe's head hurt. "I don't know how Barry does that all the time," he said.

When Howe was activated in October, the Steelers slipped him an extra game check instead of the lower practice-squad pay he should have received, but they said nothing to him about it. Howe brought it to Tom Donahoe's attention.

"Garry," Donahoe told him, "we did that just to give you a little extra money since you've been here."

"Should I go say something about it?" Stumpy wanted to know.

"No, just go cash it."

Donahoe believes Howe will stick around.

"I kept telling Bill when he first got here, I think this guy's a player," Donahoe said. "He'd look at him and say, 'He doesn't look like a player.' Even in '91, when it came right down to it, Garry should have made the team. He was as good as Keith Willis."

Another unusual success story on the Steelers' defensive line is Donald Evans. He is a 6-2, 270-pound defensive end who was drafted in 1987 by the Los Angeles Rams on the second round, as a *fullback*. The Rams waived him and Philadelphia signed him in 1988, where he played as a defensive end and linebacker. The Eagles cut him in 1989, and Evans went home to Kernersville, North Carolina, to begin his life's work as a supervisor for a trucking company.

"It was frustrating," he said, "but I stayed in shape."

Evans's problem was that he was a multitalented athlete who did not fit any of the molds at a position in the NFL. "I never did develop at one spot. It hurt me a little bit."

The Steelers have always been ones to break the mold. They convinced Evans that despite his size, he would get a chance in their defensive line, which wasn't exactly overloaded with size or talent.

He signed as a free agent in 1990 and has started 46 of the 48 games at defensive end on the right side since then. He uses his exceptional quickness to overcome his smaller size. Evans led the team with four passes batted down in '92.

"You take a guy 275, 280, and he goes against a guy weighing 315, 320," Evans said. "The guy 315 is going to win, at least that's what it's supposed to be. But what makes up the difference is how bad I want it and how much I study him, use my knowledge, my speed, and quickness to my advantage. It's how much heart you have."

Evans thought the Steelers' new defense — put together by Cowher, defensive coordinator Dom Capers, and secondary coach Dick LeBeau — had more heart than previous ones.

"Last year, we used to sit in the two-gap all the time where you read the gaps and you're not really penetrating," Evans said of the '91 defense. "We're a more penetrating defense now. Also, guys pull together and don't fuss and point fingers like we did last year. Whenever the DBs gave up a touchdown, we'd say, 'Hell, they shouldn't have given up that TD,' and they'd say, 'Hell, you all should have put pressure on a little bit more.' It was like we're not doing our job up front and you're pointing fingers at me. Last year, I got into about 15 fights in practice. This year, we pull together."

As the noise increased from the clubhouse basketball game, 6-6, 290-pound John Jackson quietly sipped a juice alone in the middle of the Steelers' locker room.

"This," Jackson said slowly, "has not been a good year for me."

His one-year-old German shepherd, Jack, died earlier that week after a $300 surgery, because he swallowed a shoelace that blocked his intestines. Jack might have been better off with *Shoeless* John Jackson as his master. At training camp, Jackson and center Dermontti Dawson discovered discrepancies in their financial report from their agent who managed their money. A subsequent federal investigation revealed that Jackson was swindled out of $142,166 while Dawson lost $389,470, tidy fortunes for offensive linemen.

In October, Jackson's father, Sam, suffered a heart attack, his third. Shortly thereafter, John temporarily lost his starting job at left tackle to Justin Strzelczyk for three games. Jackson had started 49 consecutive games, the second-longest tenure on the club to Dawson, his friend.

Back in '88, Chuck Noll wanted to cut the rookie Jackson. He was a 10th-round draft pick from Eastern Kentucky that April, and because of injuries to others, was pushed into the starting lineup in the final two exhibition games. He held his own against Lawrence Taylor in New York, but in the final exhibition game at New Orleans, Jackson was run over by linebacker Pat Swilling.

Rookies have it tough enough. Rookie offensive linemen, facing for the first time the stunts and disguises and other games played by NFL defenses, have it more difficult. Rookie left tackles who last played at Eastern Kentucky and are thrown in against L.T. and Pat Swilling have it not at all.

Most teams put their best pass rusher on the right side — the left side of the offense — because the tight end normally plays on the other side and it provides a clearer path to the quarterback. Asking Jackson as a rookie to play there in the third exhibition game was a tough task, asking him to play back-to-back against L.T. and Swilling was asking too much.

After he held Taylor off his quarterbacks, Jackson was bewildered in New Orleans. Swilling blew past him routinely that day for three sacks. Noll, forgetting the circumstances and what Jackson had done against L.T., wanted to cut him the following Monday.

But Ron Blackledge, then the offensive line coach, convinced Noll that Jackson was a 6-6, 290-pound bundle worth keeping. Jackson rewarded them by steadily improving at his craft. By the start of the 1992 season, he had helped run off Tom Ricketts, who was drafted in the first round of 1989 to be the Steelers' left tackle. Ricketts was cut before the 1992 season.

Jackson was drafted 234 spots behind Eastern Kentucky teammate Aaron Jones, the Steelers' first-round choice in 1988. By the end of '92, however, Jackson had started two-and-a-half times as many games as Jones, long ago a proven bust who was only a bit player by '92.

The November 8 game in Buffalo served as another "second chance" for Jackson. When aging Tunch Ilkin strained his back the previous week against Houston, Strzelczyk switched to right tackle and Jackson moved in at left tackle. With Ilkin still ailing, Jackson would make his first start in a month, and he would face the Bills' Bruce Smith, the best pass rusher in the AFC when he's on top of his game.

Jackson also still felt the effects of a deep cut on the calf suffered in the opener when Houston tackle Doug Smith fell on him. He didn't complain and he was never listed on the official injury report.

"The key is not to get frustrated against him," Jackson said of Bruce Smith. "He's powerful and quick. I've seen a lot of tackles get away from their technique and get out of their game against him."

Any anxiety?

"No, not really. I don't have a problem with power guys. I just have to not play too high because he clubs a lot of guys. I'll just try to be like a bad cold and stay in his face all day."

The Steelers' bus caravan pulled in front of the Hyatt Regency Fountain Plaza in downtown Buffalo early on the evening of Saturday, November 8.

What followed was a scene right out of 1979. Hundreds of squealing fans in various black-and-gold getups jammed the lobby of the Hyatt. It was so crowded, the hotel manager set up ropes so the Steelers would have a path to get to the elevators.

The Steeler Nation chanted their anthem: "Here we go, Steelers, here we go. Here we go Steelers, here we go."

Women in their 50s and 60s, their hair pushed up in beehive fashion, shoved through to greet the team. These were the same fans who first appeared in 1972 and grew in waves and decibels as the Steelers' trophy case filled up.

They were Rip Van Winkles in black and gold, reawakened by Cowher Power after a 10-year nap. Tunch Ilkin, 35, first witnessed the phenomenon as a rookie in 1980 but had grown accustomed to quiet hotel lobbies the past decade.

"It's funny, because I wasn't expecting that kind of reception in Buffalo. Usually, you walk into a hotel and there are a few fans there asking for autographs. But that lobby was packed and they had a little aisle roped off like a museum, and the fans were going nuts. Everybody was yelling, 'Tuuuuuunch' and 'Hiiiiiiiink' as we were coming in. They were clapping and screaming.

"It reminded me of my rookie year. Everywhere we went on the road was like that. I mean, there were a lot of fans in '80, '81, and '82. There still was the spillover from the Super Bowl championships, that enthusiasm. Wherever we went, there was a lot of people. I remember in Tampa Bay, my rookie year, it sounded almost like a Steeler home crowd. All you saw everywhere in Tampa was black and gold.

"That's what it reminded me of in Buffalo. It's still a thrill to see that kind of excitement generated over the Steelers. Maybe more so now than for a long time because there's been that gap where it's been 'So what..' Know what I mean?"

In the lobby crowd were quarterback Bubby Brister's parents, Walter and Frances Brister. Mrs. Brister wore a button with the number "6" on it. They had made the trip to Buffalo, even though Bubby had not played a down to that point in 1992.

Bubby's mom became a celebrity of sorts during the 1989 playoffs when television repeatedly showed her in the stands enthusiastically hooting for the Steelers. But she stopped going to games in Three Rivers Stadium on the night of October 14, 1991. That was the Monday night game in which Bubby was benched in the second half against the New York Giants in favor of O'Donnell, who rallied the Steelers from a 20-0 deficit to a 20-20 tie before the Giants won with four seconds left.

The home fans hurled four-letter insults and invectives, not only at the fallen quarterback, but at his mom in the stands. One drunken buffoon screamed that when she was pregnant with

Bubby, she should have had an abortion. Mrs. Brister did not attend another game in Pittsburgh that year.

In his contract talks with the Steelers in 1992, Brister tried to get a private box at Three Rivers Stadium included in the deal so his mom and dad and sisters could watch home games safe from the maniacs. Jim Kelly has one in Buffalo and Bernie Kosar let Mr. and Mrs. Brister and one of Bubby's sisters use his private box when the Steelers played in Cleveland. But it was no deal for Bubby in Pittsburgh.

The uproarious scene in the Hyatt lobby was to be the only good time in Buffalo for the Steelers on that weekend.

The Steelers believed they were prepared for the Bills' no-huddle offense and the noise at Rich Stadium this time. A year earlier, they were befuddled by both because of a tactical error in their preparation. When coaches and players watch videotape of opponents, they see only the plays. What they do not get is what the home viewer sees on television — the time between plays. The cameramen shooting for the club stops taping when the play ends and resumes when the next one begins.

That's fine in most situations, but the picture becomes distorted in the no-huddle. The players and coaches did not get a real feeling for the hectic pace Buffalo's no-huddle would put them through. Also, the silent video does not convey the convulsing racket in Rich Stadium.

So when the Steelers went to Buffalo in 1991, the Bills' no-huddle offense, working in concert with their fans' noise, took Pittsburgh's defense right out of its game. They could not hear their own signals being called, and because of the quickness between plays, there was no time to adjust.

They were doomed from the start. With some Steelers playing one defense and some another on many plays, Jim Kelly picked them apart. He threw a career-high six touchdown passes as Buffalo pelted the confused Steelers, 52-34.

This time, it was supposed to be different. Pittsburgh had a savvy coaching staff who fully understood the nuances of the no-huddle and put their players through practices with piped-in crowd noise. They believed they were ready.

If they could beat Buffalo, the Steelers could have a home path to the Super Bowl, as hard as that seemed to believe. It would give them the best record in the conference at 7-2, and they would hold the tie-breaker over the Bills for the home-field advantage in the playoffs. With an easy schedule — five out of their final seven at home — it was reasonable to assume they would finish with the AFC's best record.

That would mean one home playoff game followed by the AFC championship at Three Rivers Stadium. Dan Rooney merely laughed when that scenario was presented to him. Cowher reacted to it as if it were a skunk lifting its tail in his direction.

"Much too early," he shuddered, sprinting from the question. "We're still in November. Let's see where we are midway through December, then maybe we can start talking about that."

It was premature, after all. Pittsburgh still was not ready to drop Goliath on his turf. The Bills' no-huddle, recently sluggish, snapped out of it on November 8. They picked up the pace, reducing the average time between plays from 30 seconds to 17. The crowd noise, orchestrated as if Jim Kelly held a baton instead of a football, helped confuse the Steelers defense again.

Because they could not substitute with the no-huddle, Pittsburgh opened in its six-back dime defense and stayed in it. But it was a distant replay of its '91 disappearance in Buffalo. Cornerback Richard Shelton played the wrong coverage, which left James Lofton 10 yards open for a 22-yard touchdown pass. Rookie Darren Perry jumped on a short route, leaving Lofton wide open deep for an uncontested 45-yard touchdown pass. Buffalo coach Marv Levy said it was the first time he had seen "none on one" coverage.

"There were a couple of blown assignments," cornerback D. J. Johnson said. "Half the defense was playing one thing, half the defense was playing another, and it resulted in big plays."

It was a familiar refrain. The crowd was deafening, the no-huddle bewildering.

Linebacker Greg Lloyd bit on a play-action fake to Thurman Thomas, which left offensive lineman Mitch Frerotte alone for a two-yard TD catch.

"I gave up that touchdown on the goal line, the fake, to that bleeping lineman, whoever the hell he was," Lloyd snarled. "It was one of those days where things didn't go as planned."

Thomas had an easy time of it weaving through the undersized dime defense and rushing for 155 yards.

Nevertheless, the Steelers were still in the ball game, trailing by eight points midway through the fourth quarter. They had been a fourth-quarter team all season and they had a third down on their 30 as Neil O'Donnell took the snap from the shotgun. To his left, tackle John Jackson continued his day-long duel with Bruce Smith, a fight Jackson had clearly won. Smith hadn't touched the quarterback all day and was limited to three tackles.

This time, Smith charged on Jackson's left shoulder, and as the big tackle began to push him wide, Smith deftly cut inside. Jackson couldn't recover and Smith blew in on O'Donnell, dropping him for a 12-yard loss.

"I wasn't expecting him to come back inside," Jackson said. "But that was the only one he got all day. He's just a good player; you have to give it to him. We pretty much held him down all day, except for that one play."

That was enough. It was fourth-and-22. Mark Royals punted, the Bills took over on their 33 and snuffed out the final eight minutes and four seconds of the game with a long drive. Buffalo won, 28-20, to knock back the Steelers' challenge to its AFC supremacy.

"I hate to go around saying, 'Well, we played a hard game and I'll take it,'" Johnson said. "This team has big plans ahead, and we need to go ahead and win every game we can."

Cowher knew the feeling. He was the Kansas City Chiefs' defensive coordinator when they met the Bills in a playoff game the previous January in Rich Stadium. Buffalo's offense rang up 448 yards on Cowher's defense on the way to a 37-14 snow job.

"I may have the law of averages working on my side," Cowher said. "If I keep coming up here long enough, maybe I'll get a win. I'd like to come back this year. But I'd really like to play them again — at home."

12

THE BIGGER THEY ARE, THE HARDER THEY FALL

At their Monday reconvening the day after their loss in Buffalo, the Steelers received unsettling news from their coach: Tight end Eric Green was suspended for the next six games by the National Football League for violating its substance abuse policy.

"It was like a bombshell went off," cornerback D. J. Johnson described the reaction in the meeting room.

The Steelers had been, in the eyes of the public, lily-pure when it came to drugs. Until 1991, they were among several teams in the NFL that had not been tinged by a drug suspension, but they did have their share of problems.

Defensive tackle Rollin Putzier tested positive for steroids in their training camp in 1989. But he was waived and claimed by the 49ers, where he then sat out his suspension. Other modern Steelers were quietly released when their drug problems became known to the club. And long before testing, there was Joe Gilliam's battle with drugs in the 1970s and Steve Courson's steroid abuse.

Green became the third Steeler suspended in a year's time. In 1991, guard Terry Long was banned for four games for steroid use — he tried to kill himself several times when he discovered he had tested positive — and halfback Tim Worley was banished six games for using cocaine. Worley was subsequently suspended for one year in April 1992 for missing several drug tests.

No other active NFL player had been suspended during those two seasons. It made the Steelers look like the opium den of the National Football League. It was also a reminder that — new regime, new enthusiasm, or not — peril constantly lurked, and it could all unravel at any moment.

A dark cloud hangs over a team with drug problems. People scrutinize it. Errors such as dropped passes or blown assignments raise questions. Reporters turn more skeptical on injury announcements. Tardiness is viewed in a different light. The broader brush often paints the innocent. It can rip apart a team quicker than free agency.

The New England Patriots won the AFC championship in 1985 and played the Chicago Bears in the Super Bowl in January 1986. A drug scandal ensnared the Patriots and broke shortly after they crumpled to the Bears in New Orleans. The New England franchise rapidly plunged into despair and has since gone through three owners, an infamous sexual harassment furor, four coaches, and so many losses that it has become the worst franchise in the NFL.

Not all of the Patriots' problems developed because of drugs, but the drug stigma certainly played a part in the team's deterioration.

The Pittsburgh Steelers are in another league compared to the Patriots. They have been one of the NFL's honorable franchises. They have remained in the same family since Art Rooney founded them in 1933. They do not appear to have a widespread drug problem.

"Maybe we got a little lax, thinking we didn't have a problem," Dan Rooney said. "We're going to review what we have done and what we should do. We'll discuss it and make sure we have things in place. We've tried to be as aware as anyone. But by no means do we think we have all the answers."

The Steelers employ Dr. Abraham Twerski as a consulting physician on chemical dependency and substance abuse. Gateway Rehabilitation Institute in Center Township near Aliquippa provides in-residence programs for drug and alcohol abusers. Green was admitted there immediately after his suspension and Worley also spent time at Gateway.

Partly in response to the Worley and Long problems in 1991, the Steelers hired former NFL linebacker Anthony Griggs in

Offensive coordinator Joe Walton (left) ran a sophisticated offense that featured hundreds of plays and so many formations that players were frustrated and confused by its lack of focus.

Michael F. Fabus

Michael F. Fabus

At the somber press conference where Noll announced his retirement, he said, "It would have been great to have had 10 victories and been in the playoffs and have gone all the way and then said 'Good-bye,' but it didn't work that way."

Chuck Noll was the architect of four Super Bowl championship teams. Many of his players are now in professional football's Hall of Fame.

Joe Greene, player, 1969-1981 and coach, 1987-1991. Elected into the Hall of Fame in 1987.

Michael F. Fabus

Terry Bradshaw, 1970-1983. Elected into the Hall of Fame in 1989.

Michael F. Fabus

Mel Blount, 1970-1983.
Elected into the Hall of
Fame in 1989.

Jack Ham, 1971-1982.
Elected into the Hall of
Fame in 1989.

Franco Harris, 1972-1983.
Elected into the Hall of Fame
in 1990.

Pittsburgh native Bill Cowher told skeptical reporters at his introductory press conference that the Steelers' goal in his first season was "to put a fifth trophy in the case outside in the hall."

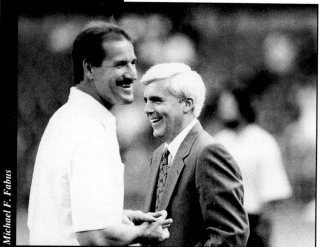

Tom Donahoe rose from scout to become the director of football operations—and the most powerful man in the Steelers' organization without the Rooney surname.

Kaye Cowher and Dan Rooney flank the Steelers' new head coach. Cowher was exhausted and near panic after his pressure-filled first day on the job.

Rod Woodson opened the scoring against Kansas City with an electrifying 80-yard punt return for a touchdown.

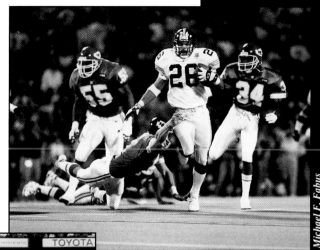

Many in Pittsburgh believe that in this age of free agency it is essential to the Steelers' quest for Super Bowl glory that Rod Woodson not get away.

Cowher says of Woodson, "He's the best in the business, the best I've ever coached, and I've been around some pretty good ones."

Michael F. Fabus

Steelers MVP
Barry Foster finished
the season with 1,690
yards rushing, and tied
the NFL record of 12
100-yard games in a
season.

Michael F. Fabus

"I put it on the line,"
Foster said. "I'm here
because I do like the game
of football. But at the
same time, it's a great
opportunity to make a lot
of money. That's what I
want to do. I'm not going
to concern myself with
fans who perceive me as a
'money player,' because
the fans aren't going to
pay my bills."

Michael F. Fabus

Foster carried the ball 30
times or more in three
games in '92, only the
seventh Steeler ever to
do so. Twice he had 33
attempts, the third
highest in team history.

Neil O'Donnell's high school coach, Ted Monica, said of his protege's exquisite technique, "I watch Neil now, and I see total concentration on the release, on cocking the ball correctly, keeping his fundamentals true, and consistency."

Neil O'Donnell won the starting quarterback job from Bubby Brister and finished third in the NFC with an 83.6 passer rating. O'Donnell played in his first Pro Bowl in just his third NFL season.

Offensive coordinator Ron Erhardt and others confer over a painful play in the December game against Seattle.

The '92 season was a difficult one for Eric Green. He battled a weight problem, unable to meet a training camp weight limit of 275, and on November 9, 1992, he received a six-game suspension for testing positive for drugs a second time.

Michael F. Fabus

Michael F. Fabus

Cowher's hands-on motivational approach to coaching is far different from Noll's. Said one player, "He's the first to high-five you when you come off the field. He's the first to talk to you when you do something bad."

March 1992 as their player development coordinator. He serves as a confidant to the players, assisting them in various matters from finding housing to getting concert tickets to providing help with personal problems.

Yet none of this prevented Eric Green from testing positive for drugs a second time and drawing his six-game suspension on November 9, 1992.

"We don't think it's an isolated situation with the Steelers," Rooney said about his team's spate of suspensions. "I'm positive there isn't a big problem here. The best proof I have is our players were totally shocked when this happened."

Not only were they shocked, they were angry at Green. They had a chance to do something special in 1992. They were young and not abundantly talented and needed all the stars they had, particularly a tight end in a tight end-oriented offense like Ron Erhardt's. They needed Eric Green and he had let them down, big time. They were torn between compassion for Green and resentment.

"Horrible news, horrible news," tight end Adrian Cooper said. "If it's not an injury, it's something else. It's killing our football team. It's tough on me, because who's behind me? Who do we have? We have (rookie) Russ Campbell and we also have Tim Jorden. They're good football players, but it's got to be tough for them, too. It just adds a little more pressure on everyone."

Cooper thought the Green suspension could hurt morale, but said, "I don't think this team will let it. We'll find a way because we're all winners and we'll find a way to win with Eric or without Eric."

Over the past two seasons, the Steelers actually had been 7-9 with Eric Green and 6-3 without him to that point. But there was no doubt they would rather play with him.

Green, a first-round draft choice, burst onto the Pittsburgh skyline late as a rookie in 1990 to supercharge a lame offense introduced by Joe Walton that season. It did not take long for the Green giant from tiny Liberty University to wrap his big paws around the NFL and twist it to his wishes.

The Steelers' offense had not scored a touchdown in the first four games of 1990. Green missed all of training camp and the first three games of the season in a contract holdout and played intermittently in the fourth. He then went out and scored the offense's first two touchdowns of the season in the fifth game. He scored five TDs on his first seven receptions. The Steelers' record for tight ends was five touchdown catches in a season and Green snapped that with No. 6 in just his fifth game.

No one in the NFL had seen anything quite like Eric Green. Ever. He was 6-5, 285 pounds, with moves like Lynn Swann. He dazzled teammates in practice with his circus catches. He was so powerful that he once injured two teammates in a game when he blocked an opposing player into them, bowling them over as if they were the 5-10 split. Walton worshipped him, anointing him after just one season in the league.

"I used to think Mike Ditka was the most complete tight end I had ever seen," Walton said in training camp in 1991. "But The Big Guy . . . He can be more special than anyone I've ever been around. He has more ability than anyone I've seen. He still has to stay healthy and hungry, of course. But if he does that, he's going to be a legitimate superstar. Hell, he's a superstar already."

The Steelers could use a few superstars. They had Rod Woodson at cornerback, an emerging Greg Lloyd at linebacker, Carnell Lake at strong safety, and Green. They had potential at other positions, as the 1992 season would show, but except for Barry Foster's coming out, those were their four big-name stars.

Green tantalized the Steelers with his talent and, when he was not injured, his performance. For years, the Steelers had ignored their tight ends, once completing just a dozen passes to them all season. Green caught 34 passes in just 13 games his rookie season. He bumped that to 41 in 1991. He had 13 touchdown catches his first two seasons.

But he also frustrated them. He had a weight problem. The Steelers listed him at 265 pounds, but he often ballooned over 290. They put him through a workout the day he signed his rookie contract, then brought him to a press conference. He perspired abundantly as he answered several questions and almost passed out from the TV lights. He finally had to excuse himself.

Green's weight continued to be an issue, and people in the organization believed that all that weight put undue stress on his legs. He tore the anterior cruciate ligament in his left knee during training camp in 1991, but he still opened the season as the starter. Despite the injury, he scored touchdowns in four consecutive games early in '91 and was having a good year. But then, safety Thomas Everett tackled him in a November practice, breaking his ankle and ending his season five games early.

When the new coaching staff put in place a "voluntary," supervised, and well-structured off-season workout program in the spring of '92, most every player attended. But Green made only cameo appearances, and the new staff did a slow burn.

"Those opportunities," Erhardt said, "can't be replaced."

"They said I should be here," Green acknowledged, "but it was a voluntary thing. You can't say something's voluntary and then demand somebody be here. That's a double standard."

Others worried that Green was wasting his talent. He was lazy, they said, and did not like to work out, yet he talked about becoming the best tight end not only in the league, but in the history of pro football.

"In my eyes, I am the best tight end in the league," he boasted in the summer of 1992. "But that's in Eric Green's eyes. Now, my focus is to put that in other people's eyes. One day, I want to be one of the best players who ever played the position in history."

They were big words from a big man. Anyone who saw him play had no doubt he had the ability to back them up. But the new coaching staff wanted to see him do it before they would crown him. Tom Donahoe, the Steelers' new boss, believed Walton and others heaped too much praise on Green too soon, and he had turned complacent.

Pat Hodgson had coached tight end Mark Bavaro of the New York Giants. As a new coach with the Steelers, Hodgson wasn't about to put Green in Bavaro's class until he proved he belonged there.

"It's easy to say what you want to do," said Hodgson. "That just doesn't happen. Anybody who wants to accomplish really good things or great things has to put a lot of effort into doing that. We'll wait and see. We're just getting exposed to Eric. Certainly, if he makes his mind up to do that, he does have that kind of potential."

Cowher gave Green a weight limit of 275 for the start of training camp. He didn't make it, but he was close, and he was angry when anyone asked.

"The weight thing!" he exploded at a writer one day. "You guys blow this thing out of proportion. When I first came into this league and scored five touchdowns in two games, you all didn't say any goddamn thing about weight. As soon as I got hurt, you say 'weight, weight, weight' and that just seems to piss me off just a little bit.

"I don't think there's an ideal weight. I think I can play at the maximum wherever I'm at, and that's just what I'm going to do. To have somebody tell me what I should play at, that's bogus."

Early on in Cowher's first training camp, a day of practice ended with 40-yard gassers. Green took his place with the rest of the tight ends and offensive linemen and offered $100 to anyone who could beat him. Guard Carlton Haselrig took the bait and as the two thundered toward the finish, Green pulled a thigh muscle in his right leg. He was off to the sidelines again.

Late in August, Green tore the right rotator cuff in his shoulder. He started the season opener in Houston, but left after the first play. The Steelers placed him on the injured reserve list, and he missed three games and the bye week. He did not return with a bang, managing 14 catches but only two touchdowns in the next five games. One of those, however, was one of the most significant of the season, a five-yarder in the fourth quarter that beat Houston, 21-20.

Eight days later, Green was suspended for six games.

Tim Worley claimed he talked to Green the night he was suspended, November 9. They had been friends, Pittsburgh's No. 1 draft picks in 1989 and 1990. At one time, both had the same agent, Doc Daniels of Los Angeles.

These were men of immense talent, players who were supposed to blossom in the '90s and help carry the new Steelers on their backs. Instead, they were in danger of blowing their careers to drugs.

Worley tested positive twice for cocaine use in 1991, once in training camp and once during the season. He was suspended for six games after the second time. He then skipped several tests the following February and, on April 29, 1992, was banished for one year by the NFL.

He got so heavily in debt, he had to borrow money from the Steelers to pay his mortgage, and his new agent even worried how he would survive when the one-year suspension hit.

"I've been on him about spending money," Jerry Albano said in March 1992. "Unless I put him on a damn budget like a child, he has a hard time keeping up with his damn money because he just writes checks like there ain't no tomorrow — and the only trouble is, he ain't got no damn money to write checks like there ain't no tomorrow. It just so happens he's spending money right now that he ain't got."

Eight months later, Worley said he was doing OK financially and that he had been "clean" for a year when he showed up at the Steelers' offices to talk to Bill Cowher about Green's predicament.

"I'm trying to get my shit together — excuse my language — and get back into the league," he said. "I'm seeing my therapist, attending (AA) meetings. I don't drink anymore, don't do nothing. I'm doing the right things. It's a pain in the ass to try to change what you're used to, but I need to do it and you got to do it to get better."

Worley weighed 240 pounds, 15 over his playing weight. Since his suspension, he had fathered a boy who lived with him and his fiancee. He had traveled between Pittsburgh, Atlanta, and North Carolina but settled in Pittsburgh to work out and get ready for what would be his return to the Steelers in 1993. He wasn't working, but said he was "comfortable" financially. He wore a big, chain-link gold necklace and carried a small, black fold-up cellular phone. He sat on a curb outside an entrance to Three Rivers Stadium, near his white Mercedes Benz. He had just come from the Clark Bar, an upscale saloon across the street from Three Rivers Stadium. Several Pirates co-owned the bar, and a group of Steelers gathered there occasionally after practice.

Water, he noted, was his drink of choice at the Clark Bar.

"Eric's one of my best friends, man. I talked to him last night. I tried to school him on what's going to happen right now and what kind of procedures he's going to have to take. He's depressed. He's very upset that he let his team down, his friends and whatever."

They never did drugs together, Worley said, just beers.

"The times I started using drugs and alcohol real heavy is when all this shit started happening to me. I got ripped off for almost $300,000. My former agent screwed me, my accountant screwed me. That's when I started drinking heavily, and all this shit just started happening.

"It's not a problem for the team. You just have to stay out of these bars and clubs. You got to stay away from these knuckleheads. You got to stay away from the groupies, because all they're going to do is get you in trouble. You just have to change your lifestyle, which is hard because that's all you know — growing up and being in the limelight. That's all you knew was clubbing and women.

"I told Eric everything he's going to face, stuff he's going to have to 'fess up to as far as getting himself better and getting back and playing in that last game and in the playoffs, the Super Bowl, whatever. I know; I'm a living example: Shit happens.

"You have a lot of people who say they're your friends, knowing you might have a drug or alcohol problem. But then they're offering you a beer, they're offering for you to smoke a joint or sniff some cocaine or something.

"I'm not like that. I'm a true friend. I tell Eric, stop hanging around these guys. You don't need to be out in these bars. Stop hanging around these places. They're not your friends, knowing you got an alcohol problem and they offer you a beer. They don't give a damn about you.

"You know how it starts. After you beat the hell out of somebody, you go out on Sunday night and drink, have a good time, run into some girls, go back to your house, and do whatever, man. That's how it goes.

"I guess we learn by our mistakes. If you don't learn from these mistakes, then I guess you're a fool. Like me, I'm done for a year. He should just look at what's been happening to me and all the shit I had to go through and the stuff I still go through. People bugging you and stuff. Look at that, man. I don't think you want to deal with that."

Dan Rooney was about to take a hard look at it himself.

His first-round draft picks were dropping like bad punts — Worley ('89), Green ('90). Darryl Sims ('85) was a horrible pick. John Rienstra ('86) had a panic disorder the Steelers did not detect until it became so severe it drove him off the field. He also revealed later that he had been attending Alcoholics Anonymous. Gabe Rivera ('83) wrecked his car while driving from a bar his rookie season and became a paraplegic.

The Steelers once consulted a psychologist about screening potential draft picks. He told them if they had checked Rivera's background, they would have found he had piled up unpaid parking tickets while a student at Texas Tech. That kind of disregard for the law, the psychologist noted, might forebode a propensity for the kind of driving that led to his crippling accident. In other words, the psychologist told the Steelers, they might have avoided him in the draft.

The Steelers told the good doctor that if the Dallas Cowboys had followed that bewildering procedure, they never would have drafted Tony Dorsett, who collected a legendary amount of unpaid parking tickets when he was a student at Pitt.

Dan Rooney dismissed that approach, but he believed there must be another.

"We maybe need to do something. These guys get so much money right away and it attracts the wrong kind of people to them."

But what could he do? Lock up his No. 1 picks? He couldn't give them less money. Put them through counseling *before* they could get into trouble? Perhaps the new rookie salary cap will help.

Worley was Exhibit A of how a No. 1 draft choice could be ill-equipped to handle his newfound wealth and fame.

He was a poor kid from Lumberton, North Carolina, who went through the University of Georgia carrying a football and few books. The ninth pick in the '89 draft, he drove at least two expensive vehicles before he ever signed his first pro football contract. Worley received a five-year, $3.05 million contract, including a $1 million check as a signing bonus.

Everything seemed fine as he led the Steelers in rushing his rookie season with 770 yards and they made the playoffs. Problems developed in 1990 when Walton put in his new system that de-emphasized the run and Tim Worley. Worley blew up at the coaches when they benched him in Los Angeles against the Raiders after he ran the wrong way on a play. He whipped his helmet against the bench in New York after they pulled him out of a game against the Jets for cutting outside instead of inside. Injuries further reduced his playing time and he finished with only 418 yards in '90.

Injuries and the coaching staff dogged him some more in 1991. In training camp, it was back pain with a Chuck Noll chaser. Noll was never the great communicator; his idea of massaging players' egos was putting his hands around their throats and squeezing. He believed in self-starters and held the old-fashioned idea that pros didn't need anyone to motivate them.

Worley was a man-child who craved a pat on the back, not an ice pick in it. But with his back ailing from a bulging disk during training camp in 1991, Noll took little pity. He told reporters he had demoted Worley to third string because he had not improved much since his rookie season.

"He has to earn his way," Noll said. "We're looking for dependable diesels, guys who keep chugging away, who can be there all the time. If you're a guy who's never around and can't be depended on, hell, you can't earn the No. 1 spot."

Informed by a writer what Noll had said, Worley smoldered after a practice in 95-degree heat at St. Vincent College in Latrobe, Pennsylvania.

"If he wants to put me there, let him put me there," Worley snapped. "I don't give a shit."

Noll had a different effect on guard Terry Long. At just 5 - 11, Long was a classic overachiever, who weighed 290 pounds. He was Chuck Noll's kind of player, the kind who would do anything to play football. He was known as a quick healer; pain did not stop him from playing. He was extremely muscular and moody.

Football meant everything to Long, so when Noll told him he had tested positive for steroids at training camp in July 1991, it devastated him. "When I looked at Chuck and saw the expression on his face, I thought my career was over then."

The Steelers left Long behind when they traveled the next day to Carlisle, Pennsylvania, for a scrimmage against the Washington Redskins, ostensibly because he had an injury. Long drove home and made several aborted attempts to kill himself in front of his panicked girlfriend.

"I just went on home and planned to do a few things stupid. There were four different things I thought about doing to myself, to pretty much end it."

Long grabbed his guns and threatened to blow his head off. He swallowed sleeping pills, then ate some rat poison he had bought on the trip from Latrobe.

"I figured I would take the sleeping pills and (along with) other things that I had accumulated in my body it would 'off' me, you know, get the job done. I seriously wanted to check out because I thought I had really destroyed everything I stood for in my life."

Long's girlfriend frantically called police and paramedics, who took him to Allegheny General Hospital. He did not return to the team for a month and was later suspended by the league for his positive steroids test.

Several days after his release from the hospital, he was on the phone talking about his problems. His biggest concern was that he had let Chuck Noll down. Over and over he repeated his anxiety, not about Noll the coach, but Noll the authority figure. When Long was 15 his father died of alcoholism.

Long also did not know what to do, whom to talk to about his predicament. I advised him during a telephone call at the time to (1) call Dan Rooney and (2) call the NFL Players Association. Noll also called Long to make sure he was OK.

When Long returned to the team, Noll approached him.

"It's good to have you back. Are you OK now?"

Long assured him he was and said, "I knew he wasn't carrying a grudge, that he was being sympathetic. Through everything, with my mom (who had suffered a heart attack) and everything, he's been a great supporter."

There was a time Worley did not think so, but today he holds no grudge himself against his former coach.

"God bless Chuck Noll. I like the guy. He did what he had to do. I'm not blaming him for nothing."

Worley did blame the Steelers offense for some of his problems on the field. He ran out of the deep I-formation at Georgia but was put closer to the line in a split backfield in Pittsburgh. He also did not carry the ball nearly as much as he had in college. To be effective, Worley needed 15–20 carries a game from a deeper set position.

The one-back offense Ron Erhardt ran in 1992 would have fit the powerful Worley perfectly.

"I feel I'm a damn good running back and given the opportunity with the offense they run now, which is my style of offense, I feel I got a good future here," Worley said.

"I watch them play but I can't come to the games because I'll probably have a heart attack in the stands. It's hard, especially when they're kicking ass and I really want to be part of it. Watching Barry Foster run, I'm like, shit, why couldn't they do that last year? That's my style of offense. A guy like Barry Foster, he's a good running back, tough, runs hard. You're supposed to give him the ball 20, 25 times a game."

Indeed, Worley never got more than 19 carries in a game, even when he was at peak performance. He averaged only 11.6 rushes a game during his first three years. Twice Foster had 33 carries in a game in 1992, the third most in Steelers history. He carried 31 times in another and finished with 1,690 yards on 390 carries, both Pittsburgh records. Only twice did he rush fewer than 21 times.

Many people believed that had Worley been treated differently on and off the field by the Steelers, he might not have gotten into his other problems. But trouble courted Worley, or vice versa. He played only in the final two games of the 1991 season because of injuries to his back and knee and his six-game suspension. He was arrested for drunken driving and he was AWOL for two days from the team in October.

His financial problems had become legendary. Agent Gary Wichard sued him for breaking a contract he had signed with him before he was drafted. Worley sued his former accountant.

He even had a fight with a parking lot attendant when he first arrived in Pittsburgh as a rookie. Worley said the only place he could find peace was back home in Lumberton.

"People at home don't treat me like people up here treat me. People up here are assholes sometimes. When I came up here I hated this place. People at home, people I grew up with knew me when I didn't have anything. They're still going to support me.

"I'm not sitting here being a baby and complaining. That stuff comes with the territory. This is the NFL; this is not college; this is not high school. I'm a grown man. You should be able to handle that kind of stuff. If you're playing shitty, they're going to treat you shitty."

Yet Worley wanted to remain in Pittsburgh and resume his football career there. So the day after Green's suspension, he popped his head into Cowher's darkened office, where the coach was watching videotape.

"What are you doing here?" Cowher said, thinking Worley was someone else, a friend.

Worley said he'd like to talk to him about Eric Green and his own situation. Cowher finally recognized Worley and listened to him for half an hour.

"We talked about the things I went through when I was having my drug and alcohol problem," Worley said. "He asked me what started it, how it begins, what gets you caught up in it.

"If I'm not here I know I can play somewhere else. But I would love to come back here. This is where I was drafted, this is where I started, and I want to finish here."

Worley saw the Steelers awash in enthusiasm and he wanted to be part of it.

"They had a way before of making you feel not a part of the team when you were hurt. This year, I see the injured guys traveling, I see the injured guys on the sidelines. They would not let us do that before. You felt funny about it.

"I'm looking at these guys on TV, at Coach Cowher, the guys look like they're very enthusiastic, they're happy to play, they're fired up. You see the coach getting into it. That's what I'm used to. When I went to college, Vince Dooley was all hype. He outran me sometimes. I love to play around that type of environment."

On May 18, 1993, Worley was reinstated by NFL commissioner Paul Tagliabue. The NFL had tested him three times a week since December and Worley passed all the urine samples. He worked out daily in Pittsburgh and his weight was down to 228. "I've been away too long," Worley said. "I'm ready to go to work again and be part of the team."

Cowher welcomed him back, and the possibility of a healthy Worley teaming with Barry Foster in the backfield was mouthwatering.

Terry Long's football career ended with Noll's retirement. The Steelers offered him help getting on a team in the World League but he turned it down. "They only pay you $28,000," Long said.

Eric Green returned to the team in time for the final game of the 1992 regular season. Despite Tim Worley's statements to the contrary, Green insisted he had not talked to him since his suspension began.

Green dropped the first pass thrown to him early in that game against the Cleveland Browns and was not thrown another either in that game or the playoff against Buffalo. Upon his return, he discovered that Cooper had supplanted him as the No. 1 tight end and the coaching staff would keep it that way until the end of the season — or longer.

Ron Erhardt acknowledged that Green's absence wounded the offense:

"That hurt us a lot. It hurt part of our total package. We never really had all of our weapons. In fact, how many games did he play? Four? We really didn't have him to really explore our tight end potential.

"He got hurt, then he got into the other thing that was his problem."

It's a problem the Steelers somehow have to solve.

13

THE FUTURE: ANOTHER ART ROONEY

Art Rooney II strolled through the back of the press box at Three Rivers Stadium and into the game-day breakfast room packed with sports writers, visiting pro scouts, club executives, pundits, game statisticians, PR men, an occasional politician, and old friends of the senior Art Rooney.

Few took notice of Dan Rooney's eldest son.

Standing alone, Art sipped a glass of orange juice. If he and his father were to compete in a game called Low Key, it might end in a draw. An acquaintance approached, shook his hand and congratulated him. Ann Rooney, his fourth child, was born the previous day, November 14.

Art Rooney II is 40 years old and blessed with good looks, a growing family, a successful law career, impressive Irish stock, and a name that is revered through most of Pennsylvania and the sporting world. Someday soon, he likely will become the next president of the Pittsburgh Steelers, maybe even their majority owner.

This former Steelers ball boy might have become vice president of the United States had he not turned down an appointment to the U.S. Senate in the spring of 1991.

That April 4, U.S. Senator John Heinz of Pittsburgh died when his small plane collided with a helicopter near Philadelphia. The replacement for Heinz, a Republican, would be appointed by Pennsylvania governor Bob Casey, a Democrat. Casey's appointee would serve until the fall and then run in a special election against Republican heavyweight Dick Thornburgh, the former governor of Pennsylvania and U.S. attorney general.

Casey's search team settled on Art Rooney II, a young man who never held political office but had all the right stuff.

"If he wanted it, it was his," said Mossie Murphy, a political analyst for WTAE in Pittsburgh and a friend of the Rooneys. "They wanted him for several reasons: One, he had the ability to raise money; two, he had a good, good political name and he had no political garbage, even more pure than Harris Wofford would have been; three, he had the energy to be able to put that together, and four, he has all the physical attributes."

Casey's team came to Pittsburgh to talk to Rooney. Leading them was the governor's political guru, James Carville, a Louisianan, and Paul Begala, a Texan. Carville and Begala would, in a little more than a year, help get Bill Clinton elected president while serving as his chief political advisers. Begala then joined the new administration in Washington. Carville, Begala, and the governor's men met with Rooney to enlighten him on what it would mean to accept the appointment to the U.S. Senate.

"It wasn't something I was considering," Art said, "but when it came up, I owed it to myself to at least give it some consideration."

The Rooney family exulted at the possibility. The Chief, Art Rooney, the late founder of the Steelers, was as much a politician as he was a sportsman. One of his best friends was David Lawrence, the former governor of Pennsylvania and mayor of Pittsburgh. The family was friendly with the Kennedys, among other big-time political connections. Dan Rooney and Bobby Kennedy had been friends. Tim Rooney, one of Dan's four brothers, and Ted Kennedy remain friends.

But for all their interest and ties to politics, only one member of the Rooney family ever held elected office: Jim Rooney, a younger brother of Art Sr., was a state senator.

Now the Chief's first grandson, Art Rooney II, had an offer to become the junior U.S. senator from Pennsylvania, and all his kin were cheering as if he were Franco Harris dashing toward the goal line with the Immaculate Reception.

"It gives you a lot of bragging rights," said his uncle Pat Rooney, who runs the family's Palm Beach Kennel Club in

Florida. "A family like ours, you'd like for someone to be a United States senator. As one of my brothers said, it's sort of on the level of being a Cardinal in the Church, you know?"

Art Rooney Jr. offered any support he could give his nephew, morally and financially. "It's not only a big thing for him, it's an honor for this family. My grandfather came over from Wales. And I don't care if you're a damn U.S. senator for six days, you know what I mean? You're a *United States Senator!* Twenty years from now, they can't change that.

"My dad was just some nice sports guy. And you're a U.S. Senator! They put it on your tombstone, 'U.S. Senator.' Man alive!"

But Art II did not like some of what Carville and Begala told him about the job description that April. After his appointment, he would virtually have to abandon his law firm, of which he was managing general partner. His young family would be uprooted, placed in the public domain and separated from Art for long periods of time. The campaign against Thornburgh, heavily backed by the Bush administration, would be brutal.

"The day he decided he was going to be appointed senator," said Murphy, Art's confidant, "everything else would have vanished and a whole new life created."

Art Rooney listened to the governor's men, thought about it for 24 hours, and turned it down on April 18. While his uncles, his father, his brothers, and other members of his extended family wanted him to take it, he did not believe it to be the best move for his wife and young children at the time.

"I know lots of politicians, I know what their lives are like," Art II said. "Their family lives are difficult at best. So it wasn't that hard of a decision, when I weighed my family life vs. the political life. It clearly was not the right thing to do for my family.

"Also, Greta is not a political type of person. Some people have wives who are interested, who would really say let's do this, we'll make it work. That's not her idea of a good family choice. When it came down to it, it wasn't that tough of a decision at all."

Most Rooneys were disappointed but supportive.

"I wish he would have done that," said Uncle John, Pat's twin brother. "We're not so far removed from being immigrant Irish, three generations. A United States senator in the family would have been very impressive."

"I'm too much into history," Uncle Art said. "I look at what it means to be a United States senator. You're doing things for the United States of America, the biggest country in the world. Wow! It's mind-boggling."

It might have been even more so. When Art II declined the governor's offer, Casey named former Kennedy aide Harris Wofford to the seat. Wofford, with Carville and Begala directing the campaign, trounced Thornburgh in November by a margin of 58 percent to 42. The following summer, Bill Clinton, the Democratic presidential front-runner, considered Wofford as his vice president before settling on Al Gore.

Had Art Rooney II accepted the appointment to the senate, he surely would have beaten Thornburgh as well. He would have run on the same platform, ridden the same national health-care hot button that fired up Wofford's campaign under Carville's production. And had Rooney won, it's possible Clinton would have chosen him over Gore as his running mate.

"Oh, sure, because he completely fit a profile," Mossie Murphy insists. "Art Rooney is not only from a very important family, but he has the name; he had that other resource, that he's Art Rooney.

"Art would have been a person that Clinton would have sought out. If Art would have been elected, he would have upset Thornburgh, he would have been a hot national thing. There would have been nine million stories done about the Rooneys. He would have become an important political person because of the way those things fall into line.

"Just by the nature of who he was. He would have been offered the job because he was a Rooney and then people would have become very interested in him because he was a Rooney. And he was the heir to Art Rooney, a name everyone interested in professional football knows."

Murphy believes Art's potential to this day in politics is unlimited.

Dan Rooney could not hide his disappointment when his son informed him of his decision.

"He doesn't talk much about it now," Dan said. "I kidded him just for a second when they talked about Wofford being a possible vice presidential pick. I told him, 'Look at that. That would have been perfect. What a place!'

"It makes for good dreams."

Having put off politics for the time being, Art Rooney II confronts another decision soon: whether to become president of the Steelers.

His verdict may determine whether the Steelers remain in Rooney hands or are sold to someone else.

"This is a unique family," Tom Donahoe said. "This is a unique operation, especially today. Very few franchises are run by one family and few where the owner is here on a daily basis and is very much involved with the team and understands football.

"Dan and Art both understand football. So to see Art around and to realize at some point in time he probably is going to be the guy who takes over and runs the operation is a reassuring fact for everybody, given the history of the Rooney family."

Before Art Rooney Sr. died on August 25, 1988, the owner-ship of the franchise was reorganized. Jack McGinley, the Chief's brother-in-law and longtime minority owner of the club, now owns 20 percent of the Steelers. The remaining 80 percent was divided equally among Art's five sons: Dan, Art Jr., Tim, and twins Pat and John. All six men are board members of the ball club and they elected Dan to run the team as president, as he has done since 1975.

The reorganization was accomplished for several reasons. The franchise that cost $3,500 in 1933 is now worth at least $140 million. The estate taxes would have been heavy after Art Sr. died, had the reorganization not taken place. Also, it simplified the process of passing on the shares after the Chief died.

But as the Rooneys advance through generations, they face problems most every other family business confronts. Each generation spawns many more heirs (and their spouses), and that can lead to monumental rhubarbs, at the least, and ugly family civil wars as members battle for control and/or money.

Such problems have already occurred with NFL franchises in Chicago, New York, and Miami.

"It's a challenge that's faced by all kinds of family busi-nesses," said Art II. "There are very few that successfully make it through the third generation. But I certainly don't view it as an insurmountable challenge. I think there clearly is a consensus among my dad and his brothers that they want the team to stay in the family."

For example, Dan Rooney has eight living children, Art Jr., four; Tim, five; Pat, seven; and John, five. That's 29 potential owners of 80 percent of the stock. And Jack McGinley and his wife, Mary Ellen Rooney McGinley have six kids.

None of the Rooney brothers wants to see his shares passed to his children through inheritance, if that means splintering the ownership.

"What does my daughter Alice care about owning the Pittsburgh Steelers?" said John Rooney, who oversees the family's dog track in Vermont from his home in Philadelphia. "Her name's Mahoney and she's trying to raise four kids. She has no interest whatsoever in that. She was born in Pittsburgh, but raised in Philadelphia."

"From a realistic standpoint," Pat Rooney said, "it's as far as it goes as a family. The next jump it goes as being almost a publicly held stock, you have so many people involved."

The Steelers franchise has run smoothly, considering five brothers and an uncle own it, with none holding a controlling interest. Brothers Tim, John, and Pat run various other Rooney Family enterprises and have never had direct involvement with the team. Tim lives in New York, John in Philadelphia, and Pat in Florida.

"When we'd go into town when my dad was alive," John says, "he'd say, 'What are you doing here?' We'd say we're going to the game, and he'd say, 'This isn't your business. Your business is the racetrack. Don't be showing up here.'

"The Chief was smart. He knew that football team was like opium. It would suck you in, you know? He didn't let us get involved."

Dan and his brother Art, however, did. Both worked for the team most of their lives, with Dan rising to president and Art to head of scouting. Dan fired his brother in 1986 because he believed Art was not communicative enough. It was a bitter split and the two did not speak for several years. But Art, who now runs the family's real estate operation from an office in suburban Upper St. Clair, did not protest publicly and he continues to support Dan as president of the ball club.

"We didn't have a palace revolt," Art Jr. said. "I left quietly."

"We get along," John Rooney said, "a lot better than probably anyone in our situation would. Anybody else that was left with this team and how crazy people are about football, I think there would have been a lot more intra-family fighting and that. There's none of that with us. Like we always tell Danny, he has the greatest owners in the world. We never bother him."

The natural, logical, and probable way for it to remain in Rooney hands is for another ownership change.

"My opinion is eventually Dan's going to have to have some way of buying us out so his son will be able to take over," John said. "It doesn't take a genius to figure that out. Down the road, if we want to keep this thing going some way, it's going to have to end up in Dan's hands."

Or, those of Art II.

"Realistically, Art's going to have to buy out the partners," Pat said. "Otherwise, you're going to end up with 35 partners. If you had 35 *monks* you couldn't get unanimity, you know?"

For that to happen, Dan and/or his son would have to gain majority control. Family sources say Dan is preparing for such a move, to buy portions of the team from his brothers. They seem agreeable to it.

"To have control is to have control; you have to have 51 percent," Pat said. "Art would have to end up with that. There are six partners in this thing and Jack McGinley's a substantial partner. It isn't like there's a couple people involved."

Even Art Rooney Jr. believes the best thing might be for Dan to acquire the controlling interest.

"I think they have a better chance if one did have it. Objectively, somewhere down the line, probably one should do it. I don't think there'd be any change to the people of Pittsburgh. It would just be Dan solidifying his position and, in truth, naming a successor, which probably wouldn't be too bad."

The financial planning for such a deal would be tricky. Fifty-one percent of $140 million, after all, is $71.4 million, and even with Dan's 16 percent ownership, that leaves a hefty $49 million to reach that point. Dan Rooney doesn't need any benefit spaghetti dinners thrown for him, but he doesn't have that kind of money, either.

With free agency having arrived and more of the profit going toward player salaries, it makes it that much more difficult.

If Dan Rooney and/or his son do not accumulate a controlling interest, the Steelers eventually would be sold to someone outside the family. Their future in Pittsburgh does not seem threatened anytime soon, and Art II believes the team can remain in Rooney hands with some creative ventures — outside financing, community involvement, a better stadium deal, and more intense marketing and commercialization.

"I think if we're going to own it, let's own it and run it. On the other hand, it's not necessary that the Rooneys own 100 percent or even 80 percent, as we own now, for that to be the case."

Art welcomed the NFL's new ownership policy that made it possible for corporations to get more involved. For example, a Rooney could maintain controlling interest in the team but have a minority partner in Pittsburgh such as the H. J. Heinz Co., a Fortune 500 company. The Pittsburgh Pirates have an ownership structure that includes such companies as Westinghouse, PPG Industries, Alcoa, and Mellon Bank. The Steelers may need outside help someday, too, although not in such a wide-ranging manner.

"If some of these small markets are going to continue to have teams," Art II said, "those kinds of ownership structures I think will become more common."

Such a move wouldn't be unprecedented for the franchise. Art Rooney Sr. after all, not only founded the ball club, he merged it, swapped it, sold it, bought it back, and had several minority owners through the years.

Change and the Pittsburgh Steelers are nothing new. The Chief would chuckle through thick cigar smoke at those who might suggest that small-market teams must find new ways to make money in order to survive. Art Rooney had been doing that since 1933. He took his ball club barnstorming through West Virginia, to New Orleans, Johnstown, Louisville — anyplace where the gate would be large enough to cover the next payroll.

The modern financial problems facing the new Steelers are just a new twist on the old ones.

"It comes down to finding some diverse sorts of revenue that we haven't had before," said Art II.

Discussions began recently between the city and both the Steelers and Pirates about producing more revenue for the teams through Three Rivers Stadium. The Steelers have one of the worst stadium deals in the country, getting little revenue from either parking, concessions, or private boxes. They want to change that.

"We need to have access to every potential source of revenue we can get our hands on," Art II said. "The city is going to have to find ways to make that work. It's probably going to require more than city government being involved. The county may have to be involved, the state. There's discussion of creating a regional asset district. Something like that is going to have to take shape here in order for this to work for the stadium tenants."

On his last St. Patrick's Day in 1988, Art Rooney Sr. worried about the Steelers' ability to remain in Three Rivers Stadium. He could not understand how the city could eliminate parking space by building the huge Carnegie Science Center in the stadium's southwest parking lots.

"There's only so much space here," the Chief said. "You have nothing but rivers and hills surrounding you and you can't park cars there."

His son, Dan, said there may come a day when the Steelers need a new stadium in order to survive. That day likely won't come soon, unless the Pirates either leave town or leave Three Rivers Stadium.

The Steelers organization, as Pittsburgh has known it, may never be the same. They have sold out every nonstrike game since 1972, so there was no need for a marketing department; they merely mailed out the season-renewal forms and counted the money as it rolled in. Their marketing was done on a more personal basis. The Steelers still do more in the community than most pro sports teams, from charitable works to public speaking. They still cart many suburban newspaper beat writers on their charter free of charge and supply them with a room, a subliminal marketing tool that started in the 1970s.

But they began to recognize the changing face of the Pittsburgh sports industry in 1992 and set about marketing the team more visibly. It was the franchise's 60th season, and it was dubbed the "Year of the Fan." They catered to season-ticket holders at training camp, held a weekend fan fest at the stadium during the club's bye week, gave away eight trips to the Super Bowl and eight trips to away games, and began a Fan Courtesy Program to eliminate offensive behavior at home games.

"We've become more attuned to what is required in today's entertainment market," said Joe Gordon, their longtime PR man and now director of communications. "We're a little late in responding for a variety of reasons. We were somewhat spoiled by the success and phenomenal loyalty of our fans."

The marketing will mushroom soon as the Steelers look for ways not only to hold onto their large season-ticket base but try to develop new fans and seek other revenue so vital to a small-market team in the free agency era.

"It is a radical change for us," Gordon said. "For too long, the typical NFL mentality was win and it takes care of everything. Not anymore."

The success of the Pirates and Penguins, not only on the field but off of it, woke up the slumbering Steelers. They stood by as aggressive marketing departments in the other two pro sports teams attracted younger fans and pilfered the Steelers' once dominant share of the sports clothing industry in Western Pennsylvania.

"Ten years ago," Gordon said, "when someone wore black and gold, nine out of 10 were Steelers apparel. Now it's split pretty evenly among the three teams. We were going in the wrong direction. We have to get a little more aggressive and pursue those opportunities."

The Pirates and Penguins changed their logos to boost sales. Don't expect the Steelers to follow suit, but Gordon would like to see them change their helmets, add a little pizzazz, and maybe even put the logo on both sides of the helmet.

Indirectly, perhaps, the seeds of the new awareness in the marketing operation might have had an effect on the new direction the football team took with the many changes that included the hiring of Tom Donahoe, adding Anthony Griggs as the players' go-between, an expanded weight room, right on through to the new coaching staff.

"We had to be more aggressive in general," Gordon said, "and part of that carries over to our team. The same kind of thing hampered our football operation for a while."

Other changes might come in the front office. Dan Rooney, observing how the new coaching staff has energized the football team, wants to do the same with the rest of the organization. Shortly after the '92 season, Rooney made his first move when he fired controller Dan McGrogan.

"Hopefully, I'm intelligent enough to see that when something's coming at you, you might as well be ready to deal with it," Rooney said about the changes free agency will force. "And it's coming."

The biggest change will be at the top.

Dan Rooney grew up with the Steelers as the owner's eldest son. He was a ball boy and ran other chores as a youth, worked in the summer at training camp and, after graduating from Duquesne University in 1955 with a degree in accounting, became a full-time club employee. He signed players to contracts while he was still a college student, but Coach Walt Kiesling had to sign for the club because Dan was not yet 21.

He officially became president of the Steelers in 1975, but in reality, ran the team in the 1960s for his father. It was Dan Rooney who fired Buddy Parker as coach during training camp in 1965. He no longer could stand by as Parker, a heavy drinker, traded away draft picks or cut players on a whim.

"I went to my father and said, 'You can't operate this way.' To this day I think Buddy was an excellent coach, but he couldn't drink. I told my dad, 'You cannot let him do things at night and do things impetuously.'"

It was Dan Rooney's first big decision of many that would include the hiring and firing of coaches and the firing of his brother Art in 1986 as head of the Steelers' scouting department.

Now it may be Dan Rooney's turn for a career change. He is 61, and his extensive duties with the league have taken him more and more away from his daily duties with the ball club. He could have had the job as NFL commissioner in 1989, but would have had to divorce himself from the Steelers to do so. Rooney was the driving force for management in reaching a new collective bargaining agreement with the players early in 1993. He and Commissioner Paul Tagliabue were the NFL's two-man team that forged the agreement.

Rooney promoted Tom Donahoe to director of football operations in order to have someone run the club in his absence, which was more evident in '92. He is on national boards of the United Way and the Ireland Fund, among his many charitable works. He would like to name a new Steelers president.

"I'm spending too much time on league matters now," Rooney said. "There's a theory, and I subscribe to it, that you can be in a job too long. You look at corporate people, they're totally enthusiastic about their jobs, then they get in and start getting a lot of other interests. With me, it's the National Football League, running the United Way campaign, getting involved with Ireland. I still try to make it a hands-on business, but there are times where I was doing other things more important for the league.

"But when you get to that point, you better start getting somebody who can pretty much do the day-to-day things."

Like his dad, Dan Rooney isn't about to leave the Steelers, but he'd like nothing better than to have Art become the next president.

"There's no question about it, he's the guy," Dan said. "He's the person who is obvious, who is capable of doing it immediately, if necessary. But a lot of things depend on that, including whether he wants it. If Art is looking for financial rewards, he's better off staying with his law business than he would coming here and making this a full-time occupation."

Art II was a ball boy and performed other work for the Steelers as a kid just as his dad had done before him. Also, like his father, he was a quarterback in high school. He came of age in the late '60s and early '70s and was somewhat of a rebel as a youth. He wore long hair and wild clothes and lived up to the image.

Mossie Murphy took him to the Democratic Convention in 1972 in Miami, where George McGovern was nominated and Art Rooney II became hooked on politics. He later became a Democratic Convention delegate. After meandering from Pitt to St. Bonaventure to construction work, Art graduated from Pitt in 1978 and from Duquesne University Law School in 1982.

He joined what is now the law firm of Klett Lieber Rooney and Schorling and virtually pulled it out of the rubble when he became its managing general partner — the youngest in Pittsburgh at the time — and reorganized the firm in 1989. He became more involved with the Steelers after the 1988 season. He helped negotiate several contracts, including No. 1 pick Eric Green's in 1990 and Rod Woodson's big contract in 1991.

"He had the ability to make decisions and he would — usually to the detriment of the person across the table," said well-known Pittsburgh sports attorney Ralph Cindrich, Green's agent.

"You could do better on a contract with Dan Rooney than with his son."

Nevertheless, Art Rooney earned Cindrich's respect for his style and fairness.

"He's tough, but not with an exterior, macho kind of personality. He's very quiet, but still a forceful advocate. You sense that and feel that, even though he's not boisterous or overly talkative."

As the Chief's eldest grandson, Art II became extremely close to his grandfather, who had a big influence on his life. Cindrich noticed that of all the people at Art Rooney's funeral, young Art was the most visibly upset.

With his dad gone, Dan Rooney turned more toward his son for advice. He took Art to NFL meetings and turned over the club's legal work to him and his firm. His name appeared in the Steelers' media guide for the first time in 1992 as the team's secretary and counsel. Art also became legal counsel for most of the other family businesses.

"He has the ability to look through things and come to the point, where a lot of people don't have that," said his uncle, John Rooney. "He is very straightforward, very honest. But he's no patsy. He and I have argued with his dad on points and he'll stick up for me if I'm right. He'll stand up to anybody."

So, does Art Rooney II want to succeed his father as president of the Steelers? Dan was off to New York or Dallas or somewhere trying to put together the NFL's labor contract as Art settled into a seat in his dad's office at Three Rivers Stadium to answer that question.

He brought along his lunch of yogurt and mineral water and he talked so low, a tape recorder next to him on his dad's desk barely picked up the words. All signs of his long-ago hippie influence had vanished — he was dressed in the conservative dark suit and shoes of most Golden Triangle attorneys, and his hair was appropriately short.

Art has not given up on a possible political career, nor that of managing general partner of his law firm. He would have to abandon both, or at least put them off, to take over the Steelers.

"I don't think I'm at the point yet where I have to make a decision," he said. "I guess I would say the shareholders certainly have some decision to make about the future makeup of the ownership and — then it falls from there — the future management of the team. I guess I would have to know more about where we're going for me to make my decision.

"And I don't think I have based my career path on walking into this office one day. There are a lot of things that have to be settled before I could be comfortable that was the right thing for me."

Those decisions ultimately will determine whether the Pittsburgh Steelers remain in Rooney hands. Many believe it's only a matter of time until Art Rooney II succeeds his father, who succeeded his father.

"I think Artie's interested," John Rooney said. "What the hell, he has to be interested. He's devoting a lot of time to it now. He's interested. He's interested, even if he doesn't know he's interested."

"He is being groomed for it," Art Rooney Jr. said. "He's plenty smart enough and his dad's giving him plenty of experience. It's a matter of commitment now. This business is a damn narcotic. So much so that perhaps Art passed up becoming a United States senator because he has a chance to be president of the Steelers."

To many in Pittsburgh, that is a more important job.

14

ALL HE WANTS IS A FOSTER HOME

Barry Foster was five years old when a pig house across the street caught on fire. Panicked pigs ran everywhere, squealing. One tried desperately to charge back into the flaming building.

"Go get him, Barry," Sharon Foster yelled to her son.

Young Barry ran it down, picked up the pig, and saved it from the fire.

"They put him on TV," his mom said. "Barry snapped that little pig up and held him in his arms. It was in the paper. Little kids wrote letters to him. He was a hero."

Twenty years later, Barry Foster is a football hero, lugging pigskins for a living on a 5-10, 217-pound Body by Brunswick. He did it better than anyone not named Emmitt Smith in 1992, better than any Steeler ever in one season. Just as Chuck Noll had built his offense around Franco Harris in 1972, Bill Cowher hitched his to Foster's rugged wagon.

He burst free of the injuries, of the shadows of Merril Hoge and Tim Worley and the shackles of Joe Walton's offense to explode into the NFL in 1992 after two years of virtual anonymity. Before '92, only six times in Steelers history had a running back carried 30 times or more in a game. Foster did it three times in '92. Twice he had 33 attempts, third highest in team history.

He ran for 190 yards in the second game of the season against the Jets, more than Franco ever had in a game. He ran for

168 yards and two touchdowns to help beat the Indianapolis Colts, 30-14, on November 22. That broke Harris's team record of seven 100-yard games in a season; Foster would go on to tie the NFL record with 12. He finished with 1,690 yards rushing, just 23 behind Dallas's Emmitt Smith for the NFL lead.

Foster had the kind of season five-year-old boys dream about. Without him, the Steelers and Bill Cowher would not have been the surprise story of '92. They had few other weapons on offense, and they rode his broad back and powerful legs to an 11-5 record and their first division title in eight years. His teammates voted him the Steelers' MVP and he started for the AFC in the Pro Bowl.

It should have been a glorious time for Foster, who could have owned the town like no other back since Franco Harris. But he often fretted over money and what he perceived as unfair treatment by team officials, reporters, and even some fans. What should have been his crowning moment when he was named the team's MVP turned into an infamous news conference in which he warned he might hold out in 1993 and even debated whether he owed the fans anything.

And if you knew where Barry Foster came from, you would understand.

"He pays all my insurance on my car," Sharon Foster explained. "My deep freeze went out and he sent me money for that. Any big bills, Barry pays. My life insurance. He pays all that kind of stuff. He sends his sisters money for different things, for their babies. He takes care of us."

Sharon and Walter Foster divorced when Barry was a toddler. Father and son see each other, but are not close.

"I love him," Barry said. "He had to do what he had to do, but at the same time, what my mom went through — that's my number one girl there."

Sharon Foster raised eight kids by herself, four boys and four girls, in Duncanville, Texas, a Dallas suburb.

"We had a lot of fun, but we went through a lot, days without eating," Barry remembered. "There would be days when you just did not eat that day. My mom, she did a hell of a job. She did it all herself. It was hard, man, but we got through it."

It seems Barry's mother knew nothing but hard times. Her father, two sisters, and a brother were murdered in separate incidents. Barry, her youngest boy, nearly died from pneumonia when he was six weeks old. They pronounced him dead, but a doctor brought him back to life after a few minutes. She often reminds him that he survived to take care of her.

Mrs. Foster worked two jobs in order to provide for her family. She was a meat cutter for 14 years. She got laid off and went to work for a box company. She would come home from that job, shower, and go on to another job as a waitress. She hurt her back lifting a bed-ridden woman for an in-home nursing service in 1986. Since then, she has had two back surgeries, two neck surgeries, a stomach operation, and a hip problem. She can no longer work, and survives off disability income and her generous son. She has 14 grandchildren, including twins who live with her and one of her twin daughters.

"I can't stand on my feet very long and I can't sit very long," she said. "My 26-year-old, Melinda Foster, drives. She's my eyes, my hands, my feet."

And Barry is her salvation. He bought his mother a new 1990 Nissan with part of the $44,000 bonus he received for signing a contract as the Steelers' fifth-round draft pick that year. He bought her a house in 1993.

"He wants to do more," Sharon Foster said. "I could call Barry right now and tell him I need some money and he'll send it. He never turns me down. He'll say, 'OK, momma, how much you need?' He's a sweetheart. He used to send me money from college, too."

Is it any wonder that money is so important to Barry Foster? He applied for the NFL draft after his junior season at Arkansas in order to provide for his family. He did not figure he would last until the fifth round, where the money is not enough to take care of two families.

"The pressure was tremendous," Barry said. "I had made this huge decision in my career to come out early. I went in the fifth round, so I was disappointed. I didn't know what was going to happen. I was afraid I wasn't going to make the team and I would go back home as a failure."

He made it, but languished for two years with the Steelers. As a rookie, he played behind both Hoge and Worley and had little chance to do anything. Given a chance in 1991, he was out by an ankle injury for nearly half the season, and some say he began brooding over his salary and his lot on the team then.

He blames the old offense under Joe Walton for his and the team's problems in 1990 and '91.

"We felt we ran the ball better than anything else we could do. We didn't think we were a passing team. The offensive schemes were really complicated; it took me two years to learn it. But he was going to make it work, regardless. He didn't want to listen to the players. We tried to tell him we couldn't understand it, that we needed to change certain things. He was just going to make his system work no matter what and that's why it failed the way it did."

Noll disputes those contentions.

"We tried to get him in. He had some good games and he was spotty. He wasn't a surprise. The question he had is putting it all together game after game, which he's doing now. Then it goes from game after game to season after season."

Foster was supposed to make $124,800 in 1992, but it was his option year and the Steelers promised to give him a new contract. In the meantime, new offensive coordinator Ron Erhardt planned to feature him in a power running game, and Foster believed his new contract should reflect his new status on the team. Unhappy with the pace of negotiations, he skipped three days of a mandatory minicamp and was fined $3,000. He boycotted the first four days of training camp and was fined $6,000. Tom Donahoe was so frustrated by Foster's stance that he began looking at alternatives. He talked to New England about John Stephens and was interested in Miami's Aaron Craver.

"We felt if we couldn't get him signed, he wouldn't be very happy," Donahoe said. "And we'd gone through that the previous year where he wasn't happy. We didn't want to create that same kind of distraction with our team. It was never a question of Barry's ability. It was whether we could get the guy straightened out on a contract situation to the point where he can at least live with what we've done."

Just before the season began, Foster and the Steelers agreed to a contract that would pay him a base salary of $363,000, a $50,000 signing bonus, and performance bonuses that could boost his take to more than $1 million in 1992. He reached virtually every incentive. But the deal tied him to the Steelers through 1994, and by the end of '92, Foster wanted more than the $460,000 base salary he was to make in '93. That was less than

Hoge's $500,000 salary and nearly identical to Worley's $450,000. Foster believed he should outdistance them both at the pay window the way he did on the playing field. Foster outgained Hoge in '92, 1,690 to 150. Foster also finished second on the team with 36 receptions.

"Money talks and everything else walks. I mean, I'm going to go wherever the money is. If it takes me to Canada, I'm going to go to Canada because you're only going to do this for so long and if you can use your body to make that kind of money, why not do it and get the most you can? No team is going to be loyal to their player because you can be gone the next season."

He sounds like a mercenary and he doesn't deny it, and he has been criticized for it. But aren't most normal people concerned about money? Look at baseball players, who are so greedy that they make their counterparts in football appear to be socialists. Why shouldn't Foster try to get what he can? What makes him different from any other red-blooded American capitalist?

Foster gained 691 yards in his first two seasons with the Steelers, then exploded for 1,690 in 1992. He was so good at what he did that he virtually became the only back Pittsburgh used to run with the ball. Before Foster, Hoge led the Steelers in rushing in three of the four previous seasons with 2,708 yards on 724 carries from 1988 through 1991. In 1992, Hoge carried 41 times for 150 yards, even though he started 11 games. Leroy Thompson was second to Foster on the team with 157 yards.

Barry Foster does not smoke, does not drink, does not do drugs, does not run around doing foolish things about town, and is not a playboy. He goes home at night, watches TV, listens to music, plays computer games — and practically every Sunday he methodically pounds out 100 yards or more. He got married in 1993. His other big passion is bass fishing.

So he wants to make scads of money so he can help his disabled mother, who hasn't exactly lived the Life of Riley. The beast! Fans talk about a lack of role models in sports nowadays, and along comes an ideal one in Barry Foster, who also happened to have the best season of any back in Pittsburgh Steelers history, and some people want to crucify him for it! They should be begging for 20 more like him.

"I put it on the line," Foster says of his playing style, which in three words can be described as full speed ahead. "I'm here because I do like the game of football. But at the same time, it's a great opportunity to make a lot of money. That's what I want to do. I'm not going to concern myself with what fans perceive me as, a 'money player,' because the fans aren't going to pay my bills."

Fans bristle at statements like that, but it is not the way Foster meant it to sound. He meant that he must look out for himself, because no one else, including the fans, will. He's the one who must fight for his money. It's not as if he is Michael Jackson and can set the price of his own concert tickets.

"I have to go out there and perform. I can't live my life according to you or anybody else. Just because you pay for a ticket, I have to ask you what I can do?"

One month after he spoke those words, Foster regretted doing so. The Steelers promised to talk to him about his contract situation.

"I learned I have to be more in control and really be responsible about what I say. I went off the handle a couple of times, said some things really out of line. I really regret saying some of the things I said at that press conference. I'm young and I'm still going to make mistakes. I'm just going to have to do a better job.

"I just hate being the bad guy. I worked so hard to win the fans over in the City of Pittsburgh and I don't want to lose that. By me losing that with a few comments in the press, I don't think it's worth it."

Yet hard feelings flamed anew when Foster skipped all of minicamp in June 1993. Cowher allowed him to miss the first three days to finish his honeymoon, and Foster promised his coach he would attend the final two days. He never showed, never called the Steelers, and Cowher was incensed by it.

Foster is a loner with no close friends on the team, although many of his teammates seem genuinely fond of him. His linemen speak glowingly of him and the Steelers sidelines erupted joyfully when he covered 100 yards on his final carry of the final game of '92 to equal Eric Dickerson's NFL record with a dozen 100-yard games. Being voted MVP by his teammates meant a lot to him because he believed they did not look upon him favorably when he caused so much commotion in training camp over his contract.

Many people think his running style and his many carries — a team-record 390 in '92 — will shorten his career. But he has a durable body, short, compact, with big hands and stubby fingers. His mother nicknamed him "Bam-Bam" when her toddler's unharnessed strength littered her living room with broken furniture. He sprained his upper back in the second to last game of the '92 season but bounced back with 103 yards on 26 carries the next week in the finale. His brothers tell him he should run out of bounds, à la Franco Harris, when the situation warrants it in order to save on wear and tear.

"As my body begins to wear down, if I really start to have problems with my body withstanding a lot of punishment, maybe I will start running out of bounds. But I feel strong and I'm just going to try to make it happen with what I have right now."

In his rookie season some players called him "Newhouse," after former Dallas Cowboy Robert Newhouse, a compact, low-to-the-ground gainer in the 1970s. Dick Haley, then the Steelers' personnel director, rolled his eyes when he heard that one.

"He's *much* better than Robert Newhouse," Haley said in training camp before Foster ever carried the ball in a real game.

Kansas City Chiefs coach Marty Schottenheimer said Foster reminds him of former Houston Oiler Earl Campbell, a Hall of Famer. O. J. Simpson, another Hall of Famer, likens him to the best runners in the game today.

"He's an explosive runner; he pops. He has a certain explosion like Thurman Thomas has," Simpson said.

After watching him run through his defense for 190 yards, New York Jets linebackers coach Foge Fazio whistled Foster's praise.

"He's a hard runner. He's not like Barry Sanders. He's a disciplined runner who follows his blocks. You can't arm tackle him, and he gets stronger as the game goes on."

Dick Hoak led the Steelers in rushing three times in the 1960s and then went on to coach for Chuck Noll. He was the lone member of Noll's staff retained by Bill Cowher. He told both his new boss and the Steelers' new offensive coordinator, Ron Erhardt, to look beyond the package when they first saw Foster.

"When you see Barry walk down the hall," Hoak said, "you're going to say, 'Well, this guy's just a power runner.' Just by his build you would think of him that way, trying to run over people. I told them he'll surprise you when he gets on the field. He has a lot of quickness and he knows how to cut and he has the ability to make people miss. When somebody's going to make contact with him, he accelerates. Very seldom do you ever see him knocked backwards. He's usually knocking the other people backwards."

Hoak says without hesitation he is the best in Pittsburgh since Franco Harris; Franco Harris says he loves watching him break his records.

"I really feel happy for Barry because of what he went through, where he really didn't come on strong right off the bat and he really didn't have a chance," Harris says. "I know it was a struggle. He didn't come out with the real big name and all the flash and all the glory. It showed me that even though things were tough for a couple years, he didn't give up. I like that kind of spirit and I really wish him the best. I just hope he's having as much fun as I had."

Maybe it's just too hard to enjoy when you know you must keep producing yards and money because that is the only thing able to save your mother from what her life was and what you want it to be.

"I don't want to be in the limelight," Barry Foster says. "I just want to do what I have to do and go home."

15

NO STEEL CURTAIN CALL

It had been building all season—for several, really — but after the Steelers crunched the Cincinnati Bengals, 21-9, on November 29 to forge a 9-3 record, the time was ripe for them to get out the spade, dig a six-foot hole, and bury the 1970s in it.

Pittsburgh football fans had lived in the '70s for more than a dozen years. They compared each Steelers team to the four-time Super Bowl champs, sized up each player against Hall of Famers who erected that dynasty.

Everywhere the contemporary player turned, the 1970s smacked him in the face. Few active Steelers received endorsements or television commercials, but there was Jack Lambert or Franco Harris or L. C. Greenwood or Joe Greene or Rocky Bleier selling something or other. During a span in the '80s, Terry Bradshaw critiqued them on KDKA-TV every Monday night. Writers who covered the Steelers of the '70s and were still on the beat in the '90s sometimes contrasted the two. When modern Steelers would get hot, broadcaster Myron Cope would on occasion whistle for the Terrible Towel to come out of the bullpen.

It was natural, but finally on November 29, 1992, the young generation screamed for it to stop. On that chilly afternoon in Cincinnati, Barry Foster broke Franco Harris's rushing record of 1,246 yards, set in 1975, and the Steelers established a one-game team record with 10 sacks of rookie quarterback David Klingler in his black-and-blue NFL debut. Afterward, someone mentioned to linebacker Greg Lloyd that the defense looked like the old Steel Curtain that afternoon.

"I don't like to be compared to those guys," Lloyd huffed. "We're the Steelers of 1992. We don't want to be compared to the Steel Curtain. We'd appreciate it if you guys would quit doing that. I know I would."

Foster rang up 102 yards to give him the NFL lead with 1,319. For the past several weeks he had been swamped with questions about Franco, and the inevitable comparisons followed. No, he said, he had never met Franco. Yes, he had seen him on TV as a kid romp all over his favorite team, the Cowboys, in a couple Super Bowls. And what did it mean to him to break this Hall of Famer's record?

"It means to me, it's a new era starting," Foster answered unexpectedly. "We've been trying to shed the image of the Steelers and the '70s for quite some time now. I think that the fall of Franco's records are just the beginning of a new era coming in."

It wasn't arrogant, and it wasn't selfish, and Foster did not want to demean Harris or the Steelers' Super Bowl teams. But ENOUGH ALREADY!

"We realize who we're following," Foster said. "They had a great team and it's hard to live that down. So until we actually get there, we're not going to live that down. We all realize that. The fans in Pittsburgh were very spoiled throughout the Bradshaw and Greene era. Sometimes, they can be very hard on us, which is not fair. But when you follow a great team those guys had, it's very tough."

Lloyd, reflecting on it later, added to the debate. He thinks today's players are better than they were 15–20 years ago.

"People can't get those four Super Bowls out of their minds," he said. "I know that's hard. But some of those guys couldn't play today because the game has gotten faster. I respect those guys and everything they did back then. Hell, they were the best back then. But nowadays it's a different ball game."

Foster and Lloyd made it clear how the new Steelers felt, and others began to pick up on it.

"I'm glad he said that," Tom Donahoe said. "This is the Steelers of the '90s. That's not saying tradition is not important here. You see the tradition's important every day you walk into this place because the first thing that hits you are four Super Bowl trophies, and that's a heck of a tradition to try to live up to.

"Your players have to say, 'Hey, we have to make our own mark,' and that's what some of our guys are starting to do. That in no way is being disrespectful to Chuck, to Franco, to Bradshaw, to Joe Greene. No way at all. But it's difficult. I thought that was one of the things we did a disservice to our players. We were always talking about the '70s and the players of the '70s and it's very, very difficult for guys to live up to that. They have to find their own niche."

Mel Blount congratulated them for doing so. He was a vital member of the Steel Curtain, performing at cornerback better than anyone before him, and was swept into the Hall of Fame. But when he joined the Steelers in 1970, the players were trying to live down a reputation that preceded them, too.

"People were saying the Same Old Steelers, guys who went out in the streets and drank and fought in the bars," Blount said. "We had the same attitude that these guys have: Don't tell us about what the Steelers did back when we were in high school or college. That's a different group of guys.

"I respect what these guys are saying: 'We want to make our own niche in Steelers history, we want our own destiny.' To me, that's a mark of a champion. 'Hey, don't tell me anything about what guys did in the '70s. This is the '90s. We're going to make our own history.'

"I think to be a great athlete, you have to have a certain amount of confidence and you have to have a certain amount of arrogance about you. Those guys have a point. They're saying, 'We respect what those guys did, but don't keep bringing it up to me.' I can relate to that."

Rocky Bleier, the little halfback who could in the '70s, also endorsed those feelings. He heard Bill Cowher's wife, Kaye, say in a meeting: "The Steelers start NOW."

"As bold as that might seem to be, that's important," Bleier said.

"I thought one of the transitional problems that had taken place through the '80s was there was no clear cut break or identity with the old and the new. The old was around for so long that an identity always was with the old. The fans and the mentality of the organization didn't allow new blood to create their own identity. There was always a holdover. It wasn't Mark Malone's team because some of the guys were still there — Stallworth, Webby, Shell. No one really created that until that ended.

"So a clean break has taken place — a great coaching staff, not a whole lot of egos involved, a mesh of experience. They adapted the system to the personnel rather than the other way around. They got rid of some deadwood in training camp that the other staff might not have and that sets a tone for everybody."

Chuck Noll also thought it was good to bury the past.

"When I came in here in '69 that's all I heard about — SOS, Same Old Steelers. We tried to get rid of the past and focus on the present and the future. That's your whole thing. You spend a lot of time trying to do that because that's important. What you've done in the past doesn't matter. It's today and what you're going to do.

"It's a distraction, whether it's good or bad. It's no different now than it was in '69 and '70 when we were trying to erase not a very good recollection of the past. A very good recollection of the past can get in the way, too."

The new Steelers actually gave Noll, Blount, Bleier, and many of their former teammates something with which to relate. They excited them. Many of the Steelers from the Super Bowl years live in the Pittsburgh area: Dwight White, L. C. Greenwood, Bleier, Harris, Andy Russell, Lambert, Lynn Swann, Jack Ham, Mike Wagner, Jon Kolb, Blount, J. T. Thomas, Larry Brown, and others. They suffered through the 1980s with all the other Pittsburgh fans, probably more so. It had been a long time in coming, but they enjoyed the 1992 season as both fans and alumni. Many of them met Bill Cowher, his coaching staff, and the players at a party for the new team and alumni before the season.

Instead of talking about the 1970s, the stars of those years prefer to speak about the new Steelers.

"This year for the first time, maybe I got caught up in the Bill Cowher thing," said Ham, the ex-linebacker who is in the coal and gas business as well as the Pro Football Hall of Fame, and broadcasts a weekly NFL game on the Mutual Radio Network. "I mean, you see guys out there busting their butt. I see Barry Foster running his butt off out there and just knocking defensive backs down and just delivering a blow rather than accepting one. I got caught up in it and I'm really pulling for these guys, more so than in the past. For the first time in a lot of years it's exciting."

Ham believes the difference was the exit of Joe Walton and the introduction of Cowher.

"It had been a team on the rise, getting better. It was a confident Bubby Brister after that 1989 season and everyone was looking forward to the following year. I think that offense not only set back the offense but after a point it even had an effect on the defense as well and the whole thing started to break down.

"That took its toll on this team, and I think now it's starting to fight its way back."

Bleier thought the clean break might have happened in 1990 had Noll done some things differently. Instead, Noll became part of the clean break that ultimately led to the success in '92.

"There's always a death and a rebirth that has to take place in the cyclical world of life, the same within an organization. The Steelers had a birth when Chuck Noll came in and it went through that whole cycle of birth and growth and excitement, and it started to die off again. It needed to have some outside regeneration again.

"I think Chuck Noll started to do that with some outside personnel, but it really didn't catch. Maybe it was the wrong personnel to give it the infusion that it needed from the coaching staff. The unfortunate thing that happened the last couple of years is that Chuck's infusion of a new influence was the wrong guy. So it was the prime time for the right person to come in."

Dwight White, a dominating defensive end of the Steel Curtain, once knocked the Steelers defense in the mid-1980s as "soft and cheesy," words that will live in team infamy.

"Those guys got very upset with me over that," said White, an investment banker in Pittsburgh. "But it was damn true. Tunch Ilkin and Gary Dunn and all those guys got pissed off at me. Hey, I'm retired. Mine is history; you guys got to do it on the field. Don't get pissed off at me, get pissed off at the guy on the other side of the line, OK?

"After I did say it, guess what? They lived right up to it because they got worse. Go look at the record. They lived right up to what I said. You were soft and cheesy, and that was putting it nicely."

White said the new Steelers don't play so nicely. He likes that.

"Playing defense is not a popularity contest. You have to be a little nasty. You got some people over there who will bring sparks on people — Greg Lloyd, Woodson. Those guys are real, real sharp-edged competitors. They're not taking any prisoners. They aren't just playing the game trying to be a good sport.

"I understand all that sportsmanship stuff; I try to teach it to my daughter and all that. But at that level, if you have a white hat on and are a nice guy, that's not going to get you squat.

"People who win and are successful are the ones who get people down, put their foot on their neck and kick them in their ass. And then you say, 'Next?'

"You get a lot of respect that way and, guess what? You win a lot of football games that way, too. You get a few penalties, too, personal fouls and stuff. But that's all right."

Franco Harris is still running. He chases down clients, pushing products in his various business ventures. Based in Pittsburgh, he runs through more airports than O. J. Simpson ever did, representing, among other things, his Super Donut, a nutritious breakfast food; his professional bike racing team, the Pittsburgh Power; and Score trading cards, of which he's a part owner.

He periodically watches a Steelers game and got caught up in the excitement of 1992. He became part of the story, also, as Foster snapped his records, bringing the Harris name alive again, 20 years after the Immaculate Reception presented the franchise with its first playoff victory.

"People remember more about the Super Bowls and us winning than if you were a leading ground gainer or something like that," Harris said as Foster was about to break his single-season rushing record. "If you can do both, it's even better, which is great and how I look at the Steelers right now. As great as Barry's doing, the team is doing great, too. So when you have that combination, that's the best of everything. There has to be a lot of momentum and a lot of enthusiasm. That seems to be contagious. I think that's going to propel and drive them to keep this going."

Andy Russell, the linebacker who witnessed the lows of the '60s and the highs of the '70s, believes Cowher had a major influence on the 1992 team.

"I'm a big Chuck Noll fan, so no way would I suggest anything negative about his abilities. On the other hand, I'm very impressed with what Cowher's accomplished. I'm excited about the whole thing. I think it's terrific. I'm impressed with what they've accomplished this year and I'm a big fan."

Russell thinks Noll might have done the same thing had he stuck around for '92 because "sometimes the raw talent needs to just age, like a wine, and they might have matured exactly the same way under Chuck."

Dwight White doesn't hold that opinion.

"I really think Cowher relates better to the players. You have talent, but it's a different day, a different generation. With us, Chuck was more of an administrator. He was not, in my opinion, a great motivator. We were the self-starters. We were very much individuals and had very strong personalities. We had, if you will, a bunch of characters on the team. If you could keep them all on the same page, you had harnessed lightning.

"And that's pretty much what Chuck was able to do. Every Sunday he would just take the muzzle off and say, 'Go get 'em, guys.'

"It worked, but I think you had a whole different demeanor of player in the '70s who didn't need to be motivated. Cowher's a little bit different. He's more current. I've always felt the best coach is the one who can get the players to feel that they don't want to let the coach down. It's not about their job, not about the win and loss. The players who go and reach down and give you that extra UNNNGGH for the coach. I think Cowher's that way. Chuck was a little different, very efficient, but it was a different personality, a different time, a different set of players."

A new era, Barry Foster called it. New, but while the players of the '90s don't want to be compared to those of the '70s, they no longer are intimidated by them, either.

A priest from Ireland told his friend, Dan Rooney, that the Steelers would forevermore have trouble winning. Rooney asked him why.

"You've got these young guys coming in here and they have to pass that deity every day," the priest revealed. "Every day they walk past those trophies. They can't overcome that."

At one point, Rooney thought about moving the four Vince Lombardi trophies from the lobby to someplace where they wouldn't be so imposing. Then he thought, why? His father founded the team in 1933 and it took him 43 seasons to win the first one. If those trophies intimidated the players, maybe they were not the kind of players who could win another one.

Bleier played at Notre Dame. He knows all about rich tradition and deities. Stashing those trophies wasn't the answer.

"Organizations, like anything else, have cultures and backgrounds. There is a certain culture the Steelers have developed, and those Super Bowls are part of that culture. So if it's an intimidating factor, it's a bullshit team. You have to look at them and say, 'Either we duplicate it and that has to be the goal or here is the precedent that has been set and the standard that has been set and we as a team and a culture will live up to it.'

"So you use that and guys who come in and see that should say, 'Hey, I'm proud of being a Steeler,' not, 'Oh, shit, I don't know if I'll ever be able to do that.'"

After their ninth victory of the season in Cincinnati, the players walked back into the Steelers' executive offices, where lunch is spread out for them each Monday. A new interior design struck them.

A mural along the wall in the lunchroom for years depicted a collage of photos from the '70s — Art Rooney holding the first Super Bowl trophy, players carrying the first trophy through the airport, photos of Blount, Ham, Greene. Now, after years there, the old mural vanished. In its place was a full-color photo of Rod Woodson bursting through a big hole while returning a kickoff against Houston in Three Rivers Stadium on November 1, 1992.

It was as if someone had heard Foster and Lloyd talking in the locker room in Cincinnati a day earlier.

The four Super Bowl trophies, all that silver like lead weights around the necks of the '80s Steelers, still whack you in the eyes when you enter the Steelers' lobby. But those who work there no longer talk about One for the Thumb anymore.

"People talk about One for the Thumb," cornerback Rod Woodson says. "We're trying to get one for any finger."

"We don't want people trying to live up to a tradition; we want them to carry it on," Rooney said. "If they win a Super Bowl, it won't be a fifth ring or this or that. It's going to be their Super Bowl trophy. They'll be carrying on the tradition."

As Barry Foster said, it's a new era. Dan Rooney has a plan for that fifth Lombardi Trophy, whenever it arrives. At that time, he will remove the large Plexiglas case that protects the original four and order five separate ones. Each trophy would stand on its own.

And when future generations talk about the Super Bowl Steelers, no one will assume they mean the ones from the 1970s.

16

ON THEIR
SCOUTS' HONOR

Tom Donahoe was a high school football coach in 1984. Today he is the Pittsburgh Steelers' director of football operations, their de facto general manager.

Doogie Howser couldn't advance as fast as Donahoe has in his profession.

He is the only man other than Chuck Noll ever given the authority by Dan Rooney to run the daily football operations, and he represents a changing philosophy throughout the organization. Bill Cowher answers to him, as does everyone else on the football team and in the scouting department.

After just one year on the job, Donahoe, 45, has become one of the brightest young executives in the National Football League. He certainly is the only one who had a crude, yellow crayon drawing of a duck taped to the lamp on his office desk for an entire season. "My good luck charm," he said of son Matthew's artistry.

Or maybe a reminder to everyone who happened by: If it looks like a duck, walks like a duck, sounds like a duck . . . it's a duck. For too many years, the Steelers had been drafting ducks, hoping they could turn them into eagles.

"Jack Butler always said, go on production," said Art Rooney Jr. "If he's a good player in college, he'll be good in the pros. We got away from that."

Part of Donahoe's new job was to make sure Pittsburgh returned to that philosophy. That is how the Steelers built their dynasty in the 1970s when Art Rooney Jr. ran their scouting department. He, scout Bill Nunn, and Butler, the head of Pittsburgh-based Blesto scouting combine, provided the information that fueled some of the bests drafts in pro football history.

But after winning a few Super Bowls, the Steelers drifted from their bottom-line philosophy on draft picks.

"Part of it was arrogance," Art Jr. says. "We thought we had great coaches and great scouts and we could teach guys. Like Greg Hawthorne (Class of '79). He played the same with us as he did in college: great athlete, made some great plays, but was inconsistent. We thought once we got him here, he would change. But what you saw was what you got. He came here and was a great athlete, made some great plays, but was inconsistent."

The Hawthorne-like reaches lasted into the '90s. The Steelers drafted linebacker Huey Richardson with the 15th pick in 1991 and cut him after one season. They drafted tackle Tom Ricketts in 1989 and cut him after three seasons. Other memorable first-round mistakes of recent vintage were Darryl Sims ('85), John Rienstra ('86) and Aaron Jones ('88). Tim Worley ('89) missed all of the '92 season with a drug suspension, and Eric Green ('90) was suspended for six games in '92 for using drugs.

"We have done an abominable job on first-round picks," Donahoe said. "We don't have any on this team, or very few."

The Steelers concluded the 1992 season with one first-round pick in the starting lineup: Rod Woodson ('87).

That a shake-up in the personnel department happened early in '92 was not surprising. It came in rapid-fire moves: Noll, the ultimate authority on draft choices, retired; Donahoe was elevated to the top; Dick Haley, the Steelers' director of player personnel since 1971, resigned to join the New York Jets in a similar capacity; Tom Modrak, a key member of the scouting department for 14 years, replaced Haley and became director of scouting; and area scout Charlie Bailey became the pro personnel coordinator.

They represented the biggest reform in the Steelers' front office since Art Rooney Jr. was fired by his brother Dan in 1986 as head of the scouting department. Now the boss is Tom Donahoe, one of the high school coaches who helped evaluate film for the

Steelers in the summer under a program developed by Art Rooney Jr.

"I had hoped one day he'd be personnel director," said Art, who hired Donahoe as a full-time Steelers scout in 1986, his final year with the club. "It's terribly exciting for me."

Donahoe, Bill Cowher, and Tom Modrak worked to build a cohesiveness that broke down under Haley and Noll, who rarely talked to each other at the end. Haley had grown frustrated with Noll and his use of high draft choices. He could not fathom why they would draft a pass-rushing defensive end like Aaron Jones from Eastern Kentucky, a 1-AA school, and try to convert him to a stand-up linebacker, which is what Noll and former linebackers coach Jed Hughes did during Jones's first training camp. Nor could Haley believe it when former defensive coordinator Dave Brazil put Richardson, another pure passrusher, at inside linebacker as a rookie.

When it came time for the Steelers to draft on the first round in 1989, they were about to pick Tim Worley. But Haley stepped in and advised them they'd be better off choosing wide receiver Andre Rison if they did not plan to use Worley properly. He is an I-back who needs to run from a deep set, he told them. They agreed, drafted him, and then put him in the split formation.

The relationship between a team's coaching staff and its personnel department often is not cozy because of the circumstances. The scouts are impatient to see their draft choices flourish; the coaches blame the scouts for not finding them better players.

In Pittsburgh, that oftentimes adversarial relationship had hardened. There was a noticeable lack of respect, not to mention a lack of communication. It finally erupted publicly on November 5, 1991. Both Haley and Donahoe criticized Noll for not using his rookies in a losing season.

"We drafted them to play," Haley said.

"We've got to try to get guys to be successful," Donahoe said, "or else trade all 12 draft choices. If you're not going to have a commitment to them, why pick them?"

Donahoe blames the communications gap between the coaching staff and personnel department for the past problems.

"Maybe it was a lack of a solid relationship with Dick and Chuck, I don't know. But I don't think there was enough communication. I don't think there was ever enough discussion of things like, 'Where's our team, where do we want to get to and what kind of players are going to help us get there?'

"That's been one of the hardest things for me until Bill came here, trying to figure out what we were or what we were looking for. I think you need to know that, because you have to give your scouts direction that the coach wants."

Donahoe cites as examples the sleek, agile, pass-rushing defensive ends the Steelers kept drafting — Aaron Jones, Huey Richardson, Kenny Davidson, etc. Once on the team, however, they would plug them into a two-gap system, which is designed for big, strong defensive ends who can control the blocker in front of him and play the gaps on both sides.

Richardson was drafted with the 15th pick in 1991 because of another communications problem. The Steelers wanted either wide receiver Mike Pritchard of Colorado or running back Leonard Russell of Arizona State. Atlanta had the 13th pick. Haley's friend, Atlanta personnel director Ken Herock, told him the Falcons would draft Pritchard but weren't in love with the guy. They were willing to switch places with the Steelers, Herock said, for a third-round draft choice.

Haley thought Herock was bluffing, so the Steelers did nothing. When it came their turn, the Falcons drafted Pritchard and New England took Russell at No. 14. The Steelers had not considered this scenario and were unprepared to draft. Thus, they wound up with one of the great busts of all time, Huey Richardson.

Under the new setup in 1992, the Steelers scouts and coaches constantly played the what-if game. What if players A, B, C, D, E, F and G are gone? Do we take H? What if team X makes a trade with team Y and drafts player Z out of the blue?

"There was very little debate on the first round," Donahoe said of the '92 draft, "because I think we had done it beforehand and worked out the potential rough spots before they existed."

Modrak welcomed the new openness.

"If we have a difference of opinion, we'll put a videotape on and talk about it right then and there. There's a lot of give-and-take."

Of course, none of this guarantees the Steelers will duplicate the kind of drafts they had in the early '70s. But they might avoid some of their disastrous draft classes of the 1980s, particularly with high choices.

The scouts always believed that Noll paid too much attention to the lower draft picks at the expense of the high ones. The low choices were players who, like him, were supposed to be too small and too slow to make it in professional football. Noll's record of success with those players is admirable. He helped develop such low-round picks as guard Carlton Haselrig, a 12th-rounder in 1989 who had not played football in college. He made the practice squad his first year as a nose tackle, but Noll moved him to guard and he became a starter in 1991 and made the Pro Bowl in 1992. Other notable low picks of recent vintage were running back Merril Hoge (10th), offensive tackles John Jackson (10th) and Justin Strzelczyk (11th), and safety Gary Jones (9th). Three of Noll's four 12th-round picks from 1987 until 1990 made the ball club.

The Steelers gladly would have traded those successes for a better record with their high picks. They spent so much time worrying about the lower-round players and proving Noll right or wrong, that it took away the emphasis where it should have been — the No. 1 pick.

Noll liked to say it did not matter in what round someone was drafted, but whether he could play or not. Indeed he proved that more than anyone through the years, from L. C. Greenwood to Carlton Haselrig. But if everyone's doing his job, the best players should be drafted first. That's why first-round picks get paid so much, why they are worth so much in trades, why so much time is spent testing them and evaluating them, why they pick them *first*. They are drafted long before the 12th-rounders because all the NFL people who get paid to evaluate them believe they are much better players. But Noll loved to prove the so-called experts wrong.

He sometimes seemed to hold grudges against his first-rounders. He saw the low choices report to training camp on time, making an average buck, while the high picks held out for more money. He detested that, saying money and agents were ruining the game. Noll believed any player who held out was cheating himself, his teammates, and his employer.

The scouts and other coaches noticed a bias Noll held for the lower-round draft picks in training camp. He was tough on his high picks, but if a low pick or free agent made a great catch, he would make sure everyone knew it.

The Steelers now have a new system in place for both drafting and developing players. Assistant coaches receive specific assignments before the draft. The cooperation between the scouts and coaching staff is no longer strained, at least not yet.

"I think everybody in this organization — coaches, personnel people — are on the same page," Donahoe said. "We know exactly what these guys are looking for and it's our job to find them. I think when you have that kind of harmony, you have a better chance to make it work.

"Now, I'm not going to guarantee that every first-round pick for the next 10 years is going to be a bonanza because there's still a human element involved. But I like our chances a whole lot better now than I did before."

For the record, Tom Donahoe is not a member of the Rooney family. "Nepotism," some wailed when Dan Rooney installed him as the organization's top football man in 1992.

Donahoe *is* Irish and Catholic, but so are many in the Steelers' front office. Somehow, people could not fathom how Donahoe rose so quickly from career high school football coach in 1984 to director of football operations for the Pittsburgh Steelers eight years later.

The Rooneys had known all about Donahoe for a while. He had been a ball boy at Steeler training camps in the 1960s. He was the grandson of former Pittsburgh mayor and Pennsylvania governor David L. Lawrence, one of the best friends of Art Rooney Sr. That, however, is not how he got his ultimate job with the Steelers.

"The influence Governor Lawrence had probably helped him become a ball boy," Art Rooney, Jr., says, laughing. "But that's where it stopped."

Donahoe, in fact, rebuffed several attempts by Butler to hire him as a pro scout and was cool toward the Steelers' initial offer. He had been a high school football coach and was content with it.

A native of Mt. Lebanon, Pennsylvania, Donahoe started two seasons at quarterback for Pittsburgh's old South Hills

Catholic. He was also a hot-shot guard on the basketball team. But there was not much demand by the colleges in either sport for someone 5-9, 155 pounds. So he went to Indiana University of Pennsylvania, graduated and, at 23, became the youngest head football coach in Pennsylvania in 1969 when he took over at Mon Valley Catholic.

Donahoe coached football and basketball at various Western Pennsylvania high schools over the next 16 years. In the summer, he and other high school coaches reviewed film of NFL players for Art Rooney Jr. of the Steelers. Many NFL scouts and personnel men got their start that way, working in the summer for Artie. They include Joe Bushofsky of Miami, Tom Modrak of the Steelers, Ron Hughes of Detroit, Chuck Connor of Atlanta, and Rip Scherer of Indianapolis.

Donahoe's work impressed Artie Rooney.

"He's very intelligent, a hard-working guy who wrote excellent reports, knew football and, boy, could he express himself well at meetings. He's a good-looking son of a gun, so he comes across well that way. He looked a little out of place. He looks like a judge or something like that. The rest of us all look like we came from the ugly stick.

"You could see when he wrote his reports on film and stuff that he knew football. He was outstanding judging personnel and stuff. There wasn't too much flying by the seat of his pants. We verified everything."

Rooney, as he had done many times with high school coaches, recommended him to Blesto's Jack Butler, who offered him a job as a pro scout. Donahoe declined. Butler offered it to him again later, and Donahoe turned him down again.

Donahoe, at the time, had made a commitment to West Allegheny High School, where he was athletic director, football coach, basketball coach, English teacher, and adviser for the student newspaper and yearbook.

"He felt he couldn't up and leave those people at that time," Butler said. "He did everything there, probably even swept the gym out. He said he couldn't leave then."

Rooney offered to talk to Donahoe for Butler.

"Tommy," he told him, "Jack doesn't come back too often. He's offered it to you twice; the next time, you better take it."

Butler made a third pass and Donahoe finally agreed. He

became an NFL scout in 1985 for Blesto. There, Butler made him an area scout, then promoted him to regional scout.

"When I hired him, I knew I would not have him very long," Butler said.

Less than two years, to be exact. Art Rooney Jr. not only had an eye for talent, he was not above stealing it. Bill Nunn, the great Steeler scout who helped dig out the talent that won four Super Bowls, was headed for semiretirement and Rooney needed to replace him. Rooney told Nunn to discreetly follow Donahoe on his scouting trips for Blesto and report back to him with his findings.

The Dallas Cowboys were also members of the Blesto Scouting Combine, and their player personnel director at the time, Gil Brandt, could see what Artie was up to.

"Art," he mentioned, "I know you have Bill Nunn traveling with Tom Donahoe, trying to talk him into working for you. I have some objections to you trying to hire the best scouts we have."

Says Rooney, "Brandt had me cold turkey."

Nunn raved about Donahoe. He told Rooney he was the best scout to come through Blesto since Chuck Connor, another former Pittsburgh high school coach who is the Atlanta Falcons' director of pro personnel. Rooney was convinced and offered Donahoe a scouting job with the Steelers. Donahoe said he'd think about it.

"I almost fell on the floor," Artie said. "Here was a chance to work for the Pittsburgh Steelers! Finally, he said he'd take it, but that he didn't want to be a scout all his life. I never had any idea he'd be the director of football operations, but Dick Haley always said he'd take an early retirement and I wanted to get a guy in there who would be a candidate to take his place."

Donahoe became the Steelers' eastern scout for three years and made an impression on Dan Rooney at meetings. He was outspoken, hard to ignore, and his opinions proved to be on target. Rooney took him out of the field in 1989, promoting him to director of pro personnel and development in the front office. His first job was helping Noll find new coaches for the ones he was ordered to fire after the 1988 season.

"He handled the little things we gave him and they turned into big things," Dan Rooney said.

Donahoe's new position and his outspokenness annoyed some in the organization. He was a rising star and they could see it. As part of his new duties, he was to evaluate the Steelers' talent throughout the season and make suggestions to Noll and his staff. He sat upstairs in the coaches booth during games and used the headphones that communicated with the coaches on the sidelines. That galled some coaches, who believed he did not belong there.

When he suggested in 1990 that fullback Merril Hoge might serve as an H-back in the Steelers new offense, he was ridiculed by a few coaches. Noll's response was they had no H-back in their playbook, so what could Donahoe be talking about?

Noll and Donahoe got along OK, but not famously. Noll used some of Donahoe's suggestions; many more were ignored. When Noll realized that Donahoe would get more control in 1992, his decision to retire became easier.

One day after Noll's retirement, Dan Rooney informally told several reporters that Donahoe would be promoted to top man in the football operation.

"There's no question there's a new era in which we're going," Rooney said.

But Donahoe still had his critics. They mocked him because of his high school background. Never mind that Charley Casserly, the Washington Redskins general manager, was a career high school football coach when he begged the late George Allen for a job in the scouting department.

George Young heard similar taunts before the New York Giants won two Super Bowls under his watch as general manager, before he was named NFL Executive of the Year three times. Young had moved from 15 years of high school coaching into the Baltimore Colts personnel department. He coached their offensive line when they won the Super Bowl. He believes Donahoe's scholastic background serves him well.

"That's probably more a plus than a criticism. That's like saying a guy can't do something because of where he's from. That's ridiculous. I always say I was a high school coach and teacher. I'm proud of that. I feel better about my 15 years in high school than I do about some of the things we're doing now. A lot of people coaching in the NFL can't coach in high school.

"Nobody was prouder of his high school coaching days than Paul Brown. He asked that he be buried in Massillon, Ohio, where he coached high school football. Coaching in high school was a big deal to him."

Donahoe's work habits are legendary. He helped break in Walt Juliff as a Blesto scout before the Dallas Cowboys stole him away from Butler. Juliff often found that he and Donahoe arrived on campus before either the sun or the college coaches.

"The guy doesn't have a weakness," Juliff said.

"You can throw all that major college stuff out the window because the guy knows football. If you get one foot in the door in this league and you're a grinder, you can move up fast."

"His mind is clear," said Blesto's Butler. "He's a logical thinker, like Thomas Aquinas. His mind is compartmentalized. He's organized. Whatever it is, he's got it. Just like Coach Noll. People believed in him, the whole bit. He just has something."

Before most people in Pittsburgh ever heard of Bill Cowher, before they even knew he was a native son, Tom Donahoe pointed him out as timber to succeed Noll. Bob Labriola, the editor of *Steelers Digest*, remembered the day Donahoe mentioned Cowher to him. Labriola's reaction was similar to those who would hear the name later. Who?

"The biggest job Tom has had in his career so far," said Art Rooney II, Dan's eldest son and heir apparent of the franchise, "was hiring the new coach. I certainly think he did a good job there.

"It might be too early to tell how good of a job Tom has done personnel-wise, because he hasn't been in control of the situation long enough to say that's his team on the field. But I have a lot of confidence in Tom."

Art II said there's more than competence that brought Donahoe to his role with the Steelers.

"It's always been important that this franchise have a certain sort of culture and Tom fits into that. My grandfather always set the tone as a low-key guy. Don't seek the limelight. Tom gets the work done and lets the actions speak for him. We've always wanted the players to feel they're part of the entire organization, not just mercenaries. That's become more difficult because there are outside pressures on the players, but that's an important element of the Steeler culture and I think Tom understands that.

"If we were hiring somebody to fill that position right now, there probably wouldn't be a lot of people to fit that description the way Tom does."

After football, the most passionate interest of Art Rooney Jr. is the Civil War. He has scoured its battlefields as intently as he once did the college practice fields. He's visited the Antietam battlefield so often, other tourists might have thought he was its curator.

Perhaps this historical perspective helped avoid a Rooney Civil War when his older brother, Dan, fired him in 1986 as head of the Steelers' scouting department. That epic move began the era of the new Steelers, although it would be another six years before the transition was nearly complete.

Art and Dan Rooney hold equal shares in the team with their three other brothers; had Art fought the firing, it might have blown into a nasty family feud. The two did not speak for several years other than at official board meetings. But it never developed into a public spat.

"They can say what they want," Artie said, "I left quietly. I thought I handled myself with the media with a little bit of dignity for the family. The Steelers were very, very important to me, and the Rooney family was very, very important to me. I really couldn't bring myself to cause a stink in public.

"I had worked all those years and made those sacrifices, being out on the road and things like that. I didn't want to tear down something."

Dan does not like to talk about it, but he believed his brother had created an autonomy in the scouting department within the organization. Dan said he wanted more communication between departments. So what happened? Art was fired, but the communication between the personnel department and the football staff did not improve until the Cowher-Donahoe team joined hands six years later. Art always thought there was nothing more important for a football team than acquiring talent and, as the chief talent scout, he constantly impressed that point on his brother. It may have been true; it also may have led to his ouster.

"I was told that I was a little bit too large," Artie said.

Was he?

"We won four Super Bowls," Artie countered, "and we went from 1972 to 1984 without a losing season. We had X number of guys in the Hall of Fame and Y number of guys in the Pro Bowl."

Dan Rooney told his brother in October 1986 that it would be his last season with the team. It followed a huge argument the two had had the previous January. According to Art, Chuck Noll told Dan sometime after the 1985 draft that Art believed his scouting department's reports on college players were "sacrosanct."

A scout's job is to scout college players and rate them. A coach's job is to coach them when they join the team. But for several months of each year, a coach becomes a scout. This occurs between the time the season ends and before the draft, when coaches visit college campuses and evaluate tapes of the prospects. What you have are scouts evaluating players all year and coaches entering the process late, often with diverse opinions. Depending on whom you believe, this can either lead to healthy discussion or bitter differences of opinion that pit coaches against scouts.

Art Rooney Jr. was aghast when his father gave Noll the final say in the draft when he hired him in 1969. Artie believed draft decisions should be left to the scouts, who spend all their time evaluating players. That, for example, is how the Washington Redskins do it today, even though they have had a strong coach in Joe Gibbs, who resigned early in 1993.

Noll's authority over the draft really did not cause much conflict early on. The coaches and scouts got along well, and many times they agreed totally on which players to draft, although the scouts won one when they convinced Noll to draft Franco Harris in 1972 instead of Robert Newhouse.

But what is interesting is that the decline in the Steelers drafts began in 1975, the year before the draft was permanently moved from January to April. Many opinions have been raised about the reason for the Steelers' rookie talent tail off. One holds that by conducting the draft nearly three months later in the year, other teams had more opportunity to catch up with the "superior" Steelers scouting operation. On the other hand, maybe it just gave the Pittsburgh coaches more time to muck things up.

It certainly provided more opportunities for the two sides to grate on each other's egos. When Noll told Dan Rooney that Art believed his reports were sacrosanct, he was telling the boss that his brother was not flexible, not willing to listen to other opinions, not a team player. Art believed the opposite might have been true, that Noll had more respect for his coaches' opinions on college players than he did for the scouts.'

"I can control the scouts, I can't control the coaches," Artie said. "I'd never seen a coach put down for doing a bad scouting job. We came in with this list, this is *our* list, the sum total of all the work we did. Now you can shoot it down if you want.

"My feeling was, hey, I don't tell him to get into the 20th century and put the tight end in the game. I never said anything like that to him at all."

Before the 1986 draft, Art said he had Tom Modrak document the number of changes that were made to the player evaluations once the coaches got involved. There were about 100. He showed the list to his brother Dan, but apparently it made no impression. Six months later, Artie was out.

"I was told by him I was doing a good job, but I had to be out of there. I never thought my situation had anything to do with Noll. It was a family situation. Dan made up his mind. It was a personal thing. You can't have the president of the team not wanting you in that job."

Today, Art Rooney Jr. has a comfortable office and a secretary in a four-story building in Upper St. Clair, Pennsylvania. He heads the Rooneys' small real estate operation and still grades tapes of college players for the team, although he's not sure anyone on the team looks at his grades. He actually employed a full-time scout until 1992, and the two of them independently scouted players in the field. Two of Artie's scouts went on to work full-time for NFL teams: Walt Juliff of Dallas and Paul Roell of Indianapolis. But Artie's scouting wasn't looked upon favorably by the real Steelers scouts.

"I had a feeling Dick Haley felt I was grooming up my white horse to come riding back in. But I did not and do not want to be personnel director of the Pittsburgh Steelers."

The extra scouting position was deleted by Dan Rooney for 1992, leaving Artie to do it himself. He no longer enters the field, preferring to watch tapes.

"I came to the conclusion I was trying to prove a point, and I didn't need to. With tapes, I can still grade about 100 guys. It takes about two-and-a-half months. I get the tapes around Thanksgiving; they bring them out."

Artie remains a significant shareholder and is a vice president of the Steelers. He faithfully attends their home games, sitting in a small private box with Jack Butler, next to the press box with several friends or high school coaches. But he never visits the Steelers' offices nor their training camp, where he prowled the sidelines for so long. He has given up any hope of resuming an active role in the team's operation.

"I'm like some military guy who reached a certain important rank and then retired. He still gets his pension, he's still referred to as 'general,' but he doesn't know everything. You're called every now and then to a board meeting, but you feel left out."

During the draft, which once had served as his yearly Super Bowl, Art Rooney usually heads for one of his beloved Civil War battlefields, to immerse himself in past conflicts, to forget about current ones. He declined an offer to work for another NFL team in October 1992. A month later, he made a quiet trip on a weekend with his wife, Kay, to view the spectacular waterfowl on Maryland's Eastern Shore.

"It was very nice," he said with quiet resignation. "But when you're used to going out Friday night to the Michigan-Notre Dame game before 100,000 people, and then to Eastern Michigan vs. Central Michigan, and then you zip home for the Steelers game, it's difficult. Once you get a taste of this, it's hard to get it out of your system. This is a narcotic. It's in your blood."

After the Steelers won their first Super Bowl in January 1975, George Halas invited Art Jr. and his wife to dinner. "Up to this time," Halas told him, "you've done the greatest job in personnel in this era."

"He may have been wrong," Artie said. "I don't give a damn if he was wrong. He was George Halas. It was like George Washington saying it.

"Everyone used to say the Rooneys were cheapskates and dumb. All those years, down the side alleys, people would say we're not too bright and we're tightfisted. Well, everyone forgot about it after the first Super Bowl. Now, they might still say we're cheapskates; but I helped prove that the Rooneys weren't exactly stupid."

17

THE MEANEST MAN
IN THE NFL

Linebacker Greg Lloyd is as subtle as a guillotine. He often wears a grey T-shirt emblazoned with a skull and crossbones, and bold letters on his broad back that proclaim, "I wasn't hired for my disposition."

But nice dispositions never become Pro Bowl linebackers with the Pittsburgh Steelers. Lloyd once head-butted a teammate so hard he caused a gash on his own forehead that had to be sewn shut; not surprising, since he wasn't wearing a helmet at the time and his teammate was.

His mood turned sour in the second half of the '92 season as Pittsburgh stumbled to victories against lightweight opponents at home. He paced the sidelines in front of the bench as the Steelers fell behind the impotent Detroit Lions on November 15, muttering and pacing, back and forth. He then led a band of defensive players that beseeched the coaches to unleash them on the blitz. It had been a big part of their success all season, but for some reason against the Lions, they had abandoned it.

The coaches acquiesced, the defense put on the blitz, and Pittsburgh won, 17-14, after a blitzing Rod Woodson sacked quarterback Erik Kramer late in the game. Kramer fumbled on the play to set up the winning touchdown.

Three weeks later they fell behind the godawful Seattle Seahawks, again at home, and this time Lloyd wasn't so diplomatic. He came off the field and smashed clean a tableful of Gatorade cups. The only way Bill Cowher was going to get a Gatorade shower on that day was by getting in the way; Lloyd then attacked the big orange bucket and sent the liquid cascading off the table. The Steelers woke up to win that one, too, 20-14.

"I don't know if I ever met anyone who has so much intensity bottled up inside him," said Marvin Lewis, the Steelers' linebackers coach. "He has an aura about him."

Lloyd saves his most poisonous venom for quarterbacks. He may not have the most sacks in the league, but it's a good bet he detests quarterbacks the most.

The NFL passed so many rules to protect quarterbacks that Jack Lambert once suggested they put dresses on them. Greg Lloyd believes they've gone beyond that.

"The game is geared for the quarterback. The quarterback can play forever in this league because of the rules. They might as well put them in a bleeping glass case back there and put in a chute that they can throw out of."

Lloyd doesn't hate quarterbacks; he merely wants to kill them: a feat that became more difficult when the NFL passed the one-step rule. Pass rushers are permitted to take one step after a quarterback releases a ball and then hit him. If they take two steps and mash him, it's a 15-yard penalty.

"I enjoy hitting them. I get pissed off when I can't hit them. If you ever see me get a shot at him, I'm going to take it. I don't care if it's one step, two steps, because when you get focused on it, how can someone tell if you were one step away? Like I'm supposed to count steps now. It's a stupid rule.

"And they say, 'Oh, you shouldn't hit him.' Well, hell, he shouldn't be back there if I shouldn't hit him. He shouldn't play this game if he doesn't want to get hit. It's a dumb-ass rule. They can fine me from now until the time I'm done playing. I don't give a shit; I'm not going to pull up on him."

Lloyd plays outside linebacker with the ferocity usually seen in highlight films of Lambert, the Hall of Famer with the four Super Bowl rings.

"In fact, I think he hits with more velocity than Lambert does," said former defensive end Dwight White, who played in front of Lambert. "He's a hell of a player."

In terms of intensity and violence, Lloyd is the closest thing to Lambert on the Steelers since Lambert retired after the 1984 season. He scowls, he seethes; he is, according to Jerry Glanville, the meanest man in pro football. But he is not Jack Lambert and he doesn't want to be. For one thing, he's bigger than Lambert, who weighed about 218.

"A 218-pound middle linebacker is unheard of now because you have linemen who can damn near run as fast as you can," Lloyd says. "You want to compare me to somebody, it's going to be tough to do because I have a different kind of game I play."

He has an unusual background as well. Greg Lloyd never met his father. When he was two years old, his mother drove from their home in Miami to her sister's in Georgia and dumped off Greg and five of his eight siblings. And that was that. Lloyd was raised by his aunt, Bertha Mae Rumph, and was one of 10 kids in a two-bedroom apartment in Ft. Valley, Georgia.

"I came from what they nowadays call a dysfunctional family," Lloyd says, "but back then it was normal. I never got an explanation why she did that. I don't even have a relationship with my mom. I call her and say hi but it's a first-name basis. I don't view her as mom. There's no mother-son relationship, but I can't blame myself for that."

As far as he knows, his father's name is James Lloyd.

"I've never seen him a day in my life. I think my sisters and them said they had seen him. But at this point in my life, it's not important to me. It doesn't really matter to me. I don't care if I ever see the man's face."

Other than living space, Lloyd was not deprived of the necessities of life. Aunt Bertha Mae, whom Greg considers his mother, was a disciplinarian.

"My aunt grew up in a time that was required that you go out and help your parents in the fields. Education was pretty much secondary, so she pretty much had a third-grade education. But she has very good common sense, very good morals and values. She was very strict.

"I can remember when the street lights were on and you weren't home, that's a whippin'. I don't care if you were down the street playing basketball, if you came home at 6:05 that was a butt-whippin'. She had old-fashioned ways. The community sort of raised you. Everybody had input on how a kid should be raised."

The only men in the house were his brothers and cousins. It was way back then that Greg Lloyd would first display the kind of ruthless play on athletic fields that would set him apart later, even in the National Football League.

"I remember growing up you wanted to know about mom and dad. You saw the other kids who had moms and dads because you participated in all the sports and either your sisters showed up or your brothers showed up, but never mom and dad. There was a void there. You always wanted them to be there but they were never there."

He compensated for it by taking it out on all the other parents who came to watch their darlings play football.

"You could take it in a negative way, but I took it in a positive way. You sort of challenged yourself. When all the other kids' moms and dads would be out there screaming for them, I'd say 'I'm going to knock the shit out of them and let's see how mom and dad like *that*.' You could channel that negative image into something positive."

Negative images abounded in the Peach County, Georgia, of the 1970s and early '80s. The white robes of the Ku Klux Klan did not flap in the night much back then but racism and segregation flourished. In each of Greg Lloyd's school years at Peach County High, they held two proms: one for the white students, one for the black. Students voted for two homecoming queens — one black, one white. At least when Lloyd graduated from high school in 1983, they held just one ceremony.

"It was just funny," says Lloyd, not laughing. "The white people had their prom at the Holiday Inn, and we had our prom at a camp out in the woods somewhere. It looked like a boy scout camp. And people accepted it. That's the way it was. When you tried to fight it, you had problems with the parents. Then the black people got to the point where they said, 'Oh, what the hell. Don't worry about it. You don't want to be with them anyway.' It was a sad thing."

It wasn't the only one.

"We had 12 o'clock lunch and all the white teachers would sit on one side and all the white students would sit over there. And the black teachers would sit on this side and the black students would sit there. Nobody said it had to be that way, but it just happened like that. All the blacks went through one line and all the whites went through another.

"I mean, it was racist to the point most people didn't mind calling you nigger in your face. I've seen and heard so much shit that you don't become numb but you get a sense you know who you are. No matter how much education you get, how many degrees, people still view you that way. You can be Greg Lloyd, All-Pro, whatever, and people still are going to view themselves as better than you are. It's sick."

Nevertheless, Lloyd would rather be called something to his face than his back. He finds the subtle racism of the North less acceptable than the open bigotry of the South. His wife, Rhonda, a national board member of the NAACP, agrees. The two have made their home in Wexford, north of Pittsburgh, for several years, but plan to buy or build a house soon back in Georgia and move there with their two young children, Gregory Leonard II and Tiara Cassandra.

"If you're a white male and you live here, then you got it made. But there's not a whole lot for people of color to do. It's been however long since the slaves have been freed, but there hadn't been any change. People here just go about it differently than down South.

"I'd rather deal with a person straight out calling me a nigger to my face because I know where he's coming from than having to deal with a person who looks at you, talks to you in your face and then as soon as you leave says something derogatory."

Each Pro Bowl coach gets one wild card choice to add to his team after the players vote for the rest of the roster. AFC coach Dan Reeves of the Denver Broncos chose Lloyd to his team for the game in Honolulu after the 1991 season and Don Shula followed by selecting him after the 1992 season.

Lloyd, a first-alternate selection both seasons, might have been voted in outright, except for two reasons. One, Steelers linebackers are required to rush, play the run, and cover receivers. Those outside linebackers voted to Pro Bowls normally are those whose primary responsibility is to rush the passer and thus pile up oodles of quarterback sacks. The other reason: Greg Lloyd's disposition might hurt his popularity among NFL voters, his fellow players.

Al Toon, the graceful wide receiver of the New York Jets, retired during the 1992 season after his ninth concussion. He suffered one of them in 1989 when then-Steelers safety Thomas Everett knocked him out with a brutal but legal smash. As Toon lay prone and the caustic New York fans fell darkly silent in Giants Stadium, Lloyd ran over to him, got on his knees — and slapped the turf three times with the palm of his hand as if he were a pro wrestling referee.

Insensitive? You bet. Apologetic? Nope.

"I've seen people get knocked out, but I hadn't been right there on top of them," Lloyd says excitedly, as if he had just spotted a UFO. "I think people were upset that I thought it was funny to see the guy get hurt. It wasn't; you don't want to see that. I just thought it was funny at the time how Toon's eyes rolled across."

Maybe Lloyd thought Toon's mom and dad were in the stands, cheering for their son.

"Then I thought back to watching NWA wrestling. It's like 'One, two, three, this guy's out.' I didn't mean anything by it. The next time we played them, I talked to Toon and told him and he laughed."

Lloyd has an old-fashioned view of his sport. It is violent, and only the strong survive. He nearly did not make it through his first two years in the league. His rookie season lasted two days of training camp before he suffered a knee injury that required major surgery. Another knee injury caused him to miss the first seven games of the next season, 1988.

Back again in 1989, he refused to wear any kind of knee brace or wrap, afraid it would remind him of his injuries. He opened the season as a starter, replacing the departed Mike Merriweather, and has started all but two games and missed only one since then.

Lloyd became the Steelers' highest paid defensive player on April 23, 1993, when he signed a new contract that would pay him $7.15 million over the next four years, through the 1996 season. His annual average salary is $1.785 million. "It's a good deal for both sides," said Dick Bell, his agent. Pittsburgh's front office recognized that while Lloyd is not in a position to be a great pass rusher, he is a cornerstone of the new Steelers.

"When I'm lined up out there, I don't think I can be blocked. I don't think anybody out there can block me. When I get blocked, I get pissed off. I think I should get to the quarterback every time I line up back there, and when I don't, I get pissed off."

The crippling injury to New York Jets defensive end Dennis Byrd in 1992 caused Lloyd to reflect on the consequences of his dangerous and violent profession, but not for long.

"It's scary as hell," he admitted, "because I know the way we fly around it could happen at any time. But you don't think about it. I got over that three years ago when I came off my knee surgery. If I go back and start thinking that I have to protect it, I'm never going to be the player I want to be. So I just let it hang out and I tell myself, if it happens, it happens.

"My wife sees me coming home after a game, sees me getting out of bed in the morning. She looks at me sometimes and shakes her head. This year, I joked around and I told her at the end of the season I'm going to retire, my body's all beat up. And she looks at me, and says, 'You should.' She's serious, but I'm just messing with her. I told her no way. As long as I can get up out of here, and I can walk to that bathroom and I can get in my car and I crank it up and I can get out of that car, I'm going to play."

He wasn't fined for counting out Al Toon, but various antics have cost him "well over $5,000," including a big one for knocking out Jets quarterback Ken O'Brien after he threw a pass in the same game that Toon was injured. No penalty was called after he hit O'Brien, but the league office later blew the whistle after a New York tabloid screamed, PITT BULLS on the back page. Lloyd was fined heavily.

"I got the justice from the referee on the field. But it's like if you spit on a guy now, they want to fine you money."

Lloyd detests hypocrisy almost as much as he does quarterbacks and racism. He growled when NFL Films widely marketed a video called "Crunch Course" that featured the most provocative violence in the NFL. It included the kinds of hits Lloyd put on O'Brien. Double jeopardy! First, the NFL fines him, then the league makes money by packaging it and selling it to the fans.

"It's really silly," he seethed. "It's violent and they push it, and then as soon as you do something like that, it's 'Oh no, we've got to fine you for that.'

"I think it's ridiculous, and it goes against everything they say they're for. It's being hypocritical. You say one thing, then you go out and condone 'Crunch Course.'"

That hypocrisy extends to the field of play, Lloyd charges.

"There's a double standard there. The only thing they do about trying to keep the violence out of the game is they just put stricter rules on the quarterback. How many games have I been in where you go in and take on a guy and you get that bleeping guy trying to take your knees out? The bleeping ref's standing right there and you point to him and go, 'Hey!!' And he says, 'Oh, that wasn't bad.'

"But if I go back there and knock the shit out of the quarterback, he comes to me immediately and goes, 'All right, that was good but be careful.' See what I'm saying. It's like the eye is always on that guy."

Joe Namath once upset him when he criticized his style of play while working a game in Pittsburgh for NBC-TV in 1991.

"Who is Joe Namath?" Lloyd sneered. "This is a guy who, if he played in the league today, I'd probably just go hit him late and see what he did, just for the hell of it. Joe Namath can go to hell; he can kiss Greg's ass."

He screams at the injustice of paying a $1,500 fine levied by the NFL office after he hurled a football into the stands at Three Rivers Stadium during the Steelers' exhilarating one-point victory over Houston. But Lloyd vows that no fine, no orders from the people in the NFL headquarters will stop him.

"No, because it's a feeling you get. If you decide to do it, you do it. They're a bunch of paper-pushing pussies who sit back there and make those rules, and they've never played a game in their life. I would like for some of them to come down on that field for just one day, and we'll suit up so we can knock the shit out of them because it's a bunch of bullshit.

"If they could keep that politics out of football and get back to the old style of play, it would make a lot of people happy."

18

LIMPING HOME

Bill Cowher Saying No. 364: "All we've done is create an opportunity for ourselves. Now we have to take advantage of that opportunity."

The opportunities, though, were slipping away faster than warm weather in Pittsburgh. The dreadful Seattle Seahawks intercepted three of quarterback Neil O'Donnell's passes on December 6 and then broke the fibula in his right leg when one of them fell on him. The Steelers dropped behind, 14-10, before Bubby Brister directed an 80-yard drive that put them in front on Barry Foster's four-yard run with 2:22 left. They salvaged a victory, however shaky.

"All I can say is we've given a new definition to winning ugly," Cowher said. "We defied the rules of the game of football."

O'Donnell would miss at least two games, but the Steelers had clinched a playoff spot, they were 10-3, and they were going to Chicago, where the Bears were wrestling with a 4-9 record, a six-game losing streak, and Mike Ditka's short fuse. It was in Chicago where the Steelers first got the idea they might be good when they beat the Bears, 28-17, in the third exhibition game.

This one put different kinds of thoughts in their heads. Middle linebacker Mike Singletary was playing in his last game at Soldier Field, and the emotional Bears wanted to make it memorable. They crunched Brister and the Steelers, 30-6.

Trashball turned to trash talk in Chicago. Bears defensive end Richard Dent kept pointing to the Steelers sidelines and screaming. Linebacker Hardy Nickerson foolishly went into his Hulk Hardy routine in the third quarter, posing with his fists thrust inward, toward his hips and his shoulders hunched. The pose was in poor taste even when Nickerson threw someone for a loss. When he did it after he tackled Neal Anderson for a one-yard gain as the Bears drove to a TD and a 20-3 bulge late in the third quarter, it was embarrassing for anyone in a Steelers uniform.

Nickerson wound up getting tossed out of the game for fighting near the end, along with Greg Lloyd. In the locker room afterward, Cowher lectured Nickerson privately for 10 minutes in front of his locker. Neither would reveal what they talked about.

"There was a message delivered," Nickerson said. "That's one unique ability Coach Cowher has, he's able to communicate with the players because he's been there."

The Bears smothered Barry Foster, who had 25 yards on 13 carries. Brister had one of his worst throwing games as a pro, completing 14 of 31 for 143 yards and two interceptions.

"We've been winning ugly and today we got our butts kicked," Brister said. "Maybe it'll make us wake up and smell the roses and get ready to take what we have an opportunity to take and not let anybody give it to us."

That night their friends, the Houston Oilers, gave it to them. Houston's loss to Green Bay clinched the first AFC Central Division title in eight years for the Steelers. But no one popped champagne in Pittsburgh.

"The most important thing still is we're not playing very well," kicker Gary Anderson said, "and we haven't played very well in a long time. I've been in the playoffs quite a few times, and you have to be playing a lot better than we're playing."

There was one division title-clinching party the following week in Pittsburgh, only it was held by the Minnesota Vikings after their 6-3 victory over the Steelers in Three Rivers Stadium. The Vikings had locked up the NFC Central Division championship.

Brister looked better in this one, but Nickerson did not. Hulk Hardy posed in front of the home fans after he missed wrapping up Minnesota's Terry Allen, who slipped off Nickerson's tackle for a two-yard gain and a Vikings first down. What would Hardy celebrate next, a Minnesota touchdown? He did not get the opportunity because no one found the end zone on December 20.

Even Franco Harris couldn't find it. Before the game, the Steelers celebrated the 20th anniversary of Franco's Immaculate Reception against the Raiders, the playoff victory that kick-started a new Steelers success story for a previous generation. They put cardboard cutouts on the playing field — where Terry Bradshaw threw the ball, where it ricocheted off Jack Tatum and Frenchy Fuqua and where Franco caught it and raced for the miracle TD.

Franco's cardboard likeness, appropriately on this day, faced the wrong way.

Pittsburgh hadn't scored a TD in two games, and Minnesota's Allen exposed their defense against the run by scorching them for 172 yards rushing. Foster got back on track with 118 yards, but his day ended frightfully when his head jammed into the turf and he momentarily lost the feeling in his legs.

"At that point," said Foster, "I thought my career was over. My legs went numb for about five to six seconds. That was about five to six seconds too long, you know?"

With the game tied, 3-3, Minnesota's Fuad Reveiz lined up for a 36-yard field goal on the last play of the game and kicked it dead-solid perfect.

"Instead of the field goal going off to the left like it did against Houston," Rod Woodson said, "it went through the uprights and we lost. What can you say?"

You could say the Steelers were in trouble. They had lost two straight to dip to 10-5, and they needed a victory to avoid playing in the first round. Everything they had accomplished was unraveling, and the Cleveland Browns would like nothing better than to pull their string in the finale.

Two days before Christmas, two announcements came in two cities: The Indianapolis Colts waived Tom Ricketts, and

Carlton Haselrig joined three other Steelers on the Pro Bowl squad.

No, no they got it wrong. Ricketts was supposed to make the Pro Bowl. Haselrig? He should be in the WWF by now, no?

This is one of those switched-at-birth draft stories that Chuck Noll loves. Ricketts played left tackle at the University of Pittsburgh, which as the scouts fly, is about four miles from Three Rivers Stadium and a mainline National Football League recruiting station. Haselrig went to another University of Pittsburgh, *at Johnstown*. Pitt-Johnstown might as well be Bangladesh to NFL scouts. They don't field a football team there; never have.

Ricketts is 6-5, 305 pounds. He became the 24th player drafted overall in 1989. The Steelers had traded holdout Pro Bowl linebacker Mike Merriweather to Minnesota during the first round and got an extra first-round choice from the Vikings in return. That pick became Ricketts, a home-grown product from the Pittsburgh suburb of Murrysville, where he went to Franklin Regional High School.

The Steelers heralded Ricketts as a natural left tackle who could anchor that critical post for years to come. Three years later they cut him. He started 13 games, none of them at left tackle. Ricketts had two rather large problems: He couldn't recover after making an initial hit on pass blocks and he couldn't stay on his feet. Why Steelers scouts couldn't see this is the great mystery; perhaps when he was playing in their backyard they closed the blinds.

Haselrig is another treasure that Chuck Noll bequeathed to Bill Cowher. He is only 6-1, undersized for an offensive lineman, but not to Noll's way of thinking. He never devalued short linemen, figuring they had bigger hearts. Noll had been an undersized offensive guard himself. Haselrig's weight is not slight, at 290 pounds, and he is the only six-time NCAA heavyweight wrestling champion in history — three titles in Division I, three in Division II. He was a Big 33 All-State football player at Johnstown High School but went to Pitt-Johnstown to wrestle.

Pittsburgh drafted him in the 12th round, even though he hadn't played football since high school. Noll assigned him to the practice squad as a nose tackle, but whenever he needed a guard, he put him there. Haselrig converted to offense permanently in 1990, made the team as a backup, and then replaced Terry Long as the starter at right guard in 1991.

He is quick on his feet and has better leverage than H. Ross Perot.

Haselrig was not quick enough on September 26, 1992, however, and he still carried evidence of it late into that season. He showed up in the locker room the week after the Steelers played in Green Bay September 27, sporting an unusual gouge on his forehead — several long, deep scratches, as if a panther had swiped him with a paw.

"What happened?" someone wanted to know.

"It's nothing," Haselrig replied nonchalantly. "My helmet just pushed down on my forehead during the game."

Nice try, Rig. He could have used that helmet in his car on September 26. Late for the team charter flight to Green Bay, Haselrig sped down a one-way road the wrong way and banged into another car. Not only did he suffer that nasty cut on his forehead, he missed the flight and was fined by Coach Bill Cowher. He made it to Green Bay in plenty of time and took his usual spot at right guard during the Steelers' first loss of the season.

But the real story stayed relatively quiet, and Haselrig even fooled some people with his cover tale. It was one of the few things that went awry for him in 1992.

"I was sitting here just thinking about the things that have gone on in my life," Haselrig said. "It's pretty wild. Making the Pro Bowl this soon surprised me."

Haselrig hopes to have more surprises in the future. His goal is to wrestle freestyle in the 1996 Olympics — and win, of course. He practices twice a week at Pitt and carries his wrestling shoes with him, just in case a match breaks out somewhere.

"The Olympics is definitely one of my goals. There are things I always wanted to accomplish. I wanted to be a national champion, play pro football, be All-Pro."

So he became a six-time national champ, skipped college ball, and made it in the NFL, then made the Pro Bowl. Go ahead, you bet that he won't win an Olympic gold medal.

Joining Haselrig in the Pro Bowl was Foster, cornerback Rod Woodson, and center Dermontti Dawson. Linebacker Greg Lloyd was voted a first alternate and was added by AFC coach Don Shula as a need player. Neil O'Donnell made it six Steelers when he was added to the roster because of an injury to Jim Kelly.

Dawson is the man who replaced the legendary Mike Webster in 1989 and has not missed a start since. Webster missed only four starts from 1976 through 1988, his last season with the Steelers. Webster could be headed for the Hall of Fame in 1996, right about the time Haselrig is wrestling in the Atlanta Olympics. Some people think Dawson might be as good as Webster, only bigger. When the Steelers got the opportunity to protect two "transitional" players under free agency in 1993, they chose Foster and Dawson, even though their contracts don't expire until after 1994.

"It's just nice to be able to step into his position and do well," Dawson said of the legendary Webster.

He is another young player with Noll's handiwork all over him. Dawson was a right guard at Kentucky and was the Steelers' second-round draft pick in 1988. On the third round, they chose center Chuck Lanza of Notre Dame. Pittsburgh's scouts figured they had the cornerstone for the offensive line of their future with Lanza at center and Dawson at right guard.

Noll, as usual, didn't follow the blueprint. He put Dawson at center and Lanza languished, trying to cut it as a backup at guard and center. The scouts were furious. Noll took a natural center and put him at guard and switched the natural guard to center. It was another Aaron Jones debacle!

But Noll saw something in Lanza he did not like. Lanza was not aggressive, not strong enough. He lost weight between his rookie season in 1988 and his last training camp in 1991, when he was listed at 265 pounds. He missed the entire 1990 season with a torn triceps muscle. The last time he made an appearance at Three Rivers Stadium came in August 1991 when, injured again, he sat in the stands with his girlfriend during an exhibition game against Washington and proposed marriage to her on the scoreboard. She said yes. A few weeks later, the Steelers said no, waiving him off the football bridle path forever.

Had Lanza somehow stayed at center and Dawson moved to right guard, perhaps Carlton Haselrig never moves to offense and is never heard from again. "I'd probably be wrestling," he said.

Instead, Chuck Noll groomed two future Pro Bowl offensive linemen. It paid big dividends in 1992 and should continue to do so. The Steelers worried about their offensive line before the

'92 season. It was mostly underweight and inexperienced. But veteran starter Duval Love came over from the Los Angeles Rams on Plan B and settled in at left guard, John Jackson played well at left tackle, Dawson and Haselrig had their best seasons, and old vet Tunch Ilkin, 35, held together at right tackle. Justin Strzelczyk, another Noll project, backed up capably at tackle and started seven games in '92, not bad for a guy who played defense at Maine before he was drafted in the 11th round.

That offensive line paved the way for Barry Foster's record-smashing 1,690 yards rushing.

"They're one of the best offensive lines in the league," Foster said.

Kent Stephenson, their coach, calls them "a bunch of try-hard guys."

"I don't think anybody thought our offensive line would come out the way it did," offensive coordinator Ron Erhardt said.

The play of Ilkin and Strzelczyk allowed the Steelers to let first-round pick Leon Searcy, their 300-pound prized rookie from Miami, ease into things. He figures prominently in the future. Ilkin signed with Green Bay as a free agent in March 1993, and Searcy was designated for his post at right tackle.

"Oh, he should definitely play a larger role, no question," Erhardt said. "That's the whole thing we wanted. We had a veteran in Tunch there and he had a chance to see him operate. I think it'll be a real good situation for him now. He's seen everything for a year."

The regular-season finale against Cleveland in Three Rivers Stadium on December 27, 1992, was crucial. Win, and the Steelers would get a first-round bye in the playoffs. Lose, and they might have to play in the first round and then go on the road.

Quarterback Neil O'Donnell began running and looked as if he might be ready. But Cowher did not want to tip his hand yet. Nevertheless, Bubby Brister told reporters on Wednesday at high noon that he knew who would start that Sunday.

"Just come watch practice and see who gets the reps," he said.

They took his advice, watched Brister take all the snaps from center, saw O'Donnell lying on a bench, and everyone reported that it looked as if Brister would start against the Browns.

The next day, Christmas Eve, Goose Goslin of KDKA radio was the only reporter to turn out. But Dan Edwards, the team's publicity director, asked him not to watch practice. Coach Bill Cowher threw a fit when he learned everyone had reported on the quarterback situation the day before, and Edwards wanted to avoid a conflict between the coach and the press.

Goslin, a respected veteran reporter, told his audience that for the first time in at least 24 years, the Steelers had closed practice. It was something Chuck Noll never had done, not in good or bad times.

The friendly relationship Cowher and the news media had for most of the season might have broken down at that point. It was a relationship rarely tested because Pittsburgh's two daily newspapers had been on strike since May 17 and because the Steelers were unexpectedly successful in Cowher's first season.

It would have been interesting to see his reaction had there been more extensive coverage and more critical commentary by the city's two newspapers to the following:

- His blowup on the practice field at St. Vincent College on August 4 when he gathered his players around him and screamed at them for 90 seconds.
- The Steelers' 0-2 start in the exhibition season, and later their two-game losing streak after opening the season with three wins.
- The holdout of veterans Thomas Everett and Louis Lipps and the players' reactions when they were cut loose.
- Greg Lloyd's revolt over being moved to inside linebacker.
- The dissension of Hardy Nickerson and Barry Foster.
- The quarterback duel.
- Eric Green's suspension.
- The decision to cut Huey Richardson.

Cowher had an extended honeymoon in Pittsburgh in 1992 and he knew it.

"There is no question a lot of things took place on this football team that could have very easily been blown into major stories," Cowher said. "We've been able to just play football."

Agent Steve Baker, for example, kept calling me in training camp, trying to drum up stories to show how purportedly unfair the Steelers were to his client, Nickerson. I informed him there was a newspaper strike in Pittsburgh and I was writing for a fax put out by the *Post-Gazette* that had a circulation around 300. Supermarket bulletin boards had wider readership. Even if I were sympathetic to his cause, I had no audience.

"This is frustrating," Baker said. "What a time for there to be a newspaper strike in Pittsburgh."

Tell me about it, Steve.

But it might have been the best thing that happened to Cowher and his young ball club.

"The issues still existed," Cowher said, "but they weren't distractions."

The success of his team could have been the biggest distraction of all.

"You could get caught up in reading how good you are," Cowher said. "You could get caught up in feeling a sense of accomplishment with what you've done. We didn't really experience that."

The potential Christmas Eve closed-practice problem eased after Cowher and Edwards talked over the situation. Practices would remain open, as they had forever with the Steelers.

It was the *Pittsburgh Press* and the *Pittsburgh Post-Gazette* that remained closed. Both papers missed the entire, unlikely story of the 1992 Steelers and their new coach. The shutdown of both papers lasted all season, before the blackout ended January 18. It never ended for one of them, however, because the *Pittsburgh Press* ceased to exist.

Two days after Christmas, the Steelers took care of business with Bubby Brister at quarterback. They defeated Cleveland, 23-13. Barry Foster tied the NFL record with his 12th 100-yard rushing game. That night their division rival, Houston, completed the dream scenario by bumping off the Buffalo Bills, who slipped to a wild-card playoff and allowed Pittsburgh to become the No. 1 team in the conference with an 11-5 record.

The Steelers had a week off and home-field advantage throughout the playoffs, the most well-traveled road to the Super Bowl. There hadn't been a playoff football game in Pittsburgh in 10 years. Two victories at home would send them to Pasadena, where they won their fourth Super Bowl in 1980.

Of the previous 22 teams with home-field advantage in the AFC, 17 of them went on to the Super Bowl. The road to the Super Bowl went through Pittsburgh again.

"We haven't played our best football yet," Bill Cowher said. "I think it's still ahead of us and I think when we do, we're going to be a very hard football team to beat."

19

A ROOM WITH NO VIEW

As he had done with his football operation, Dan Rooney reconstructed the Steelers' headquarters in 1992. Workers tore down walls, built new ones, formed offices out of storage rooms, and repositioned executives and secretaries.

One small room remained empty, except for a desk, a chair, and two paintings. No one used it. Few people even knew it existed. Once, it was among the busiest areas in the front office when it was an executive bathroom. But now it is a nondescript executive office and, like all their others, it has no windows and no name on the door.

It is the office of Charles H. Noll, Administration Advisor. That is how the Pittsburgh Steelers list him now, right up there with three Rooneys and part-owner John "Jack" McGinley at the top of their organizational flow chart. The H is for Henry, the title is for show, and the office is going to waste.

"They store things in it," Noll said, laughing.

Dan Rooney negotiated a 10-year, $1 million retirement bonus for Noll, and he wanted him to remain a part of the organization. He also wanted him to have his own office when he visited Three Rivers Stadium. Those visits were sparse in Noll's first year of retirement, and the office was never used. Noll did not want Bill Cowher to think he was looking over his shoulder, not that he would have anyway. His role with the team is undefined and, really, he can do nothing if he wants.

"I do a few things. Mostly, I guess public relations, which is my strength, right?" Noll laughed again.

Actually, the public just may be getting to know the real Chuck Noll after 23 years. Many fans perceived that Noll was a cold, calculating coach who held as much affection for his players as a plumber would for his pipes. Noll actually is a warm, witty man who detested cut-down days more than any and who jumped at chances to help former players and coaches. Tom Donahoe called him one of the most honorable and decent men he's ever met.

Noll made rare public appearances during his coaching career. He pushed no products, did no radio talkshows, stayed away from the banquet circuit. He believed that was for players, not him. But once Noll retired, he became quite the gadabout. He appeared on a few TV and radio shows, flipped the coin at the Super Bowl, threw out the first ball at the Pirates opener, accepted an honorary degree at his alma mater, the University of Dayton, was honorary chairman at a ball at the new Pittsburgh airport, and was guest of honor at a huge benefit dinner in Pittsburgh.

"I didn't have time when I was coaching," Noll explained. "If you start doing a lot of that, then you're not focusing on football. I could have been out every night when I was coaching, but then your family, which gets shortchanged anyway, gets shortchanged more. Plus, you're in more demand when you're coaching than when you're not."

Noll had never been overseas, but in the year after his retirement, he and his wife, Marianne, traveled to Japan and Germany, where he taught clinics for the NFL. Then they took a two-and-a-half-week vacation in Italy. He also spent time at his vacation condo in Hilton Head, South Carolina, and visited his son, Chris, in New Hampshire. And, oh yes, he got elected and inducted into the Pro Football Hall of Fame on his first try.

Retirement looks good on him. He has taken to it the way he might a fine Beaujolais, leisurely sipping it, enjoying its bouquet.

"I hadn't given retirement any thought," Noll said. "As a result, I think maybe it's been more pleasant because it's been a surprise, a one-day-at-a-time surprise. We're enjoying it; it's great. We're pretty much trying to get a feel for what it's like, trying to let it unfold. There aren't as many have-tos as there were before so there's more time to do the things we like to do."

So don't look for him back on the sidelines or even in a general manager's job. For one thing, he admits that the new free agency would make it extremely difficult for him to operate. When he retired, he inadvertently fueled speculation that he would someday return as a coach by refusing to say he would not. He now declares he will not. His 62nd birthday is in January 1994. He will not coach, he will not become a football administrator — in high school, college, or the pros.

"That's not in my plans at all. No. We really want to spend time doing these things."

Among the things he did in the fall of '92 was watch the Steelers play football. He attended several games, watching from the owner's box. He stood the whole time, which might be considered unusual for a fan but not for someone who stood during every Steeler game the previous 23 years. He left Bill Cowher with good talent and was impressed with what he did with it.

"I think he's doing a great job. He's sound. His record shows it. They played well. You guys maybe believe me now when I said that last year."

After watching Cowher's rookie season unfold so successfully, Noll still had no regrets about his decision to quit. It was time, as he had said. Cowher's first season convinced a lot of others it was time, too. But had Noll hired someone such as Ron Erhardt to run his offense, he might still be coaching the Steelers. No one will ever know what the 1992 Steelers might have done had Noll stayed and retooled his coaching staff. It certainly isn't something he wants to contemplate.

"I have no way of knowing," he said. "I think they've done a good job with them, using people they've had. Some of them have matured. The thing that made us happen in the '70s is that we had a group of guys who matured together. Sometimes you have a few guys who come along but you're so staggered because the old guys who carried the load are gone and you need everybody. We were fortunate in the '70s that we had a large group that matured together and stayed together. That's important."

On July 31, 1993, Chuck Noll was inducted into the Pro Football Hall of Fame. He became the eighth member of the

Steelers' four Super Bowl teams to make it. The others were Joe Greene, Jack Ham, Mel Blount, Terry Bradshaw, Franco Harris, Jack Lambert, and owner Art Rooney Sr.

Noll was the only one who went in protesting.

"This is such a team thing," Noll said, "and you get into something like this, which is an individual honor, that it's kind of embarrassing. You can't do it yourself."

But if you have a pro football hall of fame, it must include Chuck Noll, whose 209 victories rank fifth in NFL history.

"I think of all the people who were involved in the Steelers organization during our Super Bowl years," Ham said, "Chuck Noll is by far the most deserving to be inducted into the Hall of Fame."

While he swept in on his first try, a few of the 34 Hall of Fame voters actually questioned his coaching ability. Of course he was successful, they argued, he had the talent. If that were the strange criterion to judge a coach — winning only if you don't have the talent — then they should drum out Vince Lombardi, George Halas, Paul Brown, Tom Landry, Sid Gilman, and one of Noll's '93 Hall of Fame classmates, Bill Walsh. They all won with good *talent.* Imagine winning four Super Bowls without it! Look how many different coaches have tried it in Tampa Bay. More coaches have screwed up with great talent than the ones who were able to consistently produce winners with it.

"There is no question," Lambert said, "that during the Super Bowl years he had a group of guys with tremendous talent, but he kept those gifted players focused, cohesive, and on an even keel."

That was one trick that made Noll such a good coach — his ability to keep his team together and keep all those talented players' minds on the goal. Four Super Bowl victories in six years! Remember when the Chicago Bears had so much talent they were going to be the next Super Bowl dynasty? They won one. Had Mike Ditka not spent so much time in the restaurant business and selling more products on television than Procter & Gamble, he might have figured out a way to win another.

"The players know there's no monkey business there," the late Paul Brown said of Noll in 1990. "He's made it his life's work, which means he isn't trying to sell autos on the side and that kind of stuff. That would be degrading to me as a coach, to be selling stuff. You got a profession, you put your mind on it all the time. It's year-round."

Noll learned from the best. He played seven seasons for Brown in Cleveland as a messenger guard, then retired to coach defense for Sid Gillman with the Los Angeles Chargers of the new American Football League in 1960.

"I love him," Gillman said. "Chuck was destined for something good. There wasn't any question about it. He was very meticulous in everything he did, a splendid coach.

"We saw him at the University of Dayton when I was at Cincinnati and we played Dayton. He stood out like a sore thumb. Matter of fact, we recommended him to Paul Brown. Then, when I was looking for a staff with the Chargers, he called several times. He wanted to get into coaching. I felt that anyone who played for Paul and was a messenger had to be very bright.

"Boy, you talk about having convictions. He was stubborn. All the good ones are stubborn, I guess."

Another Hall of Famer was on that Chargers staff — Al Davis. At one time, the two were friends, and Davis still talks about Noll with admiration.

"He was tremendously bright, and now I would say he's wisdomed. He was tough, dedicated, very educated. He was someone I liked and enjoyed because, although we were both immersed in football — and perhaps me more than him — we could talk on a wide range of subjects. Intellectually, he was above most."

Interestingly, Davis talked to Noll about becoming the coach of the Oakland Raiders in 1969. Noll was a defensive assistant with the Baltimore Colts at the time, and they were about to lose Super Bowl III to the New York Jets. Another team also wanted to talk to Noll, the Pittsburgh Steelers.

"I was very fond of him and very impressed with him," Davis said. "Everything was positive. He was not afraid, was firm in his beliefs. I've always admired that. That's part of his success. In 1969, the choice came down, in my mind, between John Madden and him. Yes, we talked, but to go back and go through all that wouldn't be important right now. That will be in *my* book someday.

"I didn't have to interview Chuck. I lived with him; we were together about three years. but I thought the job he took was better for him, and it was a way for John to get the job with us. It worked out wonderful for both."

The two teams, Oakland and Pittsburgh, became bitter rivals in the 1970s, when they met five straight times in the playoffs, an NFL record. What might have happened had Noll gone with Davis to coach the Oakland Raiders instead? That's like asking what might have happened had Joe Paterno taken the Steelers' coaching job in 1969 when it was offered to him.

"You must remember," Davis said, "those were the greatest teams that ever played professional football. They had the greatest players, certainly. And great coaches."

Maybe some of those players became great because of who coached them. Maybe some got into the Hall of Fame because of that. Maybe some wear four Super Bowl rings today because of it.

It became fashionable in 1992 to compare the styles of Bill Cowher and Chuck Noll, and Noll always came out on the short end. Cowher was upbeat, talking to players, patting them on the back or kicking them in the fanny, slapping hands with them, encouraging them. Noll was stubborn, old-fashioned, aloof, uncommunicative, not a players' coach.

Guilty. He was the perfect coach for the perfect time. He taught his players how to do things, then expected them to do them. He did not put alarms on the dormitory exits. He looked the other way if a player broke curfew, as long as the player performed the next day. If he didn't, he would be gone.

The times changed, players changed, America changed. Players now seem to need more structure, more feedback, more enthusiasm from their coaches and alarms to help them obey curfew. That was not Chuck Noll's way.

"He never really gave us pep talks of sorts," Joe Greene said, "but we took them as pep talks. He never said the things that said 'Look at me; I'm a leader; I'm trying to lead you.' He just led us. He helped all of us to bring out the best that was in us."

"Chuck Noll," Lambert said, "was the perfect head coach for me to play for because he wasn't a rah-rah cheerleader type. He expected you to play like a professional, and as long as you did that, he treated you like one, which suited me just fine."

Art Rooney Jr. had his differences with Noll when he headed the Steelers scouting department and, indirectly, those differences might have led to Rooney's firing by his brother Dan in 1986. But when Art Rooney Jr. looks back on it all, he credits Noll with much of the Steelers' success.

"I always said, if I ever had 15 minutes of fame, 11 came from Noll and the rest from my dad. It was an honor to get into an argument with Chuck Noll."

20

UNFINISHED BUSINESS

Buffalo, as it should be.

You want to be Top Gun? You must outdraw No. 1. The Buffalo Bills had dominated the American Football Conference for two straight seasons. The Steelers had annoyed them all year from afar, toying with the best record in the AFC, even though Buffalo beat them earlier.

The Bills, in fact, almost always beat the Steelers — four times straight, six of seven since 1979. But all those Bills' victories came in Buffalo. Their only loss to the Steelers during that stretch happened in Pittsburgh in 1985. They had met once previously in the playoffs, in 1974, when the Steelers trounced the O. J. Simpson-led Bills, 32-14, on the way to their first Super Bowl victory.

So Pittsburgh had them right where it wanted them — at Three Rivers Stadium, without quarterback Jim Kelly, with Cornelius Bennett hurting, with Bruce Smith and his aching ribs, with Thurman Thomas nursing a hip pointer. It was time.

The Steelers believed that Kelly, who grew up in East Brady, a few miles up the Allegheny River, had their number. In real life, he was a Pro Bowl quarterback; against the Steelers he was the Heavenly Quarterback. In four games against the team he once idolized, Kelly had a phenomenal 110.0 passer rating. He had completed 88 of 130 passes (67.7 percent) for 1,036 yards, 11 touchdowns, and only three interceptions. Although Frank Reich had directed the Bills' stunning comeback playoff victory over Houston the previous week, Pittsburgh was more than happy to face him in the pocket instead of Kelly.

"We're loose," quarterback Neil O'Donnell said.

"I'm so excited," said Rod Woodson, "I can barely sleep at night."

Many Steelers fans did not, either. Hundreds camped out in sub-freezing weather Friday night to buy 9,000 remaining play-off tickets that would go on sale Saturday morning, one week before the game. When Dan Rooney heard about the overnight guests on the Three Rivers doorstep, he called Pizza Hut and ordered 100 pies delivered to the fans. Rooney kept this so quiet that not even his public relations guys knew about it.

Bill Cowher did not keep his quarterback decision quiet this time. He revealed it five days before the Saturday game: It would be Neil O'Donnell, whose leg had healed sufficiently to play. That was what the players had expected all along. "I like Neil," Barry Foster said. "I feel more comfortable with him."

Cowher's decision sparked a debate among Pittsburgh's fans and media. Why not go with the hot hand in Brister, a guy who had playoff experience? Cowher's answer was simple: Neil O'Donnell is our quarterback. Brister, disappointed, accepted the decision without much comment — *before* the game. But he knew it meant his days as a starter in Pittsburgh were over unless O'Donnell became injured. Had the coaches believed their two quarterbacks were close in talent and performance, Brister would have remained in the pocket for the playoffs because of O'Donnell's long layoff. Cowher's actions told Brister all he needed to know.

Playoff fever began to build in Pittsburgh. Sales of Steelers T-shirts and sweatshirts ballooned. Myron Cope, the Steelers color man and radio talk-show host, begged his listeners to pack Three Rivers Stadium with Terrible Towels. Even Cowher got into the act. "I have mine right in my office," Cowher said.

Gordon Forbes, *USA Today's* pro football columnist, put mythical odds on each of the 12 playoff teams' chances of winning the Super Bowl. He picked Pittsburgh 40-1, the longshot of the lot, even though the Steelers had a bye and the home-field advantage. Someone from the staff made copies and put one in each player's locker and another on the bulletin board four days before their game against Buffalo. It was a high school tactic, but who could argue with the results against Houston when they pulled a similar psychological maneuver?

"People doubted us the whole year," Woodson said. "No one even thought we'd be in the playoffs. Well, we're here and we won our division and we're having fun. We're going to have doubters, even if we go to the Super Bowl."

"Hey," linebacker Jerrol Williams suggested, "if you put money on us, you might win big."

The Steelers had already hit it big with Williams, a fourth-round draft pick from Purdue in 1989. He led them with nine sacks in '91, even though he started only four games. He beat out veteran Bryan Hinkle in 1992 at left outside linebacker and started every game. Williams moved to defensive end when the Steelers went to their "dime" pass defense, which featured four linemen and six backs. Teamed with Greg Lloyd, they formed one of the better pair of linebackers in the AFC.

"Jerrol Williams had one of the best years I've seen from a linebacker here in a long, long time," said Hinkle, a Steeler since 1981 and their MVP in 1986. "He didn't come off the field. If Jerrol continues to work, he'll be a Pro Bowl player. He's got to keep his mind straight and work. I think that's been his downfall."

Williams was an outstanding high school basketball player and, at 6-5, 253, has the type of speed and agility of a power forward. But he lacks the kind of strength needed to consistently rush the quarterback.

"Jerrol has a lot of potential in some areas that are still untapped," said Tom Donahoe. "He needs to get stronger. He needs to get serious about weights and the conditioning part of it. He has the size and athletic ability to be a good player."

He does not lack in confidence. Several days before the playoff game against Buffalo, Williams declared the Steelers' four starting linebackers better than the Bills' more famous quartet of Darryl Talley, Cornelius Bennett, Shane Conlan, and Marvcus Patton.

"No question. I think we're the most underrated linebacking corps in the NFL," Williams said. "We don't get recognition, but that's the meat of our team, our linebackers. I know it; people can see. Lloyd and I put pressure on the quarterback. We might not be up there in the sack totals, but we're putting on pressure that's causing our DBs to be among the top of the league in interceptions."

They would need to do that desperately against Buffalo. The Steelers ranked only ninth in the league in total offense and 13th in total defense, ratings that did not reflect their top billing in the AFC. What tipped the field in their favor was their ability to steal footballs. They led the NFL, recovering 43 turnovers; as a result, the Steelers allowed the second fewest points in the league, 225. That total was 119 points fewer than they allowed in 1991. Little surprise that their record improved.

Woodson was confident they would continue that trend in the playoff game against Buffalo: "We know anytime we play well against a good team our defense steps up to make a lot of big plays and gives the offense the ball in scoring position. That's the way we're thinking this time."

It was not to be. The Steelers did not force a turnover against Buffalo. Woodson, knocked silly on a botched punt return in the second quarter, did not recover his senses in time to save them from self-destructing.

Saturday, January 9, 1993, was a cold, overcast day with snow flurries in Pittsburgh. Cope's two-decades-old signal was heard clearly. Fans waved tens of thousands of Terrible Towels, and cornerback D. J. Johnson, following the lead of Lynn Swann in the '70s, twirled a gold towel during pregame introductions.

A unique, carnival-like atmosphere spread over Three Rivers Stadium, where 60,407 jammed their way in. It was the largest crowd ever to see a sporting event there, a thousand more than the listed capacity.

The Steelers bolted in front, 3-0, on Gary Anderson's 38-yard field goal. It was their first drive, and their only scoring drive of the day. Seven times they got to the Bills' 41 or closer, and did not score on six of them. Bill Cowher, the gambling coach who went for the jugular all season long, turned conservative and punted twice inside the Bills' 40 — from the 37 in the second period and the 36 in the third.

Woodson's mild concussion would cost them dearly. Unaware he was hurt, the Steelers left him in the game, and it was a befuddled Woodson who allowed Don Beebe to catch a 19-yard pass to the one in the second quarter. From there, guard Mitch Frerotte fooled them again. He lined up in the backfield, drifted into the end zone uncovered and caught Frank Reich's one-yard touchdown pass to put Buffalo in front, 7-3.

Frerotte, from nearby Kittanning, Pennsylvania, thus tied for second for most touchdown catches against the Steelers in the 1992 season with two, one behind teammate James Lofton.

The score remained 7-3 until midway through the third quarter when the game was decided on two plays. Sammy Walker, legally blind in one eye, had replaced Woodson at corner and was getting toasted by Beebe and Lofton. Finally, the coaches yanked Walker in favor of Richard Shelton, a former World League player. Shelton became a footnote to history when he scored the final touchdown for Chuck Noll's Steelers on a 57-yard interception return against Cleveland. He could have become more than a footnote on this day against Buffalo.

On the very play in which Shelton replaced Walker, Reich threw an out pass for Beebe near the Pittsburgh 13. Shelton broke quickly, stepped in front of Beebe and had the ball in his hands with 87 yards of clear turf in front of him. But Shelton was wearing two pairs of gloves because he hurt his hand earlier in the game, and he looked up slightly as the ball hit him.

He dropped it.

"I saw the goal line; I think that was the problem," Shelton moaned. "I was thinking last night that I may have one chance to make a big play. That was my one chance and I didn't make it. I had an open field. I think it would have been six. It would have changed the game around."

On the very next play, Shelton moved inside to the slot position and Walker went back to cornerback as the Steelers switched to their dime defense on third-and-13 for Buffalo. Reich went right after Walker and pitched a perfect pass to Lofton for a 17-yard touchdown.

It was 14-3, and the game was over no matter what the clock said. Barry Foster managed 104 yards rushing — his 13th 100-yard game — but no one else did much on offense. The final was 24-3.

"The bottom line in this business is putting points on the board," Bill Cowher said, "and we didn't do that today."

Woodson returned to the game in the fourth quarter but remembered little about it. He then broke his left hand. Still woozy from his concussion, his left hand throbbing, Woodson tried to accommodate a gaggle of reporters in the depressed Steelers locker room. One radio guy got too close and clunked Woodson on the head with a heavy microphone.

Ouch.

"It's been a hell of a day for me," Woodson sighed through a crooked smile.

They had played all season for this, surprised the football world by running up the best record in the AFC, earned a bye in the playoffs, and had a clear path to the Super Bowl. But they let it all escape without putting up much of a fight, with no big plays on defense and their offense looking as impotent as it ever had during the worst of the Joe Walton years. Over their final four games, Pittsburgh did not score a touchdown in three of them and lost all three.

It was some season; the Steelers came from nowhere, and just when it seemed they might reach the top, they discovered all too clearly that they still had more steps to climb.

"I think it was evident out there today that we need a few more people," old war-horse Bryan Hinkle said. "You lose Rod for a while, it hurts you. We need another Rod Woodson clone, if there's one out there."

Free agency would not tear up the club because the Steelers had planned well enough so that few players' contracts had expired. However, free agency did alter the look of the defense a tad. As most everyone expected, inside linebacker Hardy Nickerson high-tailed it out of Pittsburgh. He jumped at an offer from Tampa Bay of $5.1 million over three years, a shocking total the Steelers never would have matched, even had they been given the chance. Nickerson, though, did promise Cowher he would call him before signing any agreement, to give the club one final chance to keep him. Nickerson never made the call.

Also, the Steelers allowed Jerrol Williams to move to San Diego. They had the right of first refusal because he was a restricted free agent, but two things happened. First, the Chargers signed him to a one-year, $1.7 million offer sheet. That incensed the Steelers because they believed San Diego general manager Bobby Beathard had negotiated a secret deal with Williams and his agent, Eugene Parker, for a longer term that would go into effect sometime down the road if he became a Charger. Had the Steelers matched the deal, they would be guaranteed of having Williams for only one more year. Second, they became interested in outside linebacker Kevin Greene of the Los Angeles Rams.

Greene was 30 but seemed to be in his prime. His 72 1/2 career sacks are only one shy of the Steelers career record, held by L. C. Greenwood. Greene also had 10 sacks in 1992, three and a half more than Lloyd's team high.

So the Steelers signed Greene to a three-year, $5.25 million contract to play left outside linebacker and allowed Williams to go to San Diego. Williams had great potential, but Greene had done it. He gave the Steelers their best pass rusher since the glory days of the '70s. They had lost one of their most promising players but picked up a proven veteran at the same position. As free agency takes hold in the NFL, that will happen more often; as teams lose one free agent, they will replace him with another.

There were a few other minor changes because of free agency and one big one the Steelers averted.

Tunch Ilkin, one of the most popular players on the team, signed a two-year contract worth $2.2 million with Green Bay in March. Before he did, he talked to Bill Cowher, who told him if he returned to the Steelers it would be as a backup. The Steelers had allowed Leon Searcy, their first-round draft pick in 1992, to watch and learn for a year behind Ilkin. But they planned to start him at right tackle in '93.

Rather than stay in a reserve role — or perhaps get cut — Ilkin opted to sign with Green Bay, and his departure after 13 seasons with the Steelers was cordial.

Pittsburgh also lost Aaron Jones, who signed with New England for two years at $1.8 million. Jones did not start a game in '92.

Then there were the surprising developments at quarterback. Neil O'Donnell did not play well against Buffalo in the playoff at Three Rivers Stadium, but the staff left no doubt he was their quarterback, and O'Donnell felt good about the future.

"It was my first playoff," O'Donnell said, "and a lot of guys' first playoff. Now that we have a taste for it, we hope to be back a lot more. I'm hungry; I can't wait for next season."

After the playoff loss to Buffalo, Bubby Brister let O'Donnell know that he did not play well. Quiet all season about his backup role, Brister spoke up two days after the loss to Buffalo, his ego perhaps stoked by the support he received in certain quarters from the fans and media who argued he should have played.

Brister revealed a secret, that he tore a ligament in his left knee in training camp and that, he said, prevented him from playing at his best and giving a full challenge to O'Donnell for the starting job. He also said he was a better quarterback than O'Donnell.

"It's very frustrating for somebody as competitive as I am to sit there and watch somebody else play when you feel you're better then they are. . . . If I'm healthy, I think I can out-run him and out-throw him."

Brister turned the screws a little more with his next statement.

"You give me seven opportunities inside the 40, I guarantee you we'll do something. It's easy to say now, but you don't get many opportunities like that. I would like to have those opportunities, and I've been in those situations before, and I've been a big-game player. Every big game we've had around here, I've sort of come through."

Bill Cowher and Ron Erhardt both disputed Brister's assertions. O'Donnell would have won the job anyway, they said; O'Donnell is our starting quarterback.

Brister's words stung O'Donnell. Brister had been his friend, but O'Donnell could not believe the things he had said. Publicly, he tried to shrug them off, although he made a few points subtly.

"It's hard to judge," O'Donnell said coolly, "when you're on the sideline like that. I believe we're all in this together.

"Bubby says he can run better? I don't know about that. He can throw better? I don't know about that, either. I'm not going to get into a fighting match with Bubby Brister. It's been going on forever."

It would not go on much longer, however.

O'Donnell was a restricted free agent, and in March of '93 he dumped Steve Baker, his agent, in favor of high-powered Leigh Steinberg, who represents most of the better quarterbacks in the NFL. The Steelers took a gamble and made O'Donnell only a $275,000 qualifying offer, maintaining their rights under the new rules to match any free-agent offer O'Donnell would receive. By making an offer so low, however, if O'Donnell signed with another team and the Steelers did not match it, they would receive only a third-round pick in return. Had they offered him $600,000 and another team signed him, they would have received a first-round pick.

In other words, the Steelers tempted other teams to negotiate with O'Donnell because all they had to lose was a third-round pick if the Steelers did not match their offer.

And Tampa Bay took the bait. Steinberg showed up at the NFL meetings in Palm Desert, California, the week of March 21. He negotiated a contract with Richie McKay, vice-president of the Bucs, and O'Donnell signed it on March 26 for a whopping $8.175 million over three years, or an average of $2.725 million a year.

Steelers executives gulped. They had planned on signing O'Donnell to a contract for about $1 million less annually. Rod Woodson, the highest-paid player in their history, averaged only $1.45 million a year; this was nearly double that.

The Steelers had one week to match Tampa Bay's offer. Many, even within the organization, figured O'Donnell was gone. That week was one of the most intense and most publicized in the history of the franchise, excluding those before the Super Bowls. Brister, speaking from his parents' home in Monroe, Louisiana, said he was healthy, happy, and ready to return to the Steelers.

Bill Cowher, Tom Donahoe, and Dan and Art Rooney examined their options. They could allow O'Donnell to leave, receive a third-round choice in return, and start Brister, which would have been a public relations nightmare. They could let O'Donnell go, and then try to sign another proven quarterback in free agency, which would have cost them almost as much. Or they could breathe deeply and match the offer.

Cowher and offensive coordinator Ron Erhardt pushed for them to keep O'Donnell, but not even they were sure what Rooney would do. "That is," Cowher said, "a lot of money."

O'Donnell had started only 21 games, and the team's record was only 10-9 in them. The Steelers would have preferred to have a better track record to go on. But they did not, and in the end they really had no choice but to keep O'Donnell.

They matched the offer, announcing it only five hours and 20 minutes before the midnight April 3 deadline. They also came to an agreement that day with quarterback Mike Tomczak, a veteran free agent from Cleveland. Tomczak's signing meant the end of Bubby Brister in Pittsburgh. He had a $1.2 million contract, while Tomczak signed for $850,000 a year. What's more, Tomczak has accepted his role as a backup and has the mentality for it. Brister's entire makeup is that of a starter.

The Steelers tried to trade Brister, but when no one showed any interest, they finally waived him in June.

The quarterback controversy was over. The Steelers not only had weathered free agency, they may have improved themselves by signing Kevin Greene, giving Bill Cowher the kind of pass rusher he had in Kansas City with Derrick Thomas. In the course of two days, Dan Rooney shelled out nearly $13.5 million for two players over the next three seasons, surprising those who had called him cheap.

It raised even more hopes for the '93 season.

Cowher and the Steelers had accomplished so much in 1992. The honors came swiftly. Cowher was named NFL Coach of the Year by the Associated Press, something Chuck Noll somehow never won. He was picked as Pittsburgh's prestigious Dapper Dan Man of the Year, something that came Noll's way once.

What was left? Everything.

"What we have to do now is prove that we're a quality team, year in and year out," said Cowher. "That's the challenge that's ahead of us, and I like our chances."

All of Pittsburgh likes them a whole lot better than they did before the 1992 season began. It was a transitional year. It was supposed to be a year in which the new, young coach, replacing a legend, would be given the chance to get his feet wet. Instead, Bill Cowher put everyone's feet to the fire. Tom Donahoe, the Rooneys, all of Pittsburgh would have been satisfied had the Steelers turned in a competitive 8-8 season in Cowher's first year. Cowher wasn't satisfied with 11-5.

More than an unexpectedly good record was accomplished that season. The Steelers found themselves a *coach*, someone who has exceeded all the expectations they had for him on the day they hired him. He energized them — the players, the front office, the entire franchise. And the fans.

"We're going to be back," Rod Woodson promised. "We're just getting an understanding of the new system. We have a lot of talent on this team. It's going to be very tough to beat the next couple of years."

Shortly after he was named the Steelers' coach, Cowher attended a basketball game at his alma mater, Carlynton High School, and few noticed him sitting high in the corner of the gym. Not long after his first season ended, he attended a Pitt basketball game. The public-address announcer noticed him in the stands, where two of the best basketball players in Pitt history also sat — former NBA player Billy Knight and current pro Charles Smith. The two players were introduced, to polite applause. Cowher was then introduced and got a standing ovation.

He came a long way since that first day in Pittsburgh when, emotionally exhausted, he frantically tried to reach his wife to express his self-doubts. And the Steelers had come a long way as well.

Early in March, Cowher was hustling down the hallway from his office to a meeting with Donahoe at the other end. He passed by the lobby, where two fans were admiring the Super Bowl trophies. "Hey, coach," one shouted, delighted at his luck. "Can we get your picture?"

"OK," Cowher said, stopping. "But hurry, I'm on my way to a meeting."

Both men, from New Hampshire, got their pictures and Cowher was off to his meeting. Just like Chuck Noll, he appreciated the culture that Art Rooney Sr. first breathed into the franchise.

The year, 1992, may go down as one of the most pivotal in the history of the franchise. The Pittsburgh Steelers discovered a new coach, a new quarterback, and a powerful new running back, perhaps of Franco proportions. They formed an offensive line that had the makings of its best in two decades. They put a man in charge other than a Rooney for the first time, Tom Donahoe, who certainly got off on the right foot. Their president, Dan Rooney, helped forge a revolutionary new deal with the league's players that will take them into the 21st century. Not only that, it is the kind of deal that almost guarantees that the Steelers and other small-market NFL teams will be able to compete and survive in the new era of free agency.

They also mapped plans to guarantee that a Rooney or Rooneys would maintain control of the franchise.

Thanks to 1992, the future looks good for the Pittsburgh

Steelers. Their goal remains the same as always, the one Chuck Noll reached four times but never stopped pursuing. Bill Cowher set his goal in January 1992 and gave it a pretty good run. He raised everyone's expectations but his own. To him, 1992 was fulfilling in some ways, disappointing in another, because the Pittsburgh Steelers did not win the Super Bowl.

"I know that what I talked about from the beginning was realistic," Cowher said, "although I'm not sure any of them believed me at the time. They thought I was on something. I told them, 'You probably thought I was on something.'"

And he told them something else: "You're going to see how close we were."

Now he believes they are close again. Real close. It's a new season, isn't it?